RONALD COLMAN

A Very Private Person

RONALD COLMAN
A Very Private Person

A Biography by

Juliet Benita Colman

WILLIAM MORROW & COMPANY, INC.
NEW YORK   1975

Printed in the United States of America.

1 2 3 4 5   79 78 77 76 75

Library of Congress Cataloging in Publication Data

Colman, Juliet Benita.
    Ronald Colman, a very private person.

    Bibliography: p.
    1. Colman, Ronald. I . Title.
PN2287.C57C6   791.43′028′0924 [B]   74-23224
ISBN 0-688-00274-9

Book design by Helen Roberts

Foreword

At the Kaiser's "Halloween party" at Messines in 1914, amid the din of his army's band, the shellfire, whizbangs, machine-gun bullets, the shouting of Germans and British alike, came an explosion unnoticed by all except Private Colman. Shrapnel ripped through his knee and ankle, throwing him face-first into the beetroot field. Finding himself unable to put any weight upon the mangled leg, he started to crawl back, dragging the broken bones, stumbling over his kilt, and trying not to pass out. During this maneuver, it suddenly occurred to him that should the next bullet or shell be lethal, he would be found dead with his back to the enemy, and at the rate the battle was going, this was more than a strong possibility. He had every intention of maintaining the dignity both of himself and of his country, whether or not he made it to safety. Without further hesitation, he turned onto his back, and pulling with his elbows, then pushing with his good leg, he retreated from the field of battle while facing the German lines.

Although his experiences in the First World War did not weaken my father's idealistic beliefs, they certainly cultivated within him a strong sense of realism. He has for the rest of his life a contrasting combination of the realist and idealist: the man who wisely and carefully dissects Shangri-la stone by stone and yet still believes in it. The romantic exterior and dream-distant voice belied the businessman's brain. He was in fact a surprise package of many contrasts. He became mathematician and poet, photographer and painter, poultry-raiser and philosopher. He was keenly shrewd and delightfully gullible, as intricate as the vast jigsaw puzzles of which he grew inordinately fond. And he was often as difficult. He was a man's man but women's idol. He turned into a great star, yet could surprise one with his depth as an actor on the occasions he stepped out of the image that accompanied his name. Finally, he was the father who, at the end of his life and at the beginning of mine, longed to impart the secrets of the universe to his only child, but who couldn't figure out how first to capture her attention:

> *In spring, when woods are getting green*
> *I'll try and tell you what I mean.*
> *In summer, when the days are long,*
> *Perhaps you'll understand the song:* *
>
> *For this must ever be*
> *A secret, kept from all the rest,*
> *Between yourself and me.*†

I was nearly fourteen years old when Ronnie died and had known and loved him during those years as, simply, my father. It was the desire to know him better that was the incentive for writing this book. There was a great deal of learning to be done. He was already fifty-three when I was born and he had progressed through life phases that were as varied as they were numerous. I had little or no concept of him as a soldier, a shipping clerk, a husband, friend, businessman, actor, star, or indeed as an individual. Characteristics of which I had only caught a hint as a child needed to be traced to their source. His nightmare time in the First World War, his disastrous first marriage, his early starving

---

* From "Humpty Dumpty's Song," by Lewis Carroll.
† From "Evidence Read at the Trial of the Knave of Hearts," by Lewis Carroll.

days as an actor trying to secure a job in New York—those experiences were familiar to me only in the guise of his jaunty limp, his pronounced shyness with women, and his great prudence with money. There were countless sources to be investigated, and the voyage proved just as interesting to me as the discoveries.

There were dozens of films to be tracked down and seen. (Before starting the book, I had seen only seven Colman films; including the English few, he made a total of fifty-four.) The fact that nitrate film was used in the silent era does not make matters easy for would-be viewers today. Countless prints did not survive to be either copied or cared for, and as a result many films have disappeared altogether. Colman films were no exception.

Apart from delving into my own recollections of over sixteen years ago, I've tried to recall every relevant detail mentioned by my mother. (Benita survived Ronnie by nine years; she died in 1967.) There were family friends to see again, sometimes after an absence of ten to fifteen years. For the most part, I needed to discover his friends and associates and whenever possible talk to them on tape: in London, in the English provinces, in Europe, in New York, in and around Hollywood, in Santa Barbara, and—in the instance of my godfather, Tim McCoy—in Arizona. On the rare occasions when this was not feasible, letters were exchanged. Virtually everything in print concerning Ronald Colman was digested, as indeed was a great deal on the eras through which he passed. To avoid errors of secondhand information, I endeavored to uncover original sources. Each person, every event, all the sources snowballed into endless others. And then I started the actual writing.

The richest element that has emerged from the past four years of work is the heartwarming fact that I'm very happy to know Ronald Colman and even happier to know my father.

This book is dedicated to dearest J.T.,
who couldn't wait to read it,
and to my mother and father,
without whom it could not have been written—

In happiest memory.

Contents

1 ～
The Shipping Clerk at War

When Ronald Charles came into the world at the home of Marjory and Charles Colman, his parents had already been married ten years and, in the tradition of most Victorians, were fulfilling their intention of populating the empire with a large family.

Charles, an attractive man and well established as a silk merchant (following in his father's footsteps), had swept his Scottish fiancée off to St. Stephen's Church in Paddington and married her. Marjory was then thirty, and over the next fourteen years she produced five children, of which Ronald was the second son.

When he arrived, Marjory was forty—a mature, gentle woman with an aura of beauty and breeding, an outstanding sense of humor, and a remarkably impersonal outlook on life that was rarely ruffled by her large family. Her relationship with her youngest son was from the beginning one of deep fondness and warm objectivity. Emotions in those days were not worn on the proverbial coatsleeve, but were buttoned securely into understatement. When the proud mum registered his birth a couple of months later in Richmond, the clerk— who was either hard of hearing or unfamiliar with the name

—entered it as "Roland Charles," and thus it remains in the leather-bound volumes of Somerset House to this day. A prophetic beginning to a lifetime of a misspelled name, more usually with an *e* in Colman.

Ronald's two elder sisters, Edith and Gladys (then five and eight), leaped at the opportunity of playing mother to the new addition, and a rather jealous two-year-old brother, Eric, felt his limelight was stolen on the day of Ronnie's birth—the ninth of February in the fifty-fourth year of Victoria's reign. Their front gate opened onto Sandycombe Road, where the carriages clattered behind their steaming horses on the way to the splurge of Royal Botanical colors at Kew Gardens in one direction and Richmond and the river in the other.

Charles was very much the head of his family (which was increased by a final daughter, Freda, four years later), and although his second son regarded him with fondness and respect, he also held him in slight awe. A rather stern gentleman with prominent nose, bushy moustache, silvering hair, and the broad forehead that Ronnie inherited, he was inclined to believe in children being more seen than heard—doubtless a proverb he wisely adopted after the birth of his second child. The large group made too many demands on Marjory for her to spend a great length of time with each child. So Ronnie found pleasure in his privacy early in life. He wasn't particularly thrilled with the idea of fisticuffs with his brother, and his two elder sisters were not keen to share their interests or devote time to him once he was out of the nursing stage. He was not a lonely child, though. The household would not have allowed it. It was a constant hive of activity, of comings and goings—brother, sisters, friends, relations, nannie, maid, cook. . . .

When Freda replaced Ronnie in the nursery, Charles bought a rather larger house in a quieter area about the same distance from London. The double-fronted building sat on a corner of two tree-lined residential streets of Ealing. It was off the main road to London and not far from the local school in which Ronnie was enrolled. This small private school, within easy cycling distance, overlooked Haven Green and was owned by a German who had migrated to England some years before—with a degree in philosophy. Not content with that alone, he began work in his spare time for a London University art degree, which he took ten years later. When Ronnie joined the group, it consisted of forty boys, most of them sons of professional men. The school was scantily furnished and the food not particularly good, the cricket was weak and the football rough, but the boys were given a painstaking grounding by their determined and enterprising headmaster.

Ronnie's interest in reading took root here in the school library. Being of slight build and not particularly interested in the sports offered, he delved into his studies and easily emerged near the top of his form. He read as much as he could make time for, threw himself eagerly into the school plays, and bringing to mind his literary favorites, he overacted with relish.

Once a month Charles took one of the boys up to London to visit his office, through which seemed to waft the mysteries of his Oriental silks. "I enjoyed these trips enormously. They stimulated my imagination as nothing else did, and my imagination needed stimulating. . . . I didn't believe in anything I didn't see, touch, hear or taste. I remember once being told by my nurse that a certain house in the neighborhood was haunted, and I replied matter-of-factly, 'Nonsense, it just needs a coat of paint!' I had none of the dreams by day or nightmares by night which delight or horrify the highly strung child. Nursery tea was the high spot of my day. Towards buns and tea and jam were all my dreams directed!" *

* Ronald Colman interview with Gladys Hall. *Photoplay*, January, 1939.

RONALD COLMAN

It was in his father's office that he first heard tales of India, China, and Japan, enhanced by the surrounding colors and smells of the ubiquitous silks. Listening to the office talk and drinking in the atmosphere, his desire to see the world was aroused. Once home, he would rush to the atlas to trace each voyage the ships had made, and rummage through the school library to find books on the countries whence the silks came. "I assured Father I'd be in the business when I grew up, not in the London offices but as commander of one of the ships coming in from the Orient." *

It was Charles who gave him his first glimpse of a film, at the Earl's Court Exhibition. It was a catchpenny show with bands, whirligigs, fortune-tellers, and one new attraction with a sign over its entrance, ANIMATED PICTURES. The interior was stuffy and black, and on the little screen an express train rushed out of a tunnel straight at the audience, while a pianist played bass chords and a drummer wildly rubbed two pieces of sandpaper together. Ronnie was as good as tied to the railway track while he witnessed his first film. His hair stood on end. "That invention has a future," said Charles, who should have been in the business. "You watch it! Animated pictures are going to make fortunes for a great many people." *

The impression remained with Ronnie, and when he went to boarding school on the Sussex coast, he took up amateur theatricals. His more serious thought, however, had changed from ship's captain to engineer. He longed to build bridges over canyons, and he hoped very much to make it to Cambridge. There was so much knowledge he wished to embrace before channeling himself into a particular career, and Cambridge was to him the ideal springboard to broaden his education, his horizons, and himself.

* *Photoplay,* January, 1939.

The Shipping Clerk at War

A fortnight after Ronnie's sixteenth birthday, his father —then fifty-nine—became ill with pneumonia. Ronnie rushed from school to the house in Ealing and was there with his family when Charles died. Suddenly his life was jammed into another gear. There was insurance coverage sufficient to see to the needs of the deeply grieved widow and her daughters until such time as they married into their own lives, but if their house was to remain home, the sons had to help out. University was no longer a possibility. His school education was finished. Ronnie was obliged to earn his own living.

When the summer came and his term had ended, he started work as a clerk in a steamship company at $2.50 a week. Eventually knowledgeable about figure-tallying and Gregg shorthand, he was promoted to junior accountant and his salary was upped to $9.50. Though it all helped at home, the job was rather dull and routine. To add some colorful contrast, he joined the Bancroft Amateur Dramatic Society, where they acted Wilde, sang the English drinking songs, learned Gilbert and Sullivan and how to play the banjo.

Marjory was happy and relieved he was enjoying himself, knowing how much he had wanted to study at Cambridge and the deep disappointment that had followed the shock and sadness of his father's death. (Though his clerical experiences were tedious during his teens, they gave him a tremendous advantage with financial matters throughout his later career.)

When he was eighteen, he applied for and was accepted by the London Scottish Regionals, rather the *crème de la crème* of the British territorials. (His mother being Scottish, he had the requisite amount of blood in him; indeed, it had been she who first suggested he apply.) It was a kilted world of army drills, rifle practice, parades, weekend marches, and summer camps; new people, new responsibilities, and some invigorating outdoor life. As Marjory said, it made a welcome change from all those women at home, and it also made his office seem less cramping during weekdays.

Ronald's life continued on with an active and varied mixture of accounting, amateur theatricals, and soldiering over the following four years, during which time he paid for his keep at home. Every spare moment and before going to sleep each night, he read. He read everything he could lay his hands on; the lack of a university could not hamper him in that respect. If anything, he overcompensated. He knew he would not stay with the British Steamship Company all his life, much as they might appreciate it.

In the meantime, he was happy and rather proud to be contributing to the family finances in Ealing. Obviously Marjory would not want as big a house when she was on her own, but until the children went their own ways, it provided a source of security and stability for them all. She and Charles had been married for nearly twenty-seven years, and without him she felt lonely and old. The children's presence was a tonic to her and provided the happiest moments of her day. It was a bright, sunny house, surrounded by a garden which she enjoyed. The vegetables were always as fresh as the bowl of roses on the dining room table, and the rooms were as sweet-scented as they were comfortable.

Then came the summer of 1914: Germany and Russia declared war on each other. France quickly entered the conflict, and the "serious national emergency" for which the volunteers and territorials had been waiting for fifty-five years came at last. On the fourth of August, Britain was at war with Germany.

On the fifth, Ronnie went to the London Scottish headquarters in Buckingham Gate, where he was told that if 75 percent of any battalion volunteered, they would go as a unit and not be asked to serve in any other. The men were asked individually by the officers for their decision. They were a proud, eager young group with no preconceived ideas of war, and the necessary numbers were quickly obtained. The battalion, including Private Colman, would serve abroad.

The serious national emergency was treated with light-heartedness. The British were being informed daily that the vast French armies were winning consecutive victories, the Russians were about to crush Berlin, the Germans were already bankrupt with appalling losses to their men and were terrified by the sight of a British bayonet. To the young Britons, being able to go out and defend their country was rather a first-class thing, and of course the war would be over within six months. It was all exciting and a bit of a lark.

Ronnie left the British Steamship Company with a great deal of handshaking and backslapping from his elders, hugged his tearful but proud mother and sisters good-bye, and with toothbrush, shaving equipment, and books, moved into Buckingham Gate with the rest of his company. There, in a broom cupboard, Ronnie discovered Private Seton, a tall young man a couple of years his junior with much the same family background. In their secluded if claustrophobic niche, they exchanged views on the exciting business of war and finally managed some somewhat dusty sleep away from the snores of the company.

Rifles and uniforms were issued the following day, and the men eventually left for Watford and what was supposed to be a six-month training program. They were given elementary exercises and drills. Rifle practice and instructions in the art of command in the field were planned for later in the program.

As it happened, the battalion was ordered abroad at the end of the first month, untrained except for what they remembered from their peacetime operations. Seton and Ronnie, on board the old coal and cattle ship *Winifredia* at Southampton, cheerfully waved good-bye to their families amid the crowd on the dock. The London Scottish were the first territorials to serve with the Regular Army, and all eyes were going to be on their efforts and endurance. It was a great occasion for the men: fifty-five years after the formation of the L.S., the 750 were marching to war as a unit for the first time.

The *Winifredia* sailed at dark, and as she steamed through Southampton water and Spithead, searchlight after searchlight picked her up, ship after ship saluted her with a long blast on the steam whistle. The last greeting came from a headland of the Isle of Wight, flickering "Good luck" in Morse code. Seton and Colman, their exhilaration turned to exhaustion after the morning's 3 A.M. reveille, joined the others in the sleeping quarters, which consisted of uncleaned cattle stalls in the ship's hold.

The next morning they marched through Le Havre with the pipers playing *"La Marseillaise"* and their hodden gray kilts eliciting broad smiles from the French. It was a relief to be out in the fresh air again, and their ninety-pound packs were made lighter by the cheers of greeting and enthusiasm from the gathered crowds. They washed themselves in the horse troughs that evening, and on their first night in France they slept between the railway lines in the station sheds with a waterproof sheet underneath and two blankets and a greatcoat around them.

Ronnie assumed, along with many of the others, that the landing would quickly be followed by a move to the front, but he soon discovered there were other aspects of war besides actual fighting. The eight companies disbanded to carry out various assignments in the north of France; Ronnie and Seton's company was ordered to Villeneuve-Saint-Georges, about five miles north of Paris.

The billets at Villeneuve did have some beds, but they were very hard and already occupied by large numbers of lice and rats. The two men decided that the barns and hay were slightly cleaner and certainly softer, and there they made their bunks along with some of the other soldiers.

The daily routine included several jobs. They loaded and stored shells on the lines of communication, each shell weighing one hundred and fifty pounds. They put up encampments and dug blisteringly endless latrines. They were stretcher-bearers for the wounded who arrived from the front by the truckload. Most of the casualties had been totally unable to tend themselves. Gangrene and tetanus were rampant, and the wounded were treated as soon as possible. Load after load of dying and disabled men arrived from Ypres, needing the assistance of the young territorials. On several occasions Ronnie and Seton discovered each other around a corner of the billets, overwhelmed and shaking with uncontrollable tears. It was during these duties that they began to realize exactly what they were in for.

They were ordered to shave every day, which they did rather hazardously, using the water in the trough as a mirror, often reheating the same water day after day. Their only means of bathing was by using a little tin can or by hoisting a bucket of water with holes in the bottom up a tree. They took short walks whenever possible (never too far from camp in case of infiltrators) in search of the occasional puddle in which to wash.

Their clothes were soon lice-ridden, and with no others to change into, they religiously ran down the pleats of their kilts every morning with a burning cigarette end. Each man had one change of socks which he washed whenever clean water and dry weather coincided. They had been issued thick boots, the leather of which firmly refused to give. By the middle of October the weather had turned winter-cold, and Ronnie followed the others' example of smarming axle-grease on his socks before putting the boots on, both to make them bearable and to prevent frostbite.

The two friends shared everything from books and pay

to food. With bully beef and tinned butter coming out their ears, they resorted to stealing eggs from the nearby farms. On these sorties Seton carried a small bag of coke and Ronnie a bag of sticks for the fire, a pannikin in which to fry their booty hanging from his belt.

At night they played twenty-one, and later Ronnie would try to concentrate on reading the books he had brought with him from England. But neither Shaw nor Galsworthy offered respite from the chill, lice-ridden nights, from the smell of bodies in dirty clothes, from growling stomachs, strained muscles, and the dawning comprehension of war.

At the end of October, still having had no target practice, the companies finally mobilized at Saint-Omer. There, thirty-four London buses and their drivers, which only a few weeks earlier had been taking fares from these same citizens, now stood waiting to take them to the front line. It was a night drive along slippery cobblestone roads with the eastern sky bright with battle. Ronnie and Seton huddled on the crowded top deck with only their groundsheets between them and the fierce, untiring rain. By the time they arrived at Ypres nine hours later, their sodden boots had shrunk and the water had penetrated their greatcoats and kilts. They had little sleep that night in the old Cloth Hall with the roar of battle only a few miles away and with the knowledge that they would at last be part of it the following day.

Ronnie, forever prone to colds and chills, was always being told by Seton to keep his sneezes at a safe distance, but on this night of waiting they shivered together, their greatcoats damply over them, and talked. They talked about Ronnie's amateur theatricals and Seton's interest in sports, about their families, about England and their holidays, and how Ronnie liked Broadstairs and Bournemouth, and how each of them was determined to make some money after the war. They talked of dying and of never seeing their homes again, and then put it to one side in the anxiety to get to the front and have the fighting over with. After next to no sleep, the reveille sounded for 6 A.M. breakfast, and Ronnie awoke stiff and coughing to find that a rat had eaten a large hole in his greatcoat. After parade they started the march toward the front line. The mud-thick roads were filled with bundled villagers, carts piled high with belongings, children, animals, and in between straggled the endless wounded soldiers. The noise of gunfire and explosions was very loud now.

"I don't like this," admitted Ronnie under his breath to his companion.

"Neither do I, old chap, but we've got to put up with it. If there is a bullet with our names on it, we shall get it," replied the young Seton matter-of-factly.

Their feet were numbed by the well-shrunken boots, and the pressing weight of their packs only made matters worse. The greatcoats were slightly less damp, but it was the edges of their woolen kilts that were the most torturous. Drying out as the men marched, they scratched against the knees like sandpaper, making them raw. It made Ronnie forget his cold.

It is a myth that Ronnie was gassed in the war. The Germans did not use gas until later. However, he and his fellow soldiers had quite enough else to cope with on that Halloween night. As they dug themselves into the mud with their little field shovels, tripping over the beetroots and cursing, they soon appreciated the fact that not only did the enemy have stronger arms, but he outnumbered them about five to one.

Soon the shellfire, full moon, and blaze of burning Messines made every detail of the fields stand out. The London Scottish started their overdue target practice. It wasn't long before their new rifles became burning hot and began jamming. The magazines were useless; the territorials were obliged to pocket their bullets and deal with the enemy on-slaught by reloading after every shot. Behind their lines, the German band struck up *"Deutschland über Alles,"* and in the glare of the flaming windmill and farmhouse that were in the center of the field, the Germans poured toward them in waves, firing from the hip. Ronnie was spaced three yards from Seton, and their thin line advanced, firing from the shoulder. At least the Germans made easy targets by their block tactics and sheer numbers. As they closed in, it became every man for himself, and it was chaos. All Ronnie could think of was that he could not afford to make a mistake, and somehow, through the nearly overwhelming attacks of the night, they survived, and at dawn found themselves in iso-lation, for the other companies had withdrawn. So they fought their way back to the northwest, and it was then that Ronnie was hit. When one did notice a soldier missing, there was no going back, no turning around to ask if he needed help. Each man had to keep going. It was not until months later, upon his return to England, that Seton discovered his friend had not in fact been killed during the company's withdrawal.

In the field hospital the surgeons removed all the shrap-nel they could find and put his leg in a cast. Ronnie heard that Seton had survived the battle, and that the territorials' efforts on that Halloween night had enabled England to win a vital victory. The London Scottish were headlines at home. Ronnie wrote Marjory from his hospital bed, passing over the battle itself and telling her he was being sent to Scotland for clerical work as soon as he could get about on his crutches. Throughout the years he rarely referred to these war experiences. Nineteen fourteen had nothing to do with the rest of his life, and yet everything to do with it, because nobody returned home quite the same.

He had been away from England for only two months. It did not seem possible that he was still only twenty-three years old. He never felt that young again. He was filled with incredulity at being alive and with a sad bitterness given him by the reality of war.

"I loathe war. I'm inclined to be bitter about the politics of munitions and real estate which are the reasons for war. It certainly taught me to value the quiet life and strengthened my conviction that to keep as far out of the range of vision as possible is to be as safe as possible. I am not one of those veterans who look back on the war with the happy comrade feeling. There may have been gay times behind the lines— I'm sure there were—but I can't remember them." *

The leg did not heal properly and it was physically impossible for him to reenlist. Finally, in May, 1915, the medical board discharged him altogether. Decorated and limping, he returned from Scotland to the welcoming arms of home to think about a civilian job and "to get on with the business of living while the seventeen-year-old boys carried on the business of dying." *

The British Steamship Company would have happily given him back his job, but he felt that would be returning to a part of his life that was finished. In fact, he was far from deciding what career to pursue. His brief education had left him unqualified to follow up his engineering ideas. Writing had always intrigued him, but he felt neither gifted nor informed enough at this stage to attempt it professionally. The agony of war had given him a leaning toward the medical profession; however, the study of medicine was financially impossible. It was during this indecision of the summer of 1915 that the family had a visit from an uncle of Ronnie's who was with the Foreign Office in the Orient. Interested by the new horizons this gentleman brought with him to Ealing, Ronnie asked whether an appointment could be arranged

* *Photoplay,* February, 1939.

for him in the consulate. The uncle, anxious to help, was enthusiastic and promised to propose Ronnie's name.

And then Ronnie collided with the theater. Friends of his who were also friends of Lena Ashwell informed him of a sketch she was putting together at the London Coliseum and that she was looking for a "young, darkish man" for a small role. Remembering his early work with the Bancroft Society, they suggested he see her. At that time there was a sad lack of young men—either darkish or fair—in London, and Ronnie thought he might stand a chance in the auditions. He was right. The sketch was *The Maharanee of Arakan* by Tagore, and he played a herald to the princess, with absolutely nothing to say. He came on in black face, waved a flag, and tooted a trumpet.

Lena Ashwell considered him an attractive young man with a certain mature dignity about him despite his youth, shyness, and limp. They became friends, and it was she who introduced him to Gladys Cooper, who in turn needed a young man for a bit part in her new play, *The Misleading Lady*. Ronnie was only twenty-five at the time, with more war than theatrical experience behind him. He had to walk down a staircase and managed to produce the most awful racket. Every night in the theater she would say to herself, or to anyone listening, "Dear, dear, here's that handsome young man. *Why* is he so clumsy?" Indeed, at this early period there seemed no reason to assume he was ever destined for theatrical fame.

Despite his predilection for the theater, Ronnie still did not think of himself as an actor, nor had he decided on acting as his permanent career. His mother, whose opinion he respected, did not press the matter, but he was nonetheless aware that she rather wanted him to work with his uncle. He decided on indecision. Then one evening word came that his uncle had obtained the promise of a position in an

Oriental consulate. "Sitting at home, I held in one hand an encouraging review of *The Misleading Lady* and my uncle's note in the other. I knew that I had to decide then. I remember that a mere drop of the hand, a reflex action, decided it for me. Automatically, I dropped the note on my desk and went on reading the review. My choice was made." *

A strange and somewhat fatalistic beginning to a career, but there were sound reasons—however subconscious—behind that reflex action of his hand. The stage offered as wide and new a horizon as the Orient. And he wanted new horizons after his recent experiences in the war, all of which still churned through his mind each night. Also, the theater was a morale-booster to the war-weary public and an avenue through which he could reach an extensive number of his countrymen, benefiting them more than he could from the confines of a consulate. And he wanted to be of further active use to the war effort.

He was also aware that the theater was good for him. His family claimed it was the only thing that took him from his natural state of quiet into one of noisy exuberance. It did forcibly remove the barriers of shyness he usually felt with people and loosen him into easier communication. He had always wanted a far-reaching career, one in which he could excel and expand himself, and which would make him enough money to be comfortable. The theater slipped into all these categories, and so he found himself dropping the consulate and picking up the stage. (It wasn't until years later that he discovered he had theatrical antecedents dating from the eighteenth century. The two George Colmans, father and son, between them had contributed enormously to an entire century of British theater both as theater man-

* *Photoplay*, February, 1939.

agers and prolific dramatists—the father was born in 1732 and the son died in 1836.)

It was as though fate had been spying over his shoulder waiting for that decision, for shortly afterward he found himself in an important play, one in which he certainly reached a large number of people and indeed made a small name for himself.

Damaged Goods, translated from the French play by de Brieux, was for those days a brave undertaking, being the first time syphilis was discussed on the stage. Ronnie played the patient, a role that many experienced actors thought might ruin them professionally. Ronnie grabbed it as a keen young actor grabs anything to enlarge his scope and pay his rent. The nurse in the London production remembered it well:

Edith Lester Jones: "Damaged Goods was a remarkable play. It caused a furore. We played to packed, crammed houses, three matinees a week after all the controversial publicity. It started in March 1917 and ran to October. It would have gone on for much longer but for the zeppelin raids which stopped the audiences from coming. Fisher White was a very well known man, a splendid actor who came into his own playing the part of the doctor. He had a beautiful speaking voice, beautiful elocution, and he got tremendous acclaim through playing that part. Ronald replaced another actor who had first had the role of the patient. He had been totally unsuited to the part—I vividly recall his very wet handshake in the scene we had together—and we were all very glad when he was replaced by Ronald, whose whole way of playing the patient was different from the original chap. [London's largest selling theatrical newspaper, *The Stage,* said on June 7, 1917: "Ronald Colman very skillfully judges the limits and necessities of the young husband and uses them

with most commendable style and feeling."] The criticisms
that the play received were pretty good, but because of its
controversial contents the entire company was ignored at the
Theatrical Garden Party that year, which was usually represented by virtually every theatre in London!

"Fagan, the director [who also ended up in Hollywood],
was a very easygoing man, and when the raids started, he
told us to come to the theater an hour or so before the start
of the play, but one got careless about this. One night, my
family was in town and we'd been having dinner at the
Regent Palace Hotel down in the basement. When I finally
came upstairs to leave rather belatedly for the theater, there
was a terrific raid on and everyone told me not to go out in
it. But I was determined. It's quite seven or eight minutes
to go from the Regent Palace to the St. Martin's. Shaftesbury
Avenue was completely deserted. There was the sound of
guns and planes and there were bullets coming down all over
the place. I saw one deserted taxi and two people running
for shelter. I started up Shaftesbury Avenue, and there wasn't
one other soul, and I just couldn't go on! That was the only
night my understudy went on for me, and afterwards I was
always at the theater well before the curtain went up.

"There was a glass roof over the St. Martin's, and it was
not pleasant during these raids. We could hear our planes
fighting them off, and every time a gun or a bomb went off,
it sounded right on top of us. I remember when I finally got
to the theater that night, Ronnie was saying to Fisher White
that he thought it was safer being in a dugout at the Front!"

It was the first lighthearted reference he had made to
the war; his happiness with the play must have prompted it.
Its triumph and his own success went joyously to his head,
and his salary took him off to Savile Row for a "proper"
suit of wool serge. He wore it for the studio photograph he
had taken shortly afterward, a serious business. In profile,

unsmiling, fastidiously posed against the dark curtain, he looked a rather solemn member of the profession to which he was dedicated.

"The first success goes to your head terribly. That's why the second goes only to your pocketbook. You realize how ephemeral and meaningless other success is."

2

The Joy-Ride Lady

Shortly before the raids finished the play, George Dewhurst, one of the pioneers of British cinema, came to see it and later made Ronnie an offer. Ronnie had never considered the cinema as a possible means of earning his livelihood. He thought of himself as a stage actor. In any case British films were having a tough time. The cinema in England was dominated by American films (as it was to be for the decade following the war). Theater screens were blockbooked for months in advance, offering little chance for Britain's relatively sad contributions to shine through.

Common sense prevailed, however, and Ronnie asked Dewhurst how much money he was paying. It was, for the leading part, a pound a day, excluding Sundays.

"That was my foretaste of Hollywood's opulence. A pound a day . . . the man was Midas! But the film was never released. If it had been, and I had been able to see myself as others would have seen me, I'm sure I would have dashed back to my three-legged stool at the British Steamship Company in a jiffy." *

This first cinematic effort of Ronnie's was shot in a room

* *Photoplay*, February, 1939.

of an old house rigged up as a studio. Ronnie was part of the crew as well as the star, and it was altogether a pioneering effort he found difficult to take seriously.

In the beginning of the following year Ronnie took on the first of several Jewish roles. *The Little Brother* was an American play in its first production. He conquered the intonations as well as the part of George Lubin and received a "fresh and earnest" acclaim from *The Stage*. His check-ins at Bramlin's Theatrical Agency (the nerve center for all London actors) in Piccadilly were a great deal more heartening now, not only because there were fewer of them, but because each job gave him a little more confidence in himself and in his choice of profession.

Summer brought him back to the St. Martin's, this time in a spy thriller, *The Live Wire,* in which he was understudy to the lead, Donald Calthrop. From there he went directly into another American play, *The Bubble,* and his second Jewish role. This time it was a comedy, touring in the north, and he played David Goldsmith, a reporter on a financial paper. He was "convincingly and suitably rough." * Marjory hadn't been very convinced when he read her bits of the script. Although she often found it difficult to take these plays seriously, the main thing to her was that her son was happy in his theatrical involvement.

The Live Wire was to go on tour in the winter, with Ronnie taking over from Calthrop. Before refilling his lungs with the thick northern air, he took a brief holiday on the Kentish coast. The brisk November sea breezes of Folkestone were sufficient to clear anyone's lungs. He took pleasant shelter in the bookshops, and it was here an enduring relationship with the works of Robert Louis Stevenson began. "This is the particular crown and triumph of the artist—not to be

* *The Stage,* October 31, 1918.

true merely, but to be loveable; not simply to convince but to enchant." *

Stevenson offered Ronnie a clear articulation of many of his own vague and random thoughts, besides being a springboard for countless more. He discovered his own beliefs upon the pages of these books, and bought himself a pocket Stevenson with which he could conveniently confer when at work or in transit.

He returned with a new determination to live up to his confirmed ideals and took over the lead role in the touring company. He not only "enchanted and convinced" his audiences in Liverpool, but also his leading lady, one Thelma Raye. She responded with a fine performance, and promptly fell head over heels for this earnest, dedicated young man.

The fair-haired Thelma was only a year older than Ronnie, but had started in the business eight years earlier than he. Recognition and dubious acclaim had struck in *The Joy-Ride Lady,* a rather risqué 1914 musical, the title of which proved ironically prophetic of her life-style. Within a couple of years of this personal success, she was touring Australia, where she met a somewhat stagestruck and very wealthy Australian who fell for her seductive sparkle and winning ways. She was flattered by his attentions and even more so by the money behind them. They were married in Sydney in the spring of 1917. However, neither he nor the wealth of his family could compensate for Australia's lack of glamour and sophistication or for the theatrical promise and attention that was unique to London. Within a year, bored with her husband and her life, she returned home.

By the time she had found work once again, first as understudy and then as female lead in *The Live Wire,* she was already separated from her husband. Indeed, she had

* Robert Louis Stevenson, *Memories and Portraits.*

little intention of returning, having left Australia richer for the experience. She was secure in the knowledge of her attractiveness to men and in the belief of her ability to handle them. She felt, and indeed was, a good deal more worldly than Ronnie, and of the two of them considered herself unhesitatingly to be the old pro in the business—whether stage or life.

They were playing the leading roles in a production that had brought them into the private world of a touring company, and in this close focus they found each other very attractive. Without the strong theatrical bond, their affair might never have lasted. But there was a bond that smoothed over many dissimilarities of character. Thelma—impetuous, arbitrary, inclined toward flamboyance—was attracted to her antithesis in Ronnie, finding in him everything she thought she needed in a man. She mistook his gentleness for malleability, and he mistook her worldliness for maturity.

She was as convinced as Ronnie that he would succeed in the theater, and this was an enormous boost to his morale. She was gay, pretty company, something he had not had in abundance during the preceding years. She believed in him, was ready with advice, and was more than eager to listen to him expound his ideas and theories. Though Thelma's contributions lacked his intellect and intelligence, she was certainly an ever attentive audience.

By the time the tour ended and the company returned to London, they had decided to share digs. Neither had a permanent abode (the Ealing house had been sold for some time, and Marjory shared a flat with her elder daughter), and it seemed a cozy idea, as well as being financially viable. The contrast of her previous life of luxury to the more recent realities of provincial touring led Thelma to prefer vicarious rather than direct involvement with the theater. Being part of the glamour rather than the grind was quite satisfying.

They found a corner flat in Victoria and settled in to what was Ronnie's first domestic scene since Ealing. There was no doubt that life was pleasant, coming home to an attractive young woman with whom he could share his achievements and reason out his defeats. The visits to Bramlin's Agency for "Anything today?" and the work at theaters in and out of London as a result of these visits made the journey to Victoria at the end seem even more of a return home.

George Dewhurst came up with another film offer. Bramlin's had "nothing today," and Ronnie accepted the secondary role in *The Toilers* (the story of which came from an Italian song). This entailed some very cold and equally beautiful filming on location in a Cornish fishing village. Ronnie was twenty-eight years old, and this was to him a deviation from his chosen medium, interesting in its newness to him, but more of a vacation than work. He acted "theatrically," which was all he knew, the only capacity he had to offer. And everyone seemed perfectly content. The *Bioscope* (England's first film magazine of consequence) said, "From a pictorial point of view, this interesting English production is as noticeable a film as we have seen in some time." Dewhurst was given credit for the best performance as the "manly, faithful, simple Jack," and Colman (whose character was not very well developed in the scenario): "It's not Ronald Colman's fault that one can feel little interest in Bob." *

It was hardly the most auspicious beginning to a lengthy film career. He was embarrassed at his awkwardness when he saw the finished film. His name went automatically into the files of the London Casting Bureau (where the essentials and characteristics of every actor and would-be actor were listed for the benefit of agents, etc.): "Colman, Ronald.

* *Bioscope,* March 27, 1919.

Height—5 ft. 11. Weight—159. Remarks—does not screen well." (They were wrong on two out of three; he was nearer 5 ft. 10.)

Mutterings about marriage were creeping into Thelma's conversations. She was enjoying her new life, feeling rather the power behind the throne, or at least the throne-to-be. She would rush to see whatever new production Ronnie was in and offer endless advice, little of which he found useful, although he did not wish to hurt her feelings, professional or any other, by telling her so. When they had the time and money, they would go to the theater and cinema together. Ronnie was an enormous admirer of Chaplin and Fairbanks, none of whose films he missed. He was fascinated by their masterly control of movement, which he studied more and more closely. Unlike anyone else he had seen in the business, their control, precision, and grace were total. He started putting serious thought into his own. It was not difficult to see what a valuable asset movement could be to an actor—not simply to convince but to enchant. . . . He was learning.

Ronnie had no savings. The war had ended, leaving an exhausted, deflated country. His profession was as precarious as the atmosphere of his country. He strongly felt it was not the time for marriage; indeed, he did not know whether Thelma was the woman to marry. She had an irrational temper when she did not have her own way, and marriage was more and more obviously the way she had in mind, although she was still legally married to her Australian. When the subject arose, Ronnie talked of their financial insecurity. They had enough to live on, but that was all.

Marjory did not approve of Thelma leaving her husband or of Ronnie living with a married woman, but she never brought up the subject when he came to visit her. She knew he would discuss it with her if he needed to and long since believed him old enough to make his own mistakes—and cope with them.

In spring came his first separation from Thelma. Claiming she was fed up with his indecision and with the frustration of living with the man she loved who had no firm intention of marrying her, Thelma accepted an invitation from friends in Paris. Ronnie, rather depressed, soon left London to go on tour in a little play. Edmund Gwenn was the star and Ronnie played the "juve" lead.

He made friends with the young lady playing opposite him, and together they visited a well-known fortune-teller while the company was in Harrogate. The woman's explicit message for Ronnie was that he must not stay in England but go across the sea to America, that his fortune lay there. It was enough to make anyone laugh.

He returned home. After several weeks of "Nothing today," he gladly accepted another film offer. Work in the theater was scarce. English film pioneer Walter West had returned from his service with the RAC to take up work again with his studios in Walthamstow. There was nothing special about *A Daughter of Eve* except the money, which was quite definitely comforting.

Thelma returned from Paris where, disgruntled and indignant, she had made no secret of living with the man she loved. As her friends were mutual friends of her husband, the news did not take overlong to reach his ears in Australia.

The next film man to approach Ronnie was Cecil Hepworth, another of the brave English pioneers.

"Are you good in pictures?"
"Great!"
"How many have you done?"
"Two."
"What salary do you expect?"
"Thirty pounds a week."
"I'll give you six."
"Done!" *

* *Film Pictorial Annual,* 1935.

RONALD COLMAN

Hepworth, with the knowledge of hindsight, wrote in his autobiography: "His was an unknown name, and I, knowing nothing of his ability, cast him for a part of no great importance. There was, consequently, nothing very distinguished in his acting, for the part did not give him much opportunity. I also noted that he appeared to have some slight awkwardness which prevented him from walking really naturally in the film. It may have been merely temporary or he must have overcome it, for I have not noticed it in any of his films since." *

This was the shrapnel in his knee; his leg was still quite stiff. Despite this and the fact that he knew he was no great shakes on film, Ronnie made two more for West and one for Hepworth. There were not many young men around in postwar England, let alone attractive young men with professional experience in theater and film. These wartime pioneers took the best they could get, but there was not a great variety of choice.

By December Thelma's husband had petitioned for divorce, naming Ronnie as corespondent. This reinforced her barrage. She was now cut off financially. Ronnie was the reason. It would be his duty as a gentleman to marry her as soon as the divorce came through.

Theater work was suffering badly in the postwar economic slump. Ronnie had not worked for nearly a year with the exception of the five films that had fed them and paid the rent. He had a small name for himself in this medium, but there was no chance of making a fortune out of it at this particular time. Anyway, it was not his profession. He felt no love or dedication in that direction.

Finally, in the spring of 1920 came *The Great Day*, the first Drury Lane drama to go on tour since before the war. By the time he accepted the touring lead, he had made up his mind to save his money for the steamship fare to New York.

* *Came the Dawn* (London, Phoenix House, 1951).

There must be better theatrical opportunities in that golden land. It couldn't fail but offer more hope than England. After a couple of weeks, he left the tour in order to accept another film part, knowing that the salary would make up the balance needed.

Ronnie's sister Edith had married in May. Eric, a lieutenant in the RAC, had married during the war, at the age of twenty-eight. Ronnie had privately thought it an inopportune moment, engulfed as the country was with casualties and griefs, but he rarely had thoughts or interests in common with his brother. Their characters branched away from each other as did their lives. Freda, the youngest of the family, had been married for six years. In June Thelma's divorce came through. Ronnie had told her of his plan. Realizing they did not have sufficient funds to cover both their fares, she became adamant: He must marry her before he left. He had been the cause of her husband divorcing her. He was leaving the country and for all she knew would never return. She loved him. Surely he could not abandon her to a very uncertain fate; she had not worked because of him, and England in 1920 was difficult enough for those in the profession who had a current name, let alone those who had been off the boards for years. . . .

They were married in the Registry Office in Hanover Square on the eighteenth of September, 1920. Ronnie was twenty-nine. He left for New York the following month with a one-way second-class ticket, a dress suit, several letters of introduction, a small amount of money, and a fair amount of confidence. Thelma would join him as soon as it was financially feasible. They would brave the new horizons together.

He had once been told, but had forgotten, that America was where his proverbial fortune lay.

3 ❦
New York Sans Moustache

Having friends and being poor in New York is difficult; being a stranger and poor is a harsh combination. The city has a tough ferocity about it at the best of times, although its glamour can be blinding.

It seemed little time after recovering from the Manhattan skyline that Ronnie was down to small change. He was amazed that the same city that exuded wealth by the mere mention of its name could in fact be as slumped financially as London. His letters of introduction brought him no closer to a job than a secretary's office.

He had sufficient money to take a little room in Brooklyn which must have looked like the Ritz at the end of each day. Walking saved fares, and making the rounds continuously was his only hope of a job. Within a week he could step blindfolded around every steaming manhole and knew the park benches in order of comfort. There he collapsed to gather his resources and to pull up his socks for the next stretch of pavement and agents.

Autumn, poking icy fingers through the cracks of his unheated room greatly reduced its earlier charm. It was scantily furnished, on the ground floor, with a coatrack near the window. Ronnie innocently left this window open at night until someone looped a hand through and stole his coat from its hook. Unable to afford another, he was obliged to weather a New York winter without one, and he dwelt with growing fondness upon the ever-damp greatcoat that had been deserted in the trenches of Flanders.

He survived this search for theater work on dishwashing jobs and a diet consisting mainly of soup and rice pudding. He knew that by the law of averages he would eventually find a proper job. Even if he had had the fare, he would never have retreated to England, because a retreat is precisely what it would have been. He was filled with an overriding determination to succeed in this country where he was convinced everybody could; surely, with a lot of willpower, effort, and rice pudding, anyone could achieve what he wanted in America!

He was at last rewarded with a couple of walk-ons in a touring play outside New York, and returned after several weeks with seventy-five dollars, to what seemed a much brighter Brooklyn. And then another, rather more prominent walk-on got him through Christmas in Philadelphia. It was in the new George Arliss production, and though it was the smallest role in the play, it was a play destined for Broadway. The Arliss name was one of the best known in the business.

After a successful run in Philadelphia, they opened at the Booth Theater early in the new year, and a long enduring success it proved to be. Not, however, for Ronnie, who was replaced by another actor after not even one week of the bright lights. February was spent fighting depression and cold, back to rice puddings, pavements, and park benches.

He first touched on the American film world when an attractive dress suit was needed for a five-reeler in New York City. He was able to fill the need in the most insignificant part of the film and left feeling pretty insignificant himself.

In spring he landed a slightly more noticeable role in a new play that took him to Washington. He was deeply impressed by what he saw of the eastern United States between rehearsals and performances, and equally struck by the warmth and gregariousness of the people themselves. Being an Englishman, he was instantly regarded with enormous interest, and although he was a foreigner, he quickly became a foreigner at home.

The summer came, hot and hideous, heralding the worst theatrical season ever. One hundred eighty-four plays were presented on Broadway, eighty-eight of which were complete failures. The sum of one and a half million dollars was lost. Luckily for Ronnie, the role of butler in a mystery comedy swept him into orbit once again and unbelievably landed him on Broadway still firmly installed in the role. It was his first opportunity to be noticed where it counted. *Theater* magazine said he made much of a small part, and the doyen of the New York critics, Alexander Woollcott of *The New York Times,* admitted that "Ronald Colman makes a little part tell." *

Ronnie kept Thelma up to date on the proceedings, adding that although the pay was better than in London, it didn't seem to go much further. There was a good deal of steady work necessary before he could send her the fare and indeed afford for them both to live in New York. In fact, he really had to do better than an English butler before he could live as well as one.

He left the company after a couple of months, grabbing the chance to join Broadway star Fay Bainter's tour of her smash hit of several years, *East Is West.* This timely role was one up from a butler and the experience altogether a good one. While plays expired nightly on Broadway, *East Is West* played the big cities east to west and back again, defying failure of any sort. America swirled outside the train win-

* *The New York Times,* August 16, 1921.

dows, dwarfing the imagination, as Ronnie took in the flat fields of the Middle West, the Rockies, and the deserts of Arizona and New Mexico. He leaned forward in his seat automatically when the engine groaned over the Great Divide, and then finally, like some ultimate reward, came the Pacific. San Francisco roller-coastered them to the theater on cable cars through the fall fogs, occasionally allowing glimpses of the Golden Gate, and by then the U.S.A. had worked its magic on one English traveler. He was head over heels in love.

When the company chugged into downtown Los Angeles, his general state of intoxication led him on the first available morning to the doors of filmland. He had been in one American film in New York, which, being of no particular consequence, affected him little more than had its English counterparts. But Hollywood . . . if ever he were to make enough money to allow financial security, then this would be the place. It was also the magical place that had produced Chaplin and Fairbanks.

"I haunted the Hollywood studios; I had no introductions. . . . I was just on the outside. I was vastly impressed by what I saw and heard there: the range of buildings, the ceaseless commotion of little knots of people excitedly planning outdoor scenes, whole cinema villages perched on the hillsides and populated only when the camera was there. . . . That first sight of Hollywood gave me ambition. I inquired of a passerby about agents, and sought one out. He was at his desk, leaning back, reading a film magazine and steadily thickening the air with cigar smoke. I told him what I had done and I remained standing there, fumbling with my hat. He did not look up from his magazine. 'Do you think,' I ventured again, 'there might be a chance for me in Hollywood?' 'I wonder,' said he. Just that, nothing more, and I walked out." *

* *Film Pictorial Annual*, 1935.

The intoxication quavered and rolled back into the reality of the matinee. The place had made him forget that he belonged to the theater. By the time he returned to New York, it was spring.

The money he had accrued in the last months was sufficient for Thelma's fare. She arrived, dazed, in New York. The furnished room had been left for a small flat, which Ronnie had prepared with some last-minute daffodils, a supply of wire hangers from Woolworth's, and a bottle of Moët & Chandon.

After the initial excitement of their reunion and enthusiastic interchange of news, Ronnie returned to his search for work, inevitably leaving Thelma alone most of the time. Never as adaptable to new situations as her husband, she felt very much a fish out of water. She was nervous of newness, and the previous theatrical advice with which she had regaled him now lacked its early validity. When the steaming August heat enveloped them, he left for rehearsals on his biggest venture yet, the role of Henry Anderson in A. H. Woods's new production of W. Somerset Maugham's *East of Suez*. The cast included Basil Rathbone, Lucille Laverne, and Florence Eldridge. Woods's name meant box-office money, and the play was bound to be a Broadway hit. The reviews were good in Atlantic City; however, by the time the play opened in New York on September 21, tumultuous changes of cast had taken place. Ronnie was one of the casualties. Woods liked neither him nor his performance and fired him. The play was a smash, as they had all predicted, and ran for months on Broadway.

Before he had time to tear every hair from his head, he was rescued by the stage's golden girl, Ruth Chatterton, whom he had briefly met through Fay Bainter. She too was making changes in the cast of her own adaptation of *La Tendresse* (from the French play by Bataille). She needed a new man to play "the other man," and having seen Ronnie in

East Is West, thought he was physically suited and asked him to test for the part. He lived up to their hopes, so she and her co-star, Henry Miller, signed him and generally delivered him from despair. The combination of their names, the play itself, and his significant role was a unique and fortunate form of consolation prize.

He went into instant rehearsal, returning to the familiar ground of Atlantic City for his opening night. The advance notices were good, and by the time they opened at the Empire in New York City on September 25, everyone knew they had a hit. "One fine, direct and authentic performance is given by an actor named Ronald Colman," stated Woollcott.* Ronnie settled confidently into his role and prepared himself and Thelma for the tour that was due to be launched in Philadelphia one month later.

Ronnie was a very young-looking thirty-one, with no moustache and thick, almost black hair, slicked back to the sides of his head and standing rather high at the top. During the six years since he'd walked loudly and clumsily down the staircase to Gladys Cooper, he had worked hard at improving himself and his performance. The clumsiness had gone, as had the uncomfortable stiffness in his knee. His walk now had a certain jaunty assurance about it. His new overcoat had long since been worn in, Thelma was feeling her way gradually around New York, and he felt for the first time since *Damaged Goods* that his precarious profession was pleasantly so.

Fate, however, had other plans up her sleeve. Shortly after the opening, another unexpected circumstance occurred in the shape of director Henry King, who was looking— rather desperately, as it happened—for a leading man to play opposite Lillian Gish in *The White Sister.* Gish, much impressed with King's *Tol'able David,* had chosen him to direct this, her first independent film. The company was due to

* *The New York Times,* September 26, 1922.

sail in a matter of days for Italy, where the film was to be shot on location.

Henry King: "I had an agent in New York that used to get seats for various shows so that I could see the different players. There were two things on my last night: the first act of *La Tendresse* (to see a new actress) and the last act of a play at the Thirty-ninth Street Theater (to see a possible lead for *The White Sister*).

"My wife and I went to the Empire and saw the first act of *La Tendresse,* which we enjoyed very much. In the foyer at intermission, my wife said, 'You know, I'll be so happy when one day we can see a play all the way through!' We only needed to see the last act of the other play, and as we had the time, we decided to go back in to see the second act of *La Tendresse.*

"The curtain went up, and Ruth Chatterton came on stage with a young man. They played an act that ran about forty minutes, and finally a knock came at the door. She raised the window to let the young man out, and then opened the door to Henry Miller, who was playing her husband, and the curtain went down. My wife said, 'There's the man you want for Giovanni!' The name on the program was Ronald Colman.

"It was a very good scene, and he was very good in it. He made that dialogue his own material. It's when an actor makes you think that he's thought of all those things *himself* that he is good.

"I asked him up to my office the next day, and the first thing he said to me was, 'I do appreciate more than anything in the world someone calling me for an interview, but I'm no good in pictures. I have been told both in London and New York that I don't photograph well, and I've decided that I'm through with them. I'm going to stay in the theater where I know my way, and apparently I don't know my way in pictures.'

"He agreed to making a test, though insisted I was wasting my time. 'I know you won't like it when you see it!' We made the test downtown in James Abbé's studio (he was the stills photographer on *The White Sister*). All I wanted were some close-ups. I talked with him a great deal to get him to relax, because he was very tense. I said, 'I want to know if you can sit and discuss with me some questions I want to ask you, without being conscious there is a camera running over there.' 'Yes, all I have to do is concentrate, I'll do that.' The camera was running all the while.

"Then I stopped the camera and asked him if he minded if I 'took some liberties' with his appearance. His hair was too high, and with his high forehead made his face too long. So I had him comb it right down slick and then started the camera again. He was able to discount it and answered every question quite honestly and naturally, and he told me about his career. This ran about four hundred feet, and then I said, 'I want to do something else.' I took a retouching pencil and painted a moustache on him.

"We put in the balance of the afternoon on his test, until he had to go back to the theater. He said, 'You know, I've enjoyed this work very much. I'm just sorry I know you won't like it!'

"After we had looked at the film the next morning, my partner said, 'If you're pleased, I'm pleased.' We were all leaving in a few days so Ronnie rushed off to talk with Henry Miller about releasing him from the show. He was very nice about it and let him go. He took on the man at the Thirty-ninth Street Theater to replace him—the same man my agent had sent me to look at for the role of Giovanni."

Overnight, Ronnie had swung from his first good Broadway part to an astonishingly good role in a major American film. His mind had only just become attuned to a theatrical career in America, and for a while he could think of *The*

White Sister only as a most fortunate intermission. Thelma was astounded, though more at the thought of meeting Lillian Gish than at what this might mean for her husband's career.

He bid a fond and grateful farewell to Ruth Chatterton (for taking him on) and Henry Miller (for letting him go) and left the company of *La Tendresse* at the end of the same week. Passports and transportation were arranged, bags packed, and he and Thelma sailed forty-eight hours later on the S.S. *Providence* for Naples.

Among the twenty-four passengers who made up the company of *The White Sister* were director Henry King, star Lillian Gish, and the other principals, both distinguished older actors, Charles Lane and Barney Sherry. A small part of the upper deck was used for rehearsals. Ronnie, more knowledgeable about stage acting than screen, had much technique to learn and was coached throughout the course of the voyage by both director and star.

Providentially, there was as yet not much air travel, for by the time they had arrived in Naples, he had benefited from several days of film rehearsals and had grown a moustache along the vanished lines of Henry King's pencil.

4 ∾
The New Italian Actor

The White Sister was an important production in every respect. It was Ronnie's first major film role, one of the earliest American films to be shot in Italy, and the first modern religious story ever to be filmed. It was the first film that Lillian Gish, the Duse of the screen, made after leaving D. W. Griffith, as well as her first independent film. It was also the first time that Ronnie found himself in the hands of a professionally skilled film director who had the production money to back up his talents. King (and Gish) had recognized Colman's potential on stage and not only tapped it for the role of Giovanni, but carefully corrected his mistakes and taught him a good deal of screen technique.

Taken from the controversial book by Marion Crawford, *The White Sister* is the story of an Italian girl (Gish) who is separated from her lover (Colman) when he goes into the army. Believing him to have been killed in Africa, she becomes a sister in a convent and finally, despairing of his return, decides to take the final vows. (This was the first time that a reenactment of the marriage-to-the-church ceremony was ever filmed.) Meanwhile the lover, who had been held prisoner in Africa, escapes and returns to reclaim her hand, but too late . . .

Although younger than Ronnie, Lillian was a full-fledged professional in the film business and had already directed a film herself.

Lillian Gish: "I had to help him because he didn't know about films; he was new. *The White Sister* had been my choice for a film and I really worked on it. I looked at Ronnie from a director's point of view. I wanted him to take the film and make the love story work. The better the man I played opposite, the better my story and the more true the love story."

They did, in fact, run into some trouble in one particular dramatic scene. The distraught lover, having vainly tried to persuade the nun to abandon the church and marry him, has a go at physically carrying her off. At eight that night they were no nearer reaching the scene's climax or getting the Italian flavor than they had been that morning. Fortunately, Henry King was inspired. He took Ronnie out to dinner and gave him a few drinks, then came back to face the cameras once again.

Lillian: "It worked! Ronnie was so relaxed he could just walk straight. We did the scene over several times, and finally he was yelling and gesticulating as the Italians always do—however well born—when they are in a temper. (Giovanni is of noble birth.) We got the scene that is in the picture around two in the morning. The next day, he was so contrite! He kept asking people what he had said. He'd only gone so far as to say 'Damn,' but I think he was teased for some time by the men in the company. Even if he had been unconscious, though, he couldn't have ceased being a gentleman."

The magnificent interiors for the film were built in the studio on the outskirts of Rome, and the Villa d'Este was used for the convent. Roy Overbaugh's photography made the best of both—the film is visually stunning and breathes an Italian aura throughout. Even in James Abbé's stills, the soft cypress air, sunlit cobblestones, and frescoed halls glow unmistakably of Italy.

It was Ronnie's first trip to a European country where he had the chance to look around him and absorb everything peacefully. He rejoiced in the encompassing warmth of the Mediterranean. He loved the easy atmosphere after New York, the grace of the Italian buildings, the lilt of the language, and the garlic in the spaghetti. It wasn't where his father's silks had come from, but the smell and taste of the place were as fascinatingly foreign to him as Charles's office had been.

The company had been kind and helpful. The professionalism with which they tackled their work was a stimulus, and the actual mechanics of filming kept him busy with questions. The Italian crew, capable and friendly, had soon become accustomed to this seemingly mad bunch of Americans who never stopped working day or night, and they were as impressed as Ronnie when they saw the results.

Thelma was overwhelmed by the way in which matters had progressed. Due to none of her own efforts, her little-known husband was suddenly upon a path that led far beyond her wildest West End dreams. She was wildly jealous of what he was doing, the ease with which he was doing it, and the fact that she literally and figuratively played no part in the proceedings. She was not at ease amid these dedicated young American filmmakers, so serious and energetic about their work. She felt as foreign to them as she did to the Italians. Ronnie, with an ear for languages, was already picking up an understanding of Italian, and was well ahead of her in his familiarity with American expressions.

As Thelma visualized her importance diminishing, she became domineering. She saw him and the bright future he represented slipping through her fingers, and she overreacted. What started within the privacy of their hotel room now spread to public incidents of humiliation and embarrassment. On one occasion she burst screaming down the hotel corridor, "I've killed him, I've killed him!" Lillian and Henry rushed to the Colmans' room and discovered Ronnie on the floor. Soon after they'd put him on the bed, he came to and mumbled something about falling and hitting his head. They kindly pretended along with him and never established the reason for Thelma's wild actions.

She made herself increasingly unlikable to the company who had taken the reserved young Englishman to their hearts immediately, but who were hardly given the opportunity to feel the same about his wife. Ronnie naturally assumed that any kind of artistic fulfillment, not to mention an increase in their financial well-being, would be equally welcomed by his wife, and he was dismayed to see her turning rather shrewish instead, strangely opposed to success unless she herself were its very center or cause. Whereas he had the intelligence not to have his head swollen or lost over such a fortunate turn in his career, Thelma reacted in just the opposite manner. All her rationality was lost, and her husband, having tried in vain to make her see matters in perspective throughout the weeks in Italy, finally gave up the battle. It was simply not in his nature to quarrel, and she managed to twist every conversation into an argument. During the course of a masquerade party to which the company had been invited, she slapped his face, to the amazement of the assembled guests, and Ronnie simply left the room—and her.

Their marriage had been Ronnie's first total commitment to another person. Its collapse had long-lasting effects upon him. His relationships took more time to become close —whether with men or women. Without intending to, he was heading toward becoming a loner in what was to be a busier and more fulfilled life. Although he did not form any generally derogatory opinions on women, he began thinking of marriage rather as he had previously thought of films— something in which he was not at his best, where he had little confidence in the production, and was unhappy with the results.

Though Thelma and her lawyers were to plague him for many years, the Colmans never lived together again. She returned to England, and the company, aware that he wanted to avoid discussing the matter, brought his attention back to the filming, which continued rather more calmly in Sorrento, Capri, Lago Montagna, Tivoli, and Rome.

The moments during the filming he recalled with the most acute dislike were, surprisingly, unrelated to his wife. They were spent on the back of a camel. A particularly gentle and obedient camel had been selected, and Ronnie (captured during his soldiering) was obliged in one scene to gallop into the "desert" upon it. Muttering "hut hut" and other words of camel language in its ear, he found it perfectly compliant until the scene was finished—no one had told him how to stop a camel going at full tilt, and the beast was tireless. He pulled on the rope until the neck was completely doubled around, the camel looking him squarely in the eye and *still* galloping straight ahead. It was unnerving. They continued nose to nose in fierce determination, and it was several hours before the frantic company welcomed them back, steaming and exhausted, Ronnie swearing he would never approach the untrustworthy beasts again. He mentally started his "camel list"—the actor's nightmares, things that perhaps one day he could afford to avoid.

In the late spring, after six months' work and some solid grounding in Italian as well as filming, Ronnie returned to New York with the company. For a while there were difficulties in finding somebody to distribute the film. Being a modern religious story, it was met with a lot of "We get that free on Sundays, we're not going to pay for it during the week!"

Henry King: "When the president of First National saw it, he said, 'Gish is good, and who is this Italian actor playing the lead, I'm crazy about him!' but he didn't think we would get our money back on it."

Finally, Nick Schenck, then the eastern head of MGM, consented to distribute the film, which in fact made millions for both the Inspiration Company and for MGM. It had cost only $300,000 to make, including transporting the company to and from Italy. Lillian had received $1,000 and Ronnie $450 a week, which is what he had been getting from Henry Miller.

Ronnie answered Thelma's distant demands for money whenever he could. Otherwise he did not respond to her letters, which were predominantly attempts at making him feel guilty and humiliated. There was no going back, no patching up a marriage that had outgrown itself. He was learning to keep more to himself and concentrate on his work—films.

"To be what we are, and to become what we are capable of becoming is the only end of life." Stevenson continued to make a great deal of sense to him.

He was seeing films now in an entirely new light. Watching the edited print of *The White Sister,* he saw himself well photographed in a creditable role and surrounded by excellent actors for the first time. His confidence soared along with his respect for the film industry. He saw its horizons rather than just its limits and realized that here was far greater opportunity for an actor than in the theater, which he had up until then considered home. He was suddenly a film actor, and a competent one.

While Henry King was finishing work on the film, Ronnie visited him to find out whether there was anything in his next production for him. King told him of plans to film George Eliot's novel *Romola* in the fall and that both he and Lillian were keen to give him a part. But as that was some time ahead, he sent Ronnie to the old Biograph Studio where there was another picture in the making. The fact that he'd worked with Gish easily got him a small part in what turned out to be George Arliss's new film, *Twenty Dollars a Week*. He had shaved his moustache upon his return to New York, and this picture, with Ronnie in an insignificant moustache-less role, opened before *The White Sister*. As in most Arliss films, the story and everyone in it were subordinate to the star, and neither critic nor public paid much attention to anyone else.

Then, on the ninth of September, *The White Sister* opened at the Forty-fourth Street Theater, and by the twelfth everybody was paying feverish attention to this new moustached leading man and wanting to know more about him. Surely he must be a new Italian discovery made by Lillian Gish! The film was a hit, and Ronnie became a Hot Property.

Lillian Gish: "It was brought down to twelve reels to go into the Forty-fourth Street Theater, and there were two performances a day, just like a play. It ran for two hours and forty minutes. Later, when Henry had to go to Florence to assemble the costumes and sets for our next production, and I was left to cut the film from twelve reels to nine for general release, I never lost one foot of film with Ronnie in it. I thought he was so wonderful."

After a rave review of Gish's performance, the *Motion Picture Classic* echoed the sentiments of the American critics in their words on Colman: "A newcomer is Ronald Colman who plays the broken-hearted lover, and he gives a performance of quiet force and dignity. He never seems to be acting, which makes his expression all the more natural and genuine." *

Shortly after the film's opening, his role in *Romola* was

* December, 1923.

confirmed and he sailed again for Italy to rejoin Henry King, Lillian Gish, Charlie Lane, cameraman Roy Overbaugh, and art director Robert Haas. Fresh from the theater came William Powell to play the wicked but glamorous Tito, and Lillian's sister, Dorothy, joined the team to play Tessa, the other leading female role. Ronnie (moustache grown again) played the artist who was in love with Lillian—a rather ethereal, thinking man. It was a smaller and less consequential part than its predecessor, rather lost in the enormity of the epic production.

Probably the most important and enduring aspects of the film to Ronnie were that it brought him into contact with Bill Powell, who was to be one of his closest Hollywood friends, and also cemented his friendship with Charlie Lane, who had given him moral support, some worldly advice, and the perspective of humor during the tempestuous ending of his marriage to Thelma.

Bill, a tall, lean moustached American who was a contemporary of Ronnie, shared his sense of humor and to a large degree his shyness with strangers. He had been known in his youth to climb to the top of a tree to escape noisy people, and there on the highest branch, swaying in the breeze, he would gaze into the sky and ponder on the mysteries of life. Throughout later years his instinct remained much the same, and Ronnie's was hardly dissimilar. When on the ground, Bill trained at the American Academy of Dramatic Art in New York and went through the subsequent familiar periods of stage, vaudeville, joblessness, touring companies, living on apricots, wafers, and water before finally being "discovered" with the help of a good Broadway role.

Romola was his most important film to date, and at this point in his career he was best known for his villainous roles. Whether villain or, later, witty husband, the refinement and enormous *joie de vivre* with which he tackled his roles always came across to the audience.

It was during the company's work in Florence that Ronnie received word from Samuel Goldwyn, who had by this time seen *The White Sister* and was very keen to bring this new leading man to Hollywood. Ronnie's first reaction was to stick with his mentor, Henry King, whom he felt had opened a door for him that nobody else had bothered to, and who brought out the best in him on the screen. But King, involved with business problems and unsure of his next film move, urged him to accept the offer. Lane and Powell both spoke of Goldwyn being one of the sharpest young producers in Hollywood and that the offer was an exciting one, not to be missed. Securely armed with the knowledge that he could come across well on the screen, Ronnie took little more time to see this was the right move, and he confirmed his intention to Goldwyn.

Upon completion of his work on *Romola,* he sailed to New York, packed up the remainder of his belongings, and boarded the Chief in Chicago, the congratulations and encouragements of the company still bristling his moustache. He spent the three cross-country days being torn between the landscape and H. G. Wells, breakfasting on cornbread and Grape-Nuts, and savoring his Black Label at six o'clock. With ice clinking in his glass, he mulled over the thought that his imminent arrival was a great deal more auspicious than that of November, 1921.

5 〜

Hollywood and the
Early Goldwyn Years

Ronnie returned to a Hollywood that now recognized and welcomed him. *The White Sister* was his visa into the film world. Agents and producers who had barely raised their cigars at him before were now keenly interested, knowing the public soon would be. The sweet scent of success was in the air around him.

"Into the community that lives and thinks film pictures, I arrived . . . prepared to work very hard to succeed. I liked Hollywood. I like breathing space. I like green things growing around me. There isn't the feeling here of millions of people huddled together." *

Fairbanks, Novarro, and Valentino were swashbuckling across the screens; Gloria Swanson, Pola Negri, and Aileen Pringle were slinking; Keaton, Chaplin, and Lloyd, comic geniuses, were sidesplitting their audiences. The film industry, well recovered from its slump of 1920, the date of Ronnie's first visit, was now "silently" booming. Actors were kept working nonstop, often seven days a week and well into the night, for they had no union protection as yet.

The blues and greens of the Pacific were unpolluted,

* *Film Pictorial Annual*, 1935.

and the golden sands of Santa Monica were being grabbed whenever possible for thousands of dollars a square foot. Along this richest beach in the world stretched the palatial houses of Douglas Fairbanks, Sr., Sam Goldwyn, Jesse Lasky, Louis B. Mayer, and William Randolph Hearst, the biggest of them all. Breakfasts were served on the beach by butlers bearing trays of California's freshest orange juice. Few bothered to swim in the ocean as each house had its own deep swimming pool. The parties were the kind one sees now only in films, and the atmosphere of the colony was easy and joyous. Money was nothing; nobody worried about anything; prosperity was assured forever.

Up from the beach, in the sprawling lush of Beverly Hills, citrus groves grew between the streets and actors could ride to the studio, if they felt so inclined, through bougainvillea-tinted air. Hollywood was happy, irresponsible, and thriving. It may not have invented the Jazz Age, but it certainly knew how to take advantage of it!

The young Englishman was dazzled by the ubiquity of sunny luxury. After the dismal shipping office, the ordeal in France, the theatrical struggles of London and America, his early cinematic failures, and freezing in New York City, California was paradise and it was suddenly all his.

Sam Goldwyn, the man responsible for his entry to this never-never land, had already been in the film business for a decade. He had separated from MGM, the company he had helped to create, in order to form Sam Goldwyn Inc., of which he was complete monarch. As an independent producer competing in the big leagues, he had to make superior pictures or quit, and Sam's intentions were always aimed toward quality rather than quantity. He made fewer pictures than his former companies, but he worked on every detail himself, and the results were very fine. (He was in fact the first producer to establish his own wardrobe department so that he could have control of every costuming detail.) Everyone in his studio was kept constantly on his toes, for Sam was wary of contentment within his business, having seen it ruin some of the great figures in the industry. He was more generous with blame than with praise; as someone who worked for him said, "He hates yes-men, he loves no-men, but he is fond of having no-men answer him in the affirmative." * He was a hard-hitting man with an infallible eye for talent, and he had indomitable energy and stubbornness in making it pay off.

Ronnie had a great deal to learn about the business as well as about Hollywood, and he was determined to live up to the high standards his producer expected of him as a leading man. Knowing next to no one and still being financially insecure, he gratefully accepted Charlie Lane's invitation to share his apartment in Hollywood. Lane, Lillian Gish, Henry King, and Bill Powell were then—and for some time—the only friends who knew that Ronnie was married. Fortunately, no other members of the company lived in Hollywood.

So Hollywood got to know him as an attractive if somewhat remote bachelor. The tumultuous days in Italy, which resulted in his separation from Thelma, had begun a relationship with Lane that deepened over the years in closeness and understanding. Each appreciated the other's privacy and friendship, and in this totally alien atmosphere, friendship was something that Ronnie particularly prized.

Filming soon commenced on Goldwyn's recently purchased property, *Tarnish,* which starred May McAvoy. This was the first of many Goldwyn-Colman films to be adapted by Hollywood's leading scenarist, Frances Marion, and directed by George Fitzmaurice, an Irishman brought up in Paris, where he had worked at his first-loved profession, painting. His ability with lights and shadows glows throughout his films, especially those with exterior sequences.

In those days the writer (in this case Marion) remained

* *Photoplay,* August, 1937.

on the set during the shooting as an aide to the director. Often "Fitz" and Frances remarked upon the quality of their new leading man's voice. It was in great contrast to the typical American voices around him, and they thought what a pity it was that everyone couldn't hear him speaking his lines.

Frances Marion: "His voice gave us the impression of a musician playing a Chopin nocturne while a rival on the second piano was whacking out Chopsticks!"

Tarnish had been a recently successful Broadway play, written by Gilbert Emery. The story revolves around three people: Emmet Carr (Ronnie), "tarnished" because of a past escapade with a manicurist (Marie Prevost); Letitia Tevis (May McAvoy), the girl he loves; her father (Albert Gran, who had played the part on Broadway), a rather loose gentleman who had fallen for the same gold-digging manicurist. "How Letitia adjusts herself to a new philosophy of things in her love for Emmet forms the basis of the drama." *

It was a rather risqué subject even for those days; indeed, it barely slipped by Will Hays (President of the Motion Picture Producers and Distributors of America since 1922 and the industry's self-imposed PR man and censor). Generally speaking, those critics who were familiar with the Broadway production preferred it to the film. All of them, however, praised Goldwyn's new leading man. Sam, happy with Colman's personal success, gave him a long-term contract at $2,000 a week. Ronnie was pleased and relieved that *The White Sister* was not going to be a "one-shot gag" in terms of success, and felt his position becoming secure in his newly adopted home.

Goldwyn chose excellent frameworks and the best female stars for his films. Ronnie's niche—and name—was forming in Hollywood. He suddenly remembered his fortune-teller in

* *Photoplay,* December, 1925.

Harrogate six years earlier, and marveled at the fact that she had not been mad after all.

Romola was released three months later, after a total cost of nearly two million dollars, and it inspired packets of fan mail from Italy to Signor Colman, similar to those he had received after *The White Sister*. "You are quite obviously Italian, so why have you changed your name to Colman? Are you ashamed of your nationality?"

Ronnie was kept working throughout 1925 on six pictures, some of which began to give his Latin fans their first doubts about his ancestry. The first, *Her Night of Romance*, starred one of the famous Talmadge sisters, Constance, in a lively comedy-farce. Ronnie played a rather giddy English nobleman who got tight every night and happily spent borrowed money every day. Posing as a doctor, he falls in love with Talmadge, a millionairess posing as a penniless spinster. It was the first of his scripts by Hans Kraly, Ernst Lubitsch's witty scenarist.

The second was *A Thief in Paradise*, another Fitzmaurice-Marion production with more adventure than wit. Metro's luscious Aileen Pringle starred, and Ronnie had a thrilling underwater sea struggle with the "baddie." The film makes the most of its San Francisco location shooting. *The New York Times* decided it was Ronnie's best performance since *The White Sister*, which was their barometer for judging him for many months. San Francisco had lost none of its attraction to him. He took in the Golden Gate, the giant redwoods, and Fishermen's Wharf with all the gaping wonder of the enthralled tourist. The variety of the Golden State was overwhelming; California seemed to offer everything to everyone.

Thelma, who had come to the States to stay with her brother and sister-in-law in Indiana, soon heard of Ronnie's contract with Goldwyn and his personal success in *A Thief in Paradise*. She whipped out to Hollywood with a lawyer in tow, and appeared unannounced on the set one morning, demanding a sizably increased monthly allowance and half of community property. People on the lot were amazed to find there *was* a Mrs. Colman, let alone one filled with such obvious dislike for Mr. Colman! Any form of public scene, especially one about a private matter, was of the greatest distaste to Ronnie. He was as embarrassed by as he was furious with Thelma. He refused to discuss either their "marriage" or money—that was for their lawyers to debate. Thelma, however, was never one for taking hints. She was ushered off the studio lot, but one evening soon after, when he was at the theater with Lois Wilson and the Conrad Nagels, he discovered her sitting next to him when the lights came on at intermission. He catapulted out of the building, telephoning his friends later on to explain.

Separate maintenance was later agreed upon between their respective lawyers, and Thelma left with a settlement of $25,000 and an allowance of $1,500 a month for ten years, but not before she had managed to squeeze in some interviews with film magazines in the best "He done me wrong" style.

The physical confrontations with her, brief though they had been, were a sharp reminder of the nerve-jangling days in Italy. Ronnie was left shaken and all the more determined to keep her completely away from him. Wariness slipped into diffidence, and he felt a strong need to protect himself from women and indeed "people," especially now that his face was recognized all over Hollywood.

His Supreme Moment, made on loan-out to First National, was another Fitzmaurice-Marion effort. He played a role cherished in real life almost twenty years earlier: an engineer, relegated to the open spaces. In this case the engineer's life was rather more colorful than his might have been if his father had lived and Ronnie had studied at Cambridge. In the film he has an affair with a Broadway stage star (Blanche Sweet) and mines for gold in a South American camp. It was the first film in which Fitzmaurice used color sequences, and again Colman and film were widely praised.

Photoplay magazine started comparing Colman to John Gilbert—"The Rival Nordic Lovers"—"Which is the ideal screen lover? RC the Sphinx or JG the Vesuvius?" * The answering fan mail seemed to be divided equally, each man having his own wealth of adoring females. Ronnie only hoped that Thelma had not read the article and contributed her vivid opinions on the subject.

In The Sporting Venus, on loan-out to Metro, he was again Blanche Sweet's leading man, this time directed by her husband, Marshall Neilan. The film took him briefly back to Scotland for some location shots in kilts, the last time any of his films required him to leave the States. The gallant part of the Colman "image," which was later to develop in strength, first came to light in this story. A medical student (Colman) is in love with a Scottish heiress (Sweet), who is forbidden to marry him and subsequently has an unsuccessful affair with someone else. Gallantry wins as he ultimately saves his unfaithful love from suicide.

His next two films were the most successful that first year in Hollywood. The first was a comedy, Her Sister from Paris, concerning twin sisters, played by Constance Talmadge. The story revolves around the wife, who wins back her indifferent husband by posing as her dashing twin sister. Hans Kraly adapted the play by Ludwig Fulda, and the film was later remade twice—as Moulin Rouge in 1934 (with Franchot Tone in the Colman role) and as Two-Faced Woman, Garbo's last film, in 1941, with Melvyn Douglas. The story was deliciously risqué for this period, running into close shaves with the censors; however, the critics and audiences loved it. The cinema crowds started asking for Colman, and his name on a bill meant box-office success. It is one of the first indicators

* Photoplay, October, 1925.

of fame when crowds ask for a particular actor or actress; then, when they trek from their local cinema to a faraway part of town in order to see him, he's famous.

Ronnie's next film, *The Dark Angel* (again Fitzmaurice-Marion), was a landmark in his career; it was the first film in which he was not billed beneath the female star. He was no longer the leading man; he was the star. Also, the character he played embodied for the first time the gallant gentleman who places honor and self-sacrifice before his personal feelings, the character with which audiences would eventually associate him completely. Gone in this film was the Latin lover with tinges of Valentino, and it was clear that this screen character, with which Colman himself was so much at home, suited the public.

Goldwyn, ever searching for new talent and beauty, had heard of a twenty-two-year-old Hungarian actress, already popular in European films. Sam had tracked her down on his last trip to Europe, relieved her of her film commitments in Hungary, signed her, and brought her back to Hollywood with a contract of $250 a week for the first year. Vilma Banky spoke hardly any English; in fact, during *The Dark Angel* (in which she played the female lead) she spoke Hungarian, but her fair-haired looks photographed like magic, and her acting abilities were instantly apparent in her first American film.

The Dark Angel is H. B. Trevelyan's story about a young soldier (Colman) who is blinded in the war and who, because of this, decides against returning to his fiancée (Banky). Ronnie must have thought it strange irony indeed, slogging through the muddy battlefields of Flanders, Hollywood style, safely underneath the klieg lights when he had been doing the real thing eleven years before in a hodden gray kilt and wielding a jammed rifle.

Billed as "a story of blind love" in one of the advertising department's less inspired moments, it was a romantic drama that drenched many handkerchiefs across the states. The end of the film would melt the stoniest critic: The young soldier "memorizes" his room completely, with the intention of pretending he can see long enough to terminate their engagement, for fear that she might otherwise marry him out of pity. It is only when she returns to the room unexpectedly, offering him her hand, that she becomes aware of his blindness. (They *do* get each other in the end, thanks to Hollywood.) The public, who took pictures rather more seriously than we do today, sent Ronnie hundreds of letters of sympathy together with volumes of books for the blind.

Frances Marion: "I found it necessary to move the action of the play out of the confines of the small sets and also to dramatize some of the action which was contained within the play's dialogue. We saw the soldier fighting the war, for instance, and we changed the ending, which in the play had been an unhappy one and of which the public would not have approved.

"Sam, Fitz, and I went over every scene to weed out anything that smacked of bathos, or incredibility. Ronnie always made excellent suggestions, but he refused to take any credit for them, although often these suggestions became highlights of the finished picture. He had a tremendous influence on the style of acting then. His controlled performances, his lack of posturing and his economy of gesture conveyed more power to a scene than the thrashing mode a lot of actors still indulged in. Even in the most melodramatic scenes, with others in the cast whirling around like windmills in a storm, he appeared convincingly calm on the surface, yet one sensed his deep-rooted emotions."

Ronnie was a perfectionist, and since adopting films as his profession—or since *being* adopted by films—he started perfecting the way in which he moved. He had made a close film study of Chaplin and Fairbanks, having been struck by their grace, and realized there was a technique for this on film that these two had perfected. It was economy of gesture. Hands, arms, one's whole body need only hint at the movement it wished to convey completely for the camera. To make the complete movement or gesture quickly came across as clumsy and exaggerated on the screen. After Ronnie had appreciated this, it had taken only time and practice before he had become an expert in the field himself.

As far as playing a blind man was concerned, he found it more uncomfortable than difficult, due to staring into a full battery of kliegs and sun arcs most of the time. "It called for little effort. After a few moments of the lights, I felt as blind as could be desired!" Indeed, lights were for a long time an occupational hazard and actually ruined the eyes of a lot of people in the business.

Goldwyn sent Ronnie to New York for the publicity-ridden opening. It was a smash. Popular columnist Louella Parsons, known as much for her fluency with films as with gossip, wrote: "Singly, Vilma Banky would have been charming, but with Ronald Colman, she is part of a team that Mr. Goldwyn should copyright for his future pictures." * Mr. Goldwyn did virtually that. His mixture had worked, and this stunning, fair Hungarian and her dark film lover wrung the public's heart in a total of five films over the following three years.

While in New York to promote *Angel,* Ronnie had his first interview with *Photoplay,* a highly respected publication, which anyone in the profession was pleased to be included in. Ronnie could never be truly pleased about any publicity to which he was exposed, especially as it was never completely true. This was, however, part of his job, and *Photoplay* was most certainly truer than most. A young Ruth Waterbury, later to become editor of the magazine, entitled the interview "Ronald Talks At Last," and the latter part of it still echoes

* *The American,* October 12, 1925.

the sentiments of the amazed young Englishman who had arrived in Hollywood almost two years earlier:

"I'm not so terribly ambitious. I am not one of those chaps who want to play Hamlet. I'd like to earn $100,000 and invest it. That would give me $100 a week interest. The only thing is that I don't know whether one would lose his ambition if he had $100 a week without working for it. I'm extremely suspicious that I'd never stir from an easy chair again!

"Hollywood is the most physical city in the world. I don't mean sex alone. Take athletics. They all go in for them. Fine things, of course, but entirely physical. And they all have motor cars and extreme luxury. Their homes are burdened down with it.

"I love California, its beauty, and its warmth, its color, but it is almost impossible not to lose your perspective out there. There is something of the tropics about it, I suppose. When I finish a picture or whenever I can get a vacation, I go away. Down to the sea usually, but at any rate to some wild spot where I can be alone." *

Ruth Waterbury describes her second "star" interview, and Ronnie's first for *Photoplay:* "We met at the Plaza Hotel where he was staying, and I nearly fainted in the presence of his handsomeness and charm. How I got him to answer my questions and get such revelations from him as I did, I have not the faintest memory, though I presume my instant infatuation with him must have amused him and made him very kind. I was already married then, but truly quite young and naive!

"So I came home that enchanted day, wrote my story, pouring out every detail to my husband. The next day, we were walking up Fifth Avenue, when I saw a cluster of people gathering and there, sauntering along all by himself, was

* *Photoplay,* January, 1926.

Ronnie. I stood positively transfixed as he drew near me. Fortunately I could not speak, but as my bedazzled eyes met his, he looked at me without the faintest flicker of remembrance or recognition. Then and there, I learned a lesson which has been invaluable ever since. I hadn't been a person to him at all. I had been an audience, and he had given me a most delightful performance. I always felt in his debt, because I proved again and again at interviews that the people who are genuine stars—not mere personalities or weekend flashes—always did that performance instinctively on first meeting, and I was immune!"

Though the industry was in the doldrums again, with the blame put on radio, Goldwyn managed to follow *The Dark Angel* with an expensive production, *Stella Dallas*, directed by Henry King and adapted by Frances Marion. This was their first film under the United Artists banner, and the biggest production since *Romola* with which Ronnie had been involved. It cost close to half a million dollars—a large sum of money for a film that was not an epic. Goldwyn, however, was a shrewd gambler, and this bestselling novel was turned into a box-office hit.

Stella Dallas included a range of stars at varying points in their career: the virtually unknown teenager, Douglas Fairbanks, Jr., whose father was much concerned about his son's sporting a moustache in the film, which he felt added to his own years in the public eye; Colman, who was about to reach his "silent peak"; Alice Joyce, then a big star; and in the title role, Belle Bennett, brought for a star comeback. Colman's part as Belle's husband, who in his climb to success separates from his socially unacceptable wife, is relatively small. However, the standard of the production was high, and he brought refinement and sensitivity to the character of the husband-father with the upper-class background. To Ronnie, the character of Stella, his fair-haired screen wife who fails to step up the ladder of success with her young husband, was already painfully familiar.

True to custom, Thelma made an unexpected appearance, having returned to Hollywood where her estranged husband seemed to be keeping up a highly publicized success. Ronnie had gone with Henry King and the Goldwyns to see a show one night at the Biltmore Theater and, turning around in the box, he saw her sitting in the back. As soon as the lights went down, he got up and left, terrified of a recurrence of one of her public scenes. There were none that night at the Biltmore, but she became a shadow in his mind as well as in his life.

After the big box-office success of *Stella Dallas,* Ronnie went on loan to Warner's for Lubitsch's version of Oscar Wilde's *Lady Windermere's Fan,* an enormously enterprising undertaking for a German director who spoke little English and who was determined to film Wilde's story without using the author's famous epigrams. Responsible for his own casting, Lubitsch had already commenced filming with Clive Brook in the role of Darlington. After a few days, they came to the scene in which he was to meet the leading lady, and Lubitsch wanted him to click his heels and snap his head. Clive demurred, explaining this was far from an English custom. His director insisted, however, and so came a parting of the ways, much to their mutual relief. The contretemps was observed by the actress who played the part of Lady Windermere's mother:

Irene Rich: "The feeling between those two just wasn't good. Lubitsch being German, Clive English, and the war pretty recent didn't help the situation. He just didn't want to do any more and Warner's were in a state, and they thought the one person who could do the part would be Colman, who was under contract to Goldwyn. I was under contract to Warner's for five years, and it was in my contract that I was to be featured in every film, and nobody billed above me. So Sam said, 'Well, you wouldn't let me have Irene when I wanted her a few weeks ago; no, I won't let you have Colman unless he gets top billing.' And of course, a terrific sum of money. This put Warner's in a spot, as I was always supposed to have top billing. But I said I thought it was marvelous that they could get Ronnie to do the picture, and that I didn't care what happened to my name, so it was settled. Ronnie was a gentleman and you didn't find many of those! Anyway, so that's how he got the part of Darlington."

Sam then read the script and telephoned Lubitsch in a rage, saying, "Why didn't you tell me it was a villain you wanted him to play?" * Lubitsch's English was not up to explanations on the telephone, and a conference was held immediately with Sam's representative, Mr. Lehr, who demanded to know whether or not the role was that of a villain.

" 'Villain?' queried Ernst. 'I don't know what is villain. He love a beautiful girl if that is villain.' Mr. Lehr pondered for a time and then with inspiration asked, 'Does he make a sacrifice?' 'Ya, he lose the girl!' " *

Those were the magic words; he couldn't be a villain if he sacrificed his love, and Ronnie was loaned on the further condition that Lubitsch use a credit line to the effect: "Ronald Colman through courtesy of Samuel Goldwyn." Lubitsch did not let Ronnie forget this during the filming and would come up with reminders such as, "Mr. Colman, you walk across the room, you stop by the table, you pick up the book, then you look into the eyes of Miss McAvoy by courtesy of Sam Goldwyn!" *

Ronnie accepted all this good-humoredly. He was intensely relieved that the deal had finally been settled and that he was actually in this film playing Darlington. Throughout many years, Wilde had been to him not only a genius

* *Photoplay*, May, 1926.

but a joy, and he knew virtually all his works by heart. He also had great admiration for Lubitsch, who had successfully managed to "sell" the filming of one of these works to Hollywood.

Irene Rich: "Lubitsch had me dye my hair red for the role, so that I would *feel* more sophisticated and mature and rather wicked. (I was the same age as Ronnie.) He generally let you do your own part, then the moment he wasn't satisfied, he would be helpful with suggestions. He would really get into a scene; one time he was sitting on a fifteen-foot scaffolding directing a scene, and he got so excited about somebody down there, he walked right off into midair!

"I had one scene with Ronnie when I was trying to look sophisticated and he was sitting next to me. I had some lines to say, but when I turned to him, he was so beautiful that I forgot every word I was supposed to say, didn't remember a darn thing—just sat there and looked at him!"

Ronnie and Lubitsch, very polite, very professional, sailed smoothly through their scenes. He took the latter's direction, and if he didn't like the way in which he was being directed in a particular scene, he would go through the motions as Lubitsch wanted, then quietly talk it over and say, "Would you mind if I do it this way?" As Ronnie neither clicks his heels nor snaps his head in the film, one presumes that either Lubitsch had given further thought to Clive's remarks, or Colman had been more patiently and successfully persuasive on the subject.

Bert Lytell was the husband and the diminutive actress who played Esther in *Ben-Hur* was built both up and out to be the elegant Lady Windermere:

May McAvoy: "I thought everybody in the film was good except me! I didn't feel right in the part. For one thing, they had to build me up so much in height (I'm under five feet), because Ronnie was not a short man, or Bert. In the party sequence, where Lady Windermere, as the hostess, has to go around this group of people in a large room and speak to them all, they had to build a runway about eighteen inches high for me, because I was so short that if I were walking through the group, I couldn't be seen by the camera! So I walked around on this crazy runway, which couldn't be too wide because it would keep people away from me, and I was teetering on higher heels than I'd ever worn in my life. It was the same in every scene with Ronnie or any of the men, because I had to be more or less on their level to look dignified. Then they would cut to a long shot, and there I was *down* there!

"I didn't have much bosom in those days either. Bert was a great kidder and loved to have fun and would tease me about how the wardrobe department had filled me out. I'd walk onto the set and Bert would give me the eye and look directly there, and of course I'd die several deaths! Then Ronnie got into the act. He knew it embarrassed me and he and Bert would tease me together. He never started it, but he joined in, because he loved to laugh.

"Lubitsch would tell us the day before which scenes we'd be starting; we'd do two or three walk-throughs, then he'd get down to the real rehearsals. The first take might not be quite right but he didn't do ten or twelve takes like they do today. [This was just as well; Ronnie had spontaneity on the first three takes, after which he became mechanically perfect, and the screen result was dull.] We had to learn the dialogue as it was written in the script, even though it wasn't recorded, because you had to make sense in the scene. You had to mouth something or no expression would come across.

"I never knew anybody to have more beautiful manners than he had and who always did the right thing at the right time. I would like to have seen him slip just *once!* It would never have occurred to me to ask him anything personal. With somebody else, you might say, 'Well, were you ever married?' or 'Tell me something about yourself!' Although he was kind and gentle, very friendly and sweet, there was a little wall built around him, and you never got beyond that. Not that he ever put it in words, but he wanted his private life to be his own, and he had a right to it. I think it would have been much better for a lot of people if they had done that too."

The film was a medium-size success. One is conscious that it is a director's film and not the actors', all of whom are equally controlled. No star vehicle here. Happily, the film has gained attention and respect with age, and is still shown today as a silent "classic."

Ronnie's talent for light comedy (which he enjoyed doing enormously) had been well-exercised by Lubitsch, and it went into full swing in his next film, a comedy-farce. By the time he was loaned out to Joe Schenck to make *Kiki*, he was a star name, and director Clarence Brown regarded it as a triumph when they signed him. It was still, however, a Norma Talmadge (Mrs. Joe Schenck) film. Hans Kraly and Brown worked day and night on the script, taken from Belasco's comedy, which in turn had been adapted from a French play. Set in Paris (in this case, the familiar back lot of First National), the story had Colman as a Parisian theatrical producer, hounded by a would-be actress (Norma) for a job. The combination of Talmadge, Colman, Kraly, and Brown came through with such a smash that on its strength Brown landed himself a contract with MGM that lasted for thirty-two years.

The success of Norma and Ronnie as a team led to talk of another film together, a joint Goldwyn-Schenck production to be scripted by Frances Marion and directed by Henry King. Long a favorite of Norma Talmadge, *The Garden of*

Allah would have been filmed in Biskra (Algeria). The idea never went beyond the talking stage, however, due to the fact that it would have been an extremely expensive production and would have taken up a great many weeks during a period when the stars in question were much in demand in Hollywood.

Colman was going from strength to strength. Goldwyn, who had been collecting a tidy sum on Colman loan-out money, now gave Ronnie a new, better paid contract and lent him out for the last time, in what was to be the most magnificent of his silent films.

Jesse Lasky had read P. C. Wren's adventure story, *Beau Geste,* at the suggestion of his assistant (and head of Paramount's East Coast studios), Walter Wanger, and was thrilled with its film possibilities. There was the usual trouble selling it to Adolph Zukor and the East Coast financial heads, who regarded virtually every investment as an insane gamble and opposed almost all films of any importance. One of Lasky's biggest jobs was overcoming the resistance of the financial men of the company: the exhibitors and distributors were usually a reactionary, uncreative, unadventurous lot, and in this instance he finally sold the idea on the grounds that they had been having great success with Westerns, and here was a chance to do a Western with the Foreign Legion.

Lasky and Goldwyn enjoyed a rather erratic relationship, varying between friendliness and nonspeaking. Their strong personalities and ideas often clashed, especially since Sam had divorced Jesse's sister, Blanche, and Jesse sometimes suspected his ex-brother-in-law of cheating at golf. . . . The period preceding *Beau Geste* was one of their nonspeak periods, and it required strength of mind for Lasky to pick up the telephone in New York to ask Sam if he could borrow Colman for the film. Naturally, Sam was delighted, not only hearing Lasky ask him for something, but having such a pleasant opportunity for making money. The title role was one for which most actors would have given their eyeteeth, and Ronnie was suitably excited with his new venture.

Beau Geste was the first Hollywood film (with the exception of some scenes in *Greed*) to be shot right smack in the middle of the desert's no-man's land. In the section of the Arizona desert near the Mexican border, thirty miles from Yuma, there is nothing but sand—the dunes rising to a hundred and fifty feet—scorching sun, freezing nights, wind, flies, scorpions to test the endurance of all. Herbert Brenon, under contract to Famous Players-Lasky, had recently done a fine job directing *Peter Pan,* and was assigned this project, their biggest epic of the year, and one that ended by costing over a million dollars. Previously an actor himself, Brenon had established himself not only as a prominent director but also as a difficult man with a feisty Irish temper, hardly at its best under these conditions.

Camp Paramount grew from the sweat of two hundred men with material brought thirty miles by tractors from Yuma, and covered an area of four square miles to house the two-thousand-strong company and eighteen hundred animals. Floored tents sprang up—one huge mess tent, a hospital with surgeon and nurse, four post offices, a barber shop and laundry, drugstore, blacksmith and veterinary tents. Eighteen nations were represented in the camp, and many of them were ex-Legionnaires, which added even more reality to the atmosphere. Morale was boosted by the camp's nightly films, radio concerts, and orchestra. The days, however, were pretty grueling: reveille at five-thirty, breakfast at six, a seven-o'clock bugle for awaiting orders, and eight o'clock to work. Heartily reminiscent of the London Scottish. . . .

The actors could use goggles during rehearsals, but were up against the full force of sun and wind during the actual takes. Ralph Forbes (who plays John Geste) was one Englishman unaccustomed to such violent heat; he burst a blood vessel within the first week of shooting. Numerous members of the cast were injured in the thrashing desert scenes—a *mêlée* of hooves, limbs, and flying sand. As Bill Powell (playing the wicked Boldini) remarked: "War is inconvenient whether it be real or only in movies!"

Neil Hamilton plays the third Geste brother, Digby, and there is a good-looking similarity between the two that served them well in this film:

Neil Hamilton: "I had not met Ronnie before, and after a couple of weeks' work, Herbert Brenon asked me suddenly if I had any brothers or sisters, which I haven't. 'Well,' he said, 'maybe that explains the problem. I've got bad news—we have to reshoot everything we've done so far with you and Ronnie. You don't treat him like a brother. You treat him as though every time you touch him, he might fall apart! Every time you see him, you look as though you're saying, 'Yes, Mr. Colman, no, Mr. Colman.' Brothers are rough, they're intimate. In the scene coming up, you walk into the room and he is sitting there at the table and you yank the chair and give him a hug, or do something that between two brothers would be a sort of horseplay. It's an intimate scene. I don't know what to tell you to do, but you get together with Ronnie and get at it!'

"I suppose I must have been rather in awe of him up until then. Well, in those days I was a physical culture nut—wrestled every day! So I went up to Mr. Colman and asked him if he knew anything about wrestling, and when he said he'd done a good deal of it in his day, I decided what I was going to do in the scene.

"We started shooting. I walked in the room and there was my brother. 'Hiya, Beau!' 'Hello, Dig!' And I walked up to him and got a half nelson on him, but much to my surprise he didn't throw it off, and before I knew what had happened I had flung Ronald Colman to the floor with a terrific *bang*. There he lay on his back looking up at me and he said, 'Why, you son of a bitch!' I was so astonished at what had happened, I couldn't speak. He got up and rubbed himself, and I really thought for a moment there was going to be a fight, but in fact it was that half nelson that broke the ice between us. I explained to him what Brenon had said to me, and how I assumed he would know how to deal with a half nelson, and from then on we were fine. In fact, as time wore on we became good friends. Brenon saw the rushes that night and said, 'Now they are acting like brothers!'

"One of my favorite moments in the film was when the fort was attacked by the foe. There was Ronnie and I and twenty men inside, defending it. Attacking were one thousand five hundred horses and riders. (They had rounded up every out-of-work cowboy and brought them down to Yuma and put them on horses!) Groups of men on their horses were sent out with water and food to certain spots beyond the horizon to wait until later in the day when at a given signal by radio or semaphore, they'd ride in to attack the fort. The day started and finally, when the sun was exactly right and the clouds were exactly in the right position, you could see in the entire one-hundred-eighty-degrees view of the horizon little specks way in the distance. As they converged on the fort, they were recognizable as riders. It was an absolutely magnificent sight. The desert was black with them, and finally they got to within an eighth of a mile of the fort, and Brenon was seized by a stroke of genius. He picked up his megaphone and shouted, 'For every man that makes a good fall during the firing of the rifles, an extra ten-dollar check!' So they came closer and closer and when they were within one thousand feet of the fort, the signal was given for us to fire. And the twenty-two men including Ronnie and me inside the fort fired, and one thousand five hundred men fell *dead* in the desert. They couldn't use one *inch* of film.

"And then Ronnie started to laugh, and he laughed so hard I thought he was going to loose his eyeballs. The whole day's work was ruined, and there was nothing else we could do except some little shots around the inside of the fort, but even then, each time we would start, Ronnie would break up into screams of laughter to the intense disgust of Herbert Brenon.

"The next day, once only twelve men had been told to fall when we shot, the entire thing was set up again, and went off perfectly until we had fired and they had fallen off and Ronnie just exploded into hopeless laughter again and ruined the whole thing. It took us about three days to get that shot. Brenon finally said something dreadful to him like, 'If you laugh tomorrow I'm going to drag you out and have all those one thousand five hundred horses run over you!' "

Brenon's fiery temper wore very thin during the course of the filming. Later, an important press lady came all the way out into the desert camp to write a story that was to be valuable publicity for Paramount and the film. The cast were told by Brenon that they were each to give her red-carpet treatment and be on their best behavior.

Neil Hamilton: "It was as though the Queen were arriving. Dinner that evening was specially ordered food, served in a tent erected specially for the occasion, and for featured players only. And we were all under instruction to keep her entertained to the best of our ability. As dinner progressed, it was whispered around the table that Bill Powell was going to do a trick, and for us to put some salt under our plates. After much laughter and drinking, Bill got to his feet and with a low bow to the guest of honor, proceeded to show her 'How the Foreign Legion cleans up their dinner table.' With a One-Two-Three from all, the tablecloth was yanked from one end of the table to the other by Bill, leaving half of the table-setting where it was, and the other half smack in the lap of our guest. You could have heard her scream fifteen miles away. 'My new dress, it's ruined. You *bastards!*' as she tore away into the night, insisting upon being immediately returned to Hollywood. [A long ride from Yuma!]

"Brenon was furious. He discharged Bill on the spot, informing everyone that as soon as the studio could replace him, everything would be reshot, and we were told, 'Now back to your bunks and be assured your salary will be docked in order to buy her a new outfit.'

"It seemed no sooner than Ralph Forbes and I had gotten back to our tent than in came Ronnie, fit to be tied. 'Now listen, Brenon may be the director of this picture, and doing an excellent job, but he is not a general and he has no right to fire Bill or anyone else, unless they are giving a poor performance. What happened tonight was an accident, and that dame is a pain in the arse, and Bill is brokenhearted. I've seen the others, and they have agreed that in the morning we're not putting on our uniforms, because we plan to be in front of Brenon's tent as a group in our street clothes.'

"The next morning, by the time we got to Brenon's tent, the balance of the cast were standing around looking as though they'd explode if you touched them. Ronnie went inside and told him all he had to do was stick his head out and see his entire cast was returning to Hollywood with Bill. Brenon saw us all out of uniform and shouted, 'This is mutiny, *mutiny,* you hear me?' Ronnie said calmly, 'Call it what you will, sir, but we are prepared to leave and leave now. What's your answer?'

"Of course, with no cast to work with, he couldn't shoot or anything, and finally after a lot of hot air, we were told to change into our uniforms, that Powell was not going to be discharged."

So all ended well, thanks to Ronnie's *beau geste* on behalf of his friend. Despite the trials of Herbert Brenon and the discomforts of camping in the desert for three months keeping the hours of the broiling sun, Ronnie enjoyed making the film. It was a plum part in a first-rate production, and to share the experience with his good friend Powell much of the time made it more enjoyable. There was much talking, laughing, cards, and card tricks in their tent of an evening. Also, there was Ralph Forbes, whose bride, Ruth Chatterton, had been a friend of Ronnie's since the stage days of *La Tendresse*. It was, in fact, a nice group with whom to be deserted. Alice Joyce, who had played his second wife in *Stella Dallas*, plays Colman's mother in *Beau Geste*, rather a speedy age difference to have acquired within one year!

Percival Wren, author of the novel, was thrilled with both the film and Colman. The critics and public felt the same: *Beau Geste* was one of the ten most financially successful silent films ever made, much to the astonishment of the Paramount executives, who continued to believe they had a flop on their hands after the film was completed.

The Academy Awards did not come into being until the following year (1927), or no doubt *Beau Geste* would have swept off with a few honors. It did receive *Photoplay*'s distinguished Gold Medal of Honor (their seventh). This award was nominated by the readers from among the best pictures of 1926, and after the film's release Colman was second only to John Gilbert in the number of fan letters the magazine received.

The film sealed Ronnie's place on a pinnacle of success and fame; Sam Goldwyn decided not to loan out his property any longer. He had just paid a record-breaking $123,000 for the rights to the bestselling novel, *The Winning of Barbara Worth*, in which he reunited Ronnie with Vilma Banky. The publicity department was—inevitably—at work creating a romance between the two.

Ronnie braced himself to enter once again into the desert, this time in Nevada—the Black Rock. It lacked the sand dunes of *Beau Geste*'s location but made up for it in other ways. It was a dry lake about seventy miles long, one hundred miles north of Reno and halfway to the Idaho line, where there was not even a bush within eyesight. The temperatures ranged between 110 degrees in the day and 28 degrees at night. It took every ounce of self-control to get through a day without finding some reason to explode.

Ronnie was irked by the Colman-Banky "romance" that had come out of Goldwyn's publicity department. He had realized by now that Sam was one of the greatest publicity men around and that this was a permanent and, to a certain degree, necessary side to film business. But it continued to be difficult for him to accept the rumors being spread that had nothing to do with the truth. He stewed the matter over during the days of filming in the Black Rock.

When the hot and browned company returned to Hollywood after their three-month ordeal, Vilma was asked how she had enjoyed it. "So much west!", * she replied in plaintive Hungarian tones, summing up the opinion of the entire company.

Although both great effort and expense ($105,000) went into the making of *Barbara Worth,* the success of the film was nothing along the lines of its eminent predecessor, and today it is most memorable for launching Gary Cooper. Vilma received fine reviews for her portrayal of both the mother, who dies early in the story, and her daughter, the Barbara of the title.

The public adored the Colman-Banky team, and Goldwyn had shrewdly seized upon this. The following year Ronnie appeared in two more romances with Vilma. In *The Night of Love* he is a bandit who kidnaps Miss Banky on her wedding night to save her from the Duke's exercising his *droit du seigneur.* The censors threatened "the theme discussing the right of a man to the 'first night' is salacious and entirely too intimate for presentation to young people

* *Photoplay,* December, 1926.

as entertainment." The matter was taken to court, where the broad-minded judge favored the filmmakers. The setting is seventeenth-century Spain, and Ronnie with his dark curly hair romps through sunlit woods and around the castle in what is throughout a visually stunning film, thanks to Fitzmaurice's eye and hand. (It is typically Hollywood that this Englishman should be typecast as the Latin lover, and his Hungarian lady idolized as the perfect English beauty!) It was Fitz's last silent film for Goldwyn, whom he then left for First National and one of the biggest director's salaries ever paid—at that time.

Vilma and Ronnie were next teamed in *The Magic Flame*, which provided him with his first of several dual roles. This one was a costume drama set in a mythical kingdom in which he played a circus clown and a villainous count. He introduced the idea of the clown playing a banjo, being an old virtuoso from his amateur theatrical days, and serenaded the astonished company with his repertoire.

The director wanted a slight physical difference between the two characters—but the Colman face had become too well-known to allow him much digression:

Henry King: "We couldn't put wool in his cheeks because that would have made him look ridiculous, but I suggested we have some teeth made to put over his own, just to give him a different expression. He thought it was a good idea, so I sent him down to a dentist and they took a cast and made him some that gave him a tough kind of look. Then Frances Marion saw him with these on, and she and Sam couldn't believe we had done this to one of the handsomest men in pictures. I got into an awful hassle with them. Ronnie liked the teeth, he felt they gave him a character to work with. Anyway, they went on hassling for so long that we did away with the teeth and changed his moustache a bit instead."

King, who left Goldwyn to go into business for himself

after this film, always preferred *The White Sister* to the other films he made with Ronnie, and felt this was his star's opinion as well.

King: "Ronnie was a man who didn't have the great idea that he knew it all. It made me think that he was a very smart man. He didn't come in and tell you how he ought to play his part and how to direct the picture. He wanted your ideas and your help, and it established a way of working together which was very pleasant. At this stage in his career, he simply accepted a part and played it to the best of his ability. He felt that the director was the man that guided this, and he wanted to give everything in the world he possibly could to aid the director in getting the part right. He always felt that the director knew more about the part than he did. He was very frank in that respect."

And he obviously absorbed a lot of knowledge from his experiences with King.

Shortly after *The Magic Flame* was released, the Colman-Banky "romance" was permanently crushed by Vilma's marriage to Rod la Rocque. It was a gargantuan Goldwyn-staged wedding: six bridesmaids, six ushers (one of whom was Ronnie—cast by Sam), Cecil B. De Mille was best man, and Goldwyn himself gave the bride away. The fantastic wedding cake was papier-mâché, much to the guests' surprise when they tried to eat it. The whole event, with its star cast, might have been a part of one of Goldwyn's most lavish films. Press and crowds surrounded the church. When asked after the ceremony what her first child would be named, Vilma replied, "I don't know, you'll have to ask Sam Goldwyn." * (Though their marriage certainly had an extraordinarily "Hollywood" beginning, it was hardly a typical Hollywood marriage: The Rod la Rocques remained together until his

* *Photoplay,* September, 1927.

death in 1969, and Vilma was never particularly interested in film work again.)

The wedding was a classic example of Hollywood extravagance in the twenties, cropping up in films and novels of the next decade that satirized the silent era. As far as being called upon to play a role in such a publicity-centered affair, Ronnie hardly felt comfortable. It was to him Hollywood and Goldwyn at their worst.

As Ronnie came into his own with Goldwyn and his career, his finances became sufficiently stable for him to establish roots, as well as to continue to support his mother and Thelma from afar. He invested in his first property. Unlike many of his contracted colleagues, he had preferred to wait until he had sufficient savings for the down payment, rather than indebting himself earlier on by borrowing from his producer or anyone else. It was a Spanish-style, patioed house in the hills of Hollywood. Difficult to find on a winding road, secluded by walls and gardens, Ronnie's private corner was an extension of himself.

Charlie Lane was working less and heading gradually toward retirement. Returning his early kindness, Ronnie offered to rebuild the tennis house at the end of his garden into a bungalow for Lane, who accepted. So they continued together with the role of landlord reversed. Ronnie tackled tennis as well as the tennis house with determination, and though he never became an excellent player, he was a good one and certainly never lacked for competitive spirit. The tennis court at Mound Street became a very select "club." Eventually word leaked out that each weekend produced a choice selection of Hollywood's famous faces upon the Colman court, and the more enterprising and athletic fans found their way to vantage points hidden in the adjoining property. All of a sudden it was a Wimbledon crowd. Ronnie had full-length tarpaulins erected on the fencing around the court, and the thwarted fans trickled disconsolately back through the foliage.

Bill Powell, Dick Barthelmess, Clive Brook, and Warner Baxter were regulars on the court. Percy Marmont (star of, among others, the silent version of Kipling's *The Light That Failed*), came over from England to film in Hollywood.

Percy Marmont: "Tennis definitely had something to do with our friendship. He was a very keen player and so was I. Also we had a mutual friend in Charlie with whom I had worked in the east. I used to go to Ronnie's pretty well every weekend for tennis, and then in the evenings we used to meet either at his place, my place or Warner Baxter's for poker. We gambled like fury!

"One day he said, 'We have got to stop this, it's too ridiculous playing for the stakes we do!' He suggested we cut it in half the following Sunday. We did—for about half an hour—before we went back to the original big stakes, because it all got so dull! The tennis and the poker and the mutual good friends all joined us together.

"I soon discovered he would never talk about himself to people unless it was somebody he liked very much and with whom he was intimate; then he would discuss all sorts of things. But you took Ronnie into a room with a lot of people he didn't know, and he'd be perfectly genial and perfectly friendly with everybody, but there'd be no question of getting him into a corner and pumping him because he'd get out of that corner very quickly. Amid it all, though, he had this terrific humor. He'd appreciate the humor of the thing. It took quite a time to get his trust as a good friend, but it was worth it."

Another actor to join the group was one of the ten most popular Western stars ever, Tim McCoy. He was a contemporary who shared a strong character resemblance with Ronnie, though their careers were quite different. Both had the same dignity and reserve and the ever-present twinkle in the eye. A colonel from the First World War, Tim was equally at home on a horse as in a chair, and was one of the few white men to speak Indian sign language. He appeared on the Hollywood scene when Jesse Lasky hired him to supply and direct the Indians for *The Covered Wagon* (1923), the first of the large-scale Western epics. Tim also staged the prologues with the Indians for this film, both in the States and abroad. The following year he was himself signed by Paramount to appear in *The Thundering Herd*. Next he staged another prologue for Fox's *The Iron Horse* at Hollywood's Egyptian Theater, and his Indian camp in the center of Hollywood became an attraction for all the sightseers, who reported that although the braves didn't speak English, their enthusiasm for the cinema was unmistakable, a feeling Tim no doubt helped inspire.

He could relate firsthand stories of Wyatt Earp and Annie Oakley, and his knowledge of the American Indian folklore, and indeed of the folklore of the West, fascinated Ronnie. What started as a drinking and poker association emerged as a lifelong friendship with interchanged god-children. (Tim is my godfather and his son, Ronald, is my father's godson.)

Tim McCoy: "Ronnie was still living on Mound Street when our friendship began. About once a month, we would be over at Warner Baxter's where we had a great routine. We'd come in, have a drink or two, sit down and play poker until the buffet was ready. Then we'd eat, then go back and play some more poker. It was very pleasant and a lot of fun. Later, Ronnie organized this cocktail group at his place, which was almost the same bunch of fellows. We'd meet every Friday at his house. If he were on a picture or something and couldn't be there, then somebody else would take over. He made the rules and you couldn't bring just any guest. If it was someone outstanding that everyone would like to meet, then you would call Ronnie.

"So every Friday night, we would have our drinks, and anyone who had a date, or the married men who had to go home would go, and the ones left would do a pub crawl. It was just after Prohibition, and they were starting to open places along Sunset Boulevard and sometimes Ronnie and I would end up by ourselves. Dick Barthelmess was with us, when he had separated from his first wife, but Warner would have to go home to Winnie, and Bill was there when he wasn't involved in a romance. We'd eventually wind up at Ciro's and have dinner."

The company of these friends suited Ronnie, who found them stimulating and reassuring. They shared not only a wide variety of sports and games but a similar perspective on their lives. Though most of them were stars in their own right, stardom never overwhelmed any of them. They were serious at work and yet retained the wisdom and humor with which to regard its effect.

No intelligent person could remain among the movie moguls and feel indebted to them for long. Movies were as much business as art. They were all making money by benefiting from each other, and Ronnie (as well as many of his friends) had been an investment that was paying off high dividends to both his studio and himself. However, the stars' earnings often included intangible losses. Although the overlong hours at the studio offered the reward of fame and fortune, they could also confuse one's identity. There lay the ever-beckoning dream—to lose oneself to the image in the camera, which claimed many minds and indeed some lives. It was in fact the freedom of one's mind that was threatened. However, despite the push of the studio, the trumpet of publicity, and the adoration of the masses, Ronnie continued to belong exclusively to himself, his mind free from confusion. He had grown up as an independent young man, and his freedom had been threatened by the war and by his marriage. He had survived both. No suffocating embrace of Hollywood could shake his hard-won privilege. He remained firmly in charge of himself and of his dreams.

Ernest and Elsie Torrence, the hub of the English acting circle in Hollywood, gave a Christmas party in 1927, to which Ronnie and many of their mutual pals were invited.

Percy Marmont: "It was quite a big affair, with a lot of well-known people and a lot of unknowns too. We sat around their big living room after dinner, and their son distributed presents from under the tree. He'd take the present, then crack some gag like, 'This is for the man who gave that terrible performance in such and such. Now who is it?' And the man would come up and get his present. Then he said, 'This is for the best-looking man in Hollywood!' and there was a *rush* to the tree of Ronnie, Warner Baxter and me. Actually, it turned out to be my present, and both of them were joking to Torrence, 'There must be something wrong with your eyes!' We became absolute children, but it was wonderful!"

When Ronnie spent time alone, away from films, poker, tennis, and friends, it was invariably with a book in hand. His education having been forcibly limited in his youth, he had made up for it with copious reading and became well-versed in a wide range of subjects from history to astronomy. The house in Mound Street offered, for the first time, space for his own library, and his collection developed from the classics, through the entire works of Shakespeare, Dickens, Hugo, Stevenson, Wilde, and Shaw to Lewis Carroll and Edward Lear. With each month the library grew larger, the rare first editions and the signed copies more numerous.

Goldwyn, in a publicity bid for what was to be his romantic team's last film together, appealed to the public for story suggestions and offered a prize of $2,500. Out of the forty thousand entries came Baroness Orczy's *Leatherface,* an idea recommended by the scenarists after they had read the novel. Again in costume, the story is set in The Netherlands during the Spanish occupation of the sixteenth century, and ideally suited the Banky-Colman image. Fred Niblo, whose biggest triumph had been *Ben-Hur* three years earlier, directed, and the film (retitled *Two Lovers*) did well in 1928, the year in which the first feature-length movie with spoken dialogue was made.

It was a timely decision between Goldwyn, Colman, and Banky that this be the last film using the famous team. Vilma had become a star in her own right, and neither she nor Ronnie were content in this fifty-fifty position any longer. It was very difficult finding ideas that satisfied them both. Either it was a man's story, with which Vilma was dissatisfied, or a woman's, and Ronnie would be indifferent to his part.

Also, in Sam's opinion their combined salaries were too much for each picture to bear. *Two Lovers* was costing nearly a million dollars, and Sam wanted to have each of them star in two films a year, separately. Ronnie was happy with the split and looked forward to some light comedy again, and eventually his ideal role—Sydney Carton. "There is always the possibility that our work may become mechanical. Perhaps it is now. We are so thoroughly familiar with each other's reaction to any situation a script may call for that quite unconsciously we may anticipate such reactions. We can't be certain that we're not playing scenes today quite in the manner we played certain scenes in *The Dark Angel*." *

Goldwyn tried to rid Vilma of her strong Hungarian accent in preparation for sound. She subsequently starred in three films, but being happily "housewifed," she did not really care about losing her accent or continuing her career

* *Motion Picture,* April, 1928.

any longer. Eventually Sam terminated her contract. During their association, however, Colman and Banky had become (with Garbo and Gilbert, Gaynor and Farrell) one of the famous romantic teams of the silent era.

When *Two Lovers* was completed, Ronnie left for his first vacation from Goldwyn and Hollywood, at what was virtually the end of his career in silent films. Talkies were taking over, and the Goldwyn studio people were already consulting about how to introduce their number-one star into this new medium.

He sailed for Southampton with friend and fellow-English-actor, Philip Strange. The voyage was a sharp contrast to his penniless one of seven years before. The few days on board ship were made particularly enjoyable by the presence of a young lady from New York by the name of Dorothy Feiner. A dark, attractive, intelligent woman, she was delightful company during the journey and obviously made an impact on Ronnie, who got up at five in the morning to say good-bye to her as she disembarked at Cherbourg.

The boat docked in Southampton to crowds of waving fans, including a group of Ronnie and Philip Strange's old pals, one of whom had brought along a young English director friend, Alfred Hitchcock. They took the train to Waterloo, only to discover that every platform ticket seemed to have been sold to Colman enthusiasts, and it took the huddled group a quarter of an hour to inch themselves along the few yards to a taxi. Not associating this sort of demonstration with his native land, Ronnie was astounded and rather pleased.

Marjory, now in her seventies, was the chief reason for his trip. She was waiting at the hotel, safely away from the fans with whom she hardly associated her younger son. When he finally arrived, the only noticeable differences in him as far as she was concerned were his healthy nut-color, his moustache, and his slightly American intonation. When, several days later, *Two Lovers* was about to open in town, Ronnie thought it would amuse his mother to take her to the opening night in the West End. Crowds surged around their car, which crawled slowly forward to the entrance. "My dear Ronnie, what in the world are all these people doing here? Has there been an accident?" "And that," related Ronnie several years later, "is about how seriously my family took me!"

After such a long absence, it was a rewarding stay, both from the point of view of having time with his mother and family and receiving such a warm welcome from his countrymen. Marjory sailed for Australia soon afterward, where she joined her other married children, Freda and Eric, who had emigrated there. The London visit was also important for a rather fate-ridden first meeting—or perhaps "sight" would be more appropriate. It was during lunch in a London restaurant that he was first dazzled by a certain dark English beauty at a neighboring table. No words were exchanged, and he did not know who she was, but they stared surreptitiously at each other throughout the meal. She was a young English actress, already a well-known name in her own country—Benita Hume.

Ronnie was brought back to Hollywood by a telegram from Sam saying he had acquired the rights to Joseph Conrad's novel, *The Rescue*. Colman was to play the hero, Tom Lingard, opposite Sam's new French discovery, Lily Damita. This was Ronnie's last silent film and the first in which he received exclusive star billing. Although it was a literary departure from his romantic teamwork with Banky, the problem faced by the hero was one with which he was already familiar—that of a man faced with the unenviable choice between love and duty. This time he played a trader who falls in love with the wife of an English Member of Parliament. The story is set on the Java coast and was filmed on Santa Cruz island off Santa Barbara, under demanding conditions of bad weather, mounting production costs, and Herbert (*Beau Geste*) Brenon's bad temper, which was not helped by his breaking an ankle during the filming. The company lived for three months in rough shacks, sharing the questionable companionship of the island's goats. Despite all this, some brilliant photography was achieved of the boats and ocean storms, and both the film and Colman had good reviews.

"Ronald Colman . . . is right out of the Conrad pattern, one that suffers deeply without any flamboyant emotion . . . The repressed acting of Colman makes the figure very real. . . . Spectacularly beautiful scenes, amazing water shots. It isn't another *Beau Geste,* but director Herbert Brenon has brought out in Colman the same quality that characterized him in that earlier work." *

When the waterlogged and bedraggled company finally returned to Hollywood, Ronnie wrote to Dorothy Feiner in New York asking for a signed photograph and a letter from her. "I've just finished a production. The craze for sound pictures has upset all arrangements, and it is possible that they may remake a part of the picture just completed with talking (which would involve a trip east)." However, the synchronized sound effects did not actually include Colman, being mostly vocal chorus numbers. By Ronnie's next visit east Dorothy had become Mrs. Richard Rodgers. (She was married in March, 1930.) He remained a friend of hers, as well as of her parents and husband, for a long time.

The previous year Arthur Hornblow had joined Goldwyn as a writer. However, he soon became involved with production and with the task of being a buffer between Goldwyn and Colman, a significant step in this producer-actor relationship. The complete antitheses of one another, Goldwyn and Colman would hardly have been destined for friendship under the best of circumstances, and certainly their

* *Photoplay,* March, 1930.

professional relationship was often strained. A brilliant businessman who had created one of the finest and most select studios, Goldwyn was fiercely determined and rather unsubtle of character. He had an explosive temper and all the words to go with it. He was conscious of the use of publicity for his stars, not minding what the department drummed up as long as it got space. All of Ronnie's innate English correctness and restraint were at odds with his boss, though he appreciated him as a first-rate producer. Hornblow, who possessed knowledge as well as coherence, bridged their personality gap. But it was not a bridge that could survive a great deal of stormy weather.

6

Sound—Not Simply to Convince but to Enchant

The Goldwyn people were understandably cautious about Ronnie's first talking vehicle. He was their golden boy, and the ax of sound was falling swiftly upon a number of heads. Sam, who justly prided himself on being a good prophet, had said that talkies would revolutionize love sequences, and he was right. The hisses and crackles of early sound equipment robbed the prolonged clinches of any romance and were equally rough on the voices. Besides this, audiences still preferred what they were used to—silence and their imagination. As far as they were concerned, talking did not go with necking and such sequences elicited snickers rather than sentiment. Sam was not about to allow Colman into this vulnerable situation. He took his number-one romantic star and put him into melodrama tinged with light comedy, another forte of Ronnie's and one in which he delighted. There were going to be no more passionate love scenes until sound was smoothed out.

Arthur Hornblow, on the lookout in New York, found that *Bulldog Drummond,* then a famous property, was available for sale, and distinguished playwright Sidney Howard, who was a keen admirer of Colman, agreed to do the script.

Goldwyn okayed the idea and they returned triumphantly to Hollywood. Howard was the first playwright to do a Hollywood screenplay (referred to as "titles" within the business for years after talkies were in), which in itself added prestige to the production. Up until then directors, actors, and scenarists had all been pitching in on the scripts.

The fact that Colman was hardly physically suited to Sapper's hero, nicknamed "Bulldog" as much for his looks as for his character, did not prevent him from playing the part, any more than it stopped the wealth of other good-looking actors who played Drummond on both sides of the Atlantic during the twenties and thirties (Carlyle Blackwell, Ralph Richardson, Jack Buchanan, John Howard). Drummond was certainly—typically—tailored both in looks and character to fit Colman, rather than the reverse. His Drummond was the honorable gentleman who had already proved himself in such well-received films as *Beau Geste* and *The Rescue*. The combination of the story, Howard and Colman was a surefire premise of success. Colman's voice proved at once to be a natural complement to both his looks and the role of a gentleman. A lovely, unknown blonde, Joan Bennett, whose voice had come through best of those auditioned, was the heroine, and Lilyan Tashman played the slinky, witty villainess.

Each scene was rehearsed endlessly, so that actual shooting was rapid and needed few takes. Hardly a line changed from the course upon which they had decided at rehearsals, hardly a scene revised. Filming the long hours and the night work became more of a strain with the added worries sound had brought with it. Suddenly all the usual clatter and verbal instructions that had accompanied old-style filmmaking were brought to complete silence for every take. The sound man with his earphones and dials was in control. Mikes were hidden at various points in the set, in between which were "dead spots" where the actor's words could not be heard.

Not only was his voice important, but so was the precise location where the actor used it. The sets of *Drummond* were of cloth, which helped deaden the sound and eliminated any chance of echoes. (Cloth or felt on the set was, in fact, a primitive version of the mattress-lined sound studios of today.)

The lights necessary to the new medium reduced actors to pools of sweat within minutes. Whereas silent film was a mere sixteen frames per second, sound passed through the synchronized camera at twenty-four, requiring twice as much light exposure and producing almost three times as much heat. Eventually Eastman Kodak saved the perspiring crowds with faster emulsions that needed much less light.

Along with all his colleagues, Ronnie suffered in his first adventure with sound, but in his case it was only in the actual filmmaking rather than the result. Sound required far more concentration, and the actors were exhausted at the end of each overlong day. Mid-film, Lilyan and Ronnie discussed the situation between scenes in no sugary terms. They exchanged a few choice words concerning Sam Goldwyn and his methods of picture-making, only to discover that the mikes on the sound stage were open and that Sam was sitting in the recording room listening to every word. There were clearly many sound contingencies with which to reckon!

The damsel-in-distress story of *Bulldog Drummond,* its snappy dialogue, fine cast, and the excitement of sound, made up for the film's hilariously static direction. As with most early talkies, one can almost feel the weighty immobility of the soundproof camera in its "sweat box" and the plotting as to where to hide the microphone next. At the time watching a talking film was rather like watching a stage play through a keyhole.

The film opened in New York, and Sam asked Ronnie to promote it with a personal appearance. Wearing his black tie and tight smile, he arrived with Frances Goldwyn and Percy Marmont, as much for protection as for moral support.

He received a thundering ovation from the audience at the end of the film. The two men, after sufficient bowing and smiling, dashed out to do their best to avoid the crowds, as previously arranged with Frances.

Percy Marmont: "We had arranged for the car to be at the stage door, as there was a vast crowd out front, since everyone knew Ronnie was there. We were going to burst through the back door into the car, and the chauffeur had instructions to start the engine the minute he saw us. We dashed out of the door and there was no car but a vast crowd waiting. We couldn't go back because the stage door wouldn't open inward. Ronnie just said, 'Jesus!' and we rushed along the side of the cinema until we found a side door we could open, pushed in and slammed it to. It was a dreadful ordeal getting through that mob of people. Ronnie was shaking like a leaf. Eventually we got a message through to Sam, and the car came around to the front of the house. It was an awful experience for him, and it might have been one of his reasons for not attending opening nights later in his career when there was no pressure."

Both public and critics acclaimed the film: "*Bulldog Drummond* gives him a new personality. It is apparent that comedy will be his forte, as well as drama, from this initial adventure. He loses nothing by the transition but rather gains a great deal. He has a cultivated and resonant voice, and an ability to color words which will probably permit him a large range in his future career. He is one of the most successful in accomplishing the change." (The Los Angeles *Times,* August 15, 1929.) "He's suave and easy before the terrorizing mikes. Voice gives him a new charm. *Bulldog Drummond* puts Ronald Colman right at the top. . . . Goldwyn took a lot of pains with the film. It is intelligently and tastefully done [which gives one an idea of the standard of other talkies around at the time!]. The sound is highly expert." (*Photoplay,* July, 1929.) "It is the happiest and most enjoyable entertainment of its kind that has so far reached the screen. This latest combination of voices and shadows has been produced with remarkable savoir faire. . . . The voices in this production are particularly well registered. Mr. Colman is as ingratiating when he talks as when he was silent." (*The New York Times,* May 3, 1929.)

Sam's shrewdness and care with his star's first talkie paid excellent dividends. Luckily Ronnie's voice, which became as famous as his moustache, was a natural resource that only had to be tapped effectively, and of *that* his producer made certain. Goldwyn prophesied, "What Chaplin is to the silent film, Colman will be to sound!" *

As he was entering this new phase of his career, Ronnie received news from Freda in Australia that their mother had died there. She was nearly eighty, and he could only be happy that he had been able to spend time with her in England before she had left, and that she had lived to see her younger son achieve success in his career. He invited Freda to California for a holiday from her home, husband, and the tensions that build up in nursing someone old. She sailed from Australia and stayed in Mound Street, where Ronnie and tennis and the combination of familiar English friends wth congenial Americans made her feel quickly at her ease in this famed and distant city. It took her little time to realize that Hollywood is more in one's heart—or mind—than a part of any map. Everyone has a different conception of Hollywood, perhaps the more extreme with the greater distance away from it. Australia was a fair distance, and she had been unsure of what to expect. Freda became acquainted with Ronnie's Hollywood, which, despite having turned him into a heartthrob of millions seven years earlier, had not changed him into a glittering name-dropper or snob. He was minding his own business as usual, while the heartthrobbing millions

* *Film Weekly,* June 10, 1929.

minded the business of his image. If more wary than in his youth, he was certainly more fulfilled and more aware of his potentialities. He had made his home where his business was centered; the working hours were longer than in any office, but the way in which he conducted his life was as normal as any successful businessman's. He was doing all the things he wanted to do and enjoyed doing, from films to fishing. In fact, to Freda's surprise, his Hollywood was very down-to-earth for a never-never land. His friends were equally so, and she soon forgot that she was talking to what had up until then been inaccessible names in lights. Sometimes she even beat them at tennis.

Bulldog Drummond won Ronnie an Oscar nomination for Best Actor (1929–30) as did his next venture with sound, *Condemned*—more for his voice than for anything else. As a French prisoner on Devil's Island, he is a lot more Colman than convict in the Papillonesque story of *Condemned*. However, there was already less rigidity in this film than in *Drummond;* sound was being handled with a little more experience and fluidity, although the story itself is rather slow and lumbering. Louella Parsons gushed in her best Hollywood froth: "You may wonder how a prisoner can be as blithe and gay as Ronald Colman. But you only wonder briefly, for Mr. Colman has so much charm you forget to be logical. His gaiety, his absolute indifference to danger, and his happy insouciance are merely attractive, and who cares about common sense when there is an actor with Colman's appeal in the offing?" *

Ronnie had a second brush with the more dangerous aspects of his profession in this film. During a scene following his prison escape, he hides beneath a floating bridge while the guards walk over it. The exact amount of space was measured to fit his head between the water level and the bridge, so that he could surface when he had run out of breath. Action: The guards approach. He takes a deep breath

* Los Angeles *Examiner,* December 6, 1929.

and submerges, holding it as long as possible, then finds that their weight upon the bridge has lowered it, leaving no space for his head to come up. Some astute man on the set sensed something was wrong, climbed into the water, and dragged out the choking star. He recovered, of course, and mentally added underwater scenes to his "camel" list. The bridge was heightened several inches, and the sequence reshot successfully.

He again did his duty in attending the glittering first night of the film. This time the premiere took place at Grauman's Chinese Theater in Hollywood, and he was accompanied by Ann Harding (heroine), Dudley Digges (villain), and Wesley Ruggles (director). "A thronging audience attested their interest in the star and the continued approval for big picture openings. Such gala inaugural ceremonies of film-land are coming with greater frequency now, but seemingly without any lessening of glitter in most cases. What with the boulevard arrayed in its Christmas trappings, the spectacle of the first night was more elaborate than usual and drew an especially large street crowd, that came to hear the stars introduced in front of the playhouse, and talk over the radio in a national broadcast." *

Now safely across the sound barrier, Ronnie ventured his opinions on this revolutionary new medium: "The talkies are doing one very great thing. They are bringing drama—good drama—created by people who know how to do it—to everyone in the world at a price which is within everyone's reach. . . . Talking pictures will never . . . take the place of the stage to those people who are . . . in a position to enjoy the latter. But they will mean a great deal to people who are not in that position—and still more to those who never have been."

As to its effect on the individual actor: "It has lifted William Powell out of mediocre parts into distinguished

* Los Angeles *Times,* December 6, 1929.

ones. . . . It has let me play a character who has a sense of humor! I have played sombre roles for so long—it was a relief to play a man who smiled not only at the things about him but also a little at himself. . . . Even in *Condemned,* my role is handled much more lightly than it would have been in a silent version, although it is a rather heavy part.

"I believe in comedy. I believe that properly handled, it may contain all the essentials of drama. This is on the surface a light-hearted and courageous generation. People do not go about beating their breasts and being tragic in public when they suffer. At least I am certain that Anglo-Saxons do not! Why not, then, let us show characters on the screen who are like the people we know—who meet their difficulties with poise and perhaps the tongue in the cheek a little?

"For some reason, it seems easier to do this in talking pictures than it did in silent ones, and I am glad." *

"From the actor's point of view, there are naturally advantages and disadvantages. Certainly there is change. The greatest change is the actor's screen personality. His acting is different, of course. To get an idea across with words one automatically uses different techniques. In a talking picture, I might say very quietly, 'I have some bad news for you.' Such a procedure on the silent screen would be unintelligible. The line would be registered by facial expression and gesture. Under the new regime, it will undoubtedly be a case of the survival of the fittest. Good screen actors who can master the new conditions and good stage stars with screen personality will take the place of those who for some reason cannot make the grade, and this holds true of all of us, not only actors, but everyone in the business." †

Around the time of transition into sound, Ronnie's friends and fellow actors Neil Hamilton, the Torrences, Warner Baxter, Ruth Chatterton, Bill Powell, and Dick Barthel-

* *Film Weekly,* November 18, 1929.
† *Film Weekly,* May 27, 1929.

mess all leased beach frontage in Malibu, a far cry from the highly developed and not too distant Santa Monica; thirty feet of Malibu oceanfront for ten years was then leasing for $30 per month. Less than an hour from the studios, Malibu was ideal for weekends and for investment; at that time few people lived on the beach, which stretched for miles of pristine sand, with the narrow, quiet old coast road running parallel to it.

Ronnie was also caught up with the idea and leased some frontage near Warner Baxter's. The crop of cottages was soon flourishing. Whenever his film schedule allowed, he drove down during the spring and summer months to spend days swimming and sunning, and evenings with his neighboring pals. He took up waterskiing with Bill Powell and Dick Barthelmess (the popular trio were soon dubbed "The Three Musketeers" by the film colony) and tried his hand at sailing and deep-sea fishing. It was a healthy release after the days of studio heat and lights; they returned to work browned, salted, and needing next to no makeup.

Ronnie's only constant worry was Thelma. Every time it was publicized that he had signed a new deal, Thelma was in touch. The only people who knew about the situation in any detail were his closest friends—Lane, Marmont, Bill, Dick, Warner, and Tim McCoy. He was determined to maintain his privacy on the subject and above all to avoid public scandal and embarrassment. Occasionally she would, by letter or telephone, hysterically threaten to "expose" him with some new flagrant publicity, cashing in on being Mrs. Ronald Colman, finding another way of "getting even." She seemed totally unable to accept the fact that their marriage was long since dead.

Subjected to this form of blackmail, Ronnie could only pacify her with his monthly checks from a safe distance, with his lawyer running interference. He continued to believe that she would find somebody else and quietly, willingly divorce him. He shuddered at the thought of the inevitable publicity entailed in fighting to divorce her in the United States. Better to continue separated, keeping her quiet and cared for, and wait. He was certainly in no rush to remarry.

When the occasion arose to escort a lady to a restaurant or to his box at the horse races, he made certain to be always a member of a foursome rather than a couple, mostly because of his genuine desire to keep his private life from the press, and partly to avoid giving Thelma possible cause for action. Any entertaining of a lady on her own was done well out of the public eye.

He was developing the need for a human shield, a permanent protection from the public as well as from Thelma, and he found one in Tommy Turner—a bespectacled gentleman a few years his junior and as mousey as his Dickensian name implies. Tommy had all the natural talents of a gentleman's gentleman, secretary, chauffeur, bag-carrier, and valet. He scurried about dealing with everything in eager obedience rather than with a mind of his own. He empathized with his employer's life to the point of whispering hoarsely when Ronnie developed laryngitis. Quiet, capable, unobtrusive, and reliable, Tommy managed diplomatically to remain as secretive about Colman as Colman himself, and at the same time be a staunch buffer. In short, he fulfilled every qualification that Ronnie desired, and he was an enduring success.

As he had Tommy protecting him in his day-to-day life, he needed the similar, shielding company of a friend whenever he went on a trip. On one such occasion, when one of his cohorts was unable to accompany him to England, Arthur Hornblow sensibly inquired why he didn't go on his own. "Are you *mad?*" responded Ronnie. "What do you think would happen to me on the boat?"

The need for this protective armor was physical as well

as emotional; anyone who is famous is threatened with various forms of infringement by their public. Once, for instance, a woman arrived on Ronnie's doorstep surrounded by her suitcased possessions with the firm intention of moving in, based upon the equally firm conviction that she had been invited. She installed herself amid her goods and chattels and staunchly refused to budge. Finally abandoning both argument and diplomacy, Tommy sent for the fire department.

On another occasion Ronnie returned home with Joan Blondell and her fiancé (a close friend of Ronnie's), cinematographer George Barnes, to hear a sireny "Ronieeee" wafting down upon the breeze. There was a woman on his roof.

Joan Blondell: "He got George and me into the house very quickly and then told us the police were coming. By God, they found a very naked, very unattractive woman. She fought the police to get at the most glamorous star of them all. He had such a dignity about him, even that crazy night. He arranged with the officers privately that she was to be given some money, sent home, and that nothing be done to her. The poor thing was so frightened and desperate to have a place in the life of that fantastic Ronald Colman.

"When I met my future husband, George Barnes, I had been one of those kid fans of Ronald Colman, the way everybody was. George looked very like him: he had the same velvet huge brown eyes, but was shorter and thinner. Then I found out that my husband-to-be was a friend of Ronnie's, and he took me to the house on Mound Street, way up in the hills. Now, it's no longer an elegant neighborhood, but then it was. It was a lovely Spanish place with a huge outside door. His secretary looked through the peephole before he let you in. He led you down a beautiful corridor into an outside arbor. The evenings were fabulous there. His close friends were around—Dick Barthelmess and his wife, the

Clive Brooks, Warner Baxters, and Bill Powell. George and I were just going together and I was the youngest of the group, and they were all so darling to me. I saw for the first time how perfectly and in what good taste people could live. The drinks that were poured were always on a huge table on one side of a flower-filled room that overlooked the garden and the tennis court. The liquor was in the most beautiful cut-glass bottle. I always remember those crystal shiny bottles and beautiful paper-thin glasses. Then they'd go out and play tennis, come back and have their Scotch and soda or whatever, and the soda came from a great round container that you squirted with a silver chain link around it, not in soda bottles.

"To me, Ronnie's home was the most homey I'd seen. I still want to call him Mr. Colman, because that's what I used to call him. I'll never forget he set up a security for me, a life insurance policy, whereby at the age of forty I would never have to work again. And another policy, so that if I ever had an accident, whatever I was being paid at that moment, I'd get for the rest of my life. What a terrific thing that was to do for a kid starting out, to take her aside and say, 'You're going to be in this profession a long time, so from every paycheck you get, put money into this policy. When you are forty, you'll be free!'

"He had a costume party one night at his house, and George and I were invited. George dressed as an old-fashioned sailor with a soup-strainer moustache and I was a burlesque queen in a very tight little short outfit with the long hose and aigrettes in my hair. We all sang, and I played the drums. It was the Hollywood I had dreamed about. That—to me—being part of Ronald Colman's life, was even more memorable than the life I had at Warner Brothers. He and his friends were so distinguished, and he had divine humor. We'd all tell stories, and sometimes he'd get up and act them out while we'd all be sitting cross-legged on floor and couch. Those were beautiful, wonderful evenings. . . ."

Quickly following up the success of *Bulldog Drummond,* Goldwyn secured a similar property. *Raffles* (spiritual forefather of *The Pink Panther*) is based on E. W. Hornung's stories of a high-class English cricketer who does some sleuthing on the side, a role already distinguished by Gerald du Maurier and John Barrymore. Like Colman's Drummond, Raffles handles his adventures with undaunted style and aplomb. (This film is most probably the source of Ronnie's erroneous image as an avid cricket player.) Sparklingly adapted for the screen by Sidney Howard, the story had all the promise of a natural hit. Goldwyn signed Harry D'Arrast, a brilliant director who made only nine films in his exceptional career. *Raffles,* however, was not to be among them, though his preproduction work on the script exhibited itself in the film finished by another.

It was Goldwyn's habit to sit in on the rushes of all his films, and when he saw something of which he didn't approve to dispense the more coherent and diplomatic Arthur Hornblow to deal with it. On the third day when, as it happened, Hornblow was not around, Goldwyn went from the rushes to the set and delivered the complaint himself, in his rather tactless, unsubtle manner. D'Arrast's own hot Basque temper flared: "You and I don't speak the same language, Mr. Goldwyn." "I'm sorry, Mr. D'Arrast, but it is my money that's buying the language!" Hornblow returned to find that D'Arrast had been fired on the spot and replaced by George Fitzmaurice.

Fitz was not only a fine director but a man of sagacity who knew how to handle people, and who understood Goldwyn. They would quarrel but not fight, and they managed to have a long and successful association. Colman, who had made seven films with Fitz, had a healthy respect for his ability as a director which Goldwyn shared. A pleasant atmosphere reigned once again on the set, and the filming continued without a hitch.

In the three years since the debut of sound, progress on improving equipment and so forth had moved with the breakneck speed only money can buy. Now the camera covers were much lighter, and the machinery that accompanied sound was being made to move far more silently and with greater ease. Fitz directed with snappy, tongue-in-cheek decisiveness, completely in accord with Howard's witty screenplay. The high-ceilinged sets of the equally high-class English manor house go well around the shoulders of Colman, Kay Francis, and the elder generation—Alison Skipworth as Lady Melrose, with her unashamed penchant for brandy, pug dogs, and handsome young men, and veteran English actor Frederick Kerr as her husband.

The clear-sighted and sophisticated film magazine *Cinema* (which appeared monthly during 1930 only) had the following to say on the film: "Those who look for the white-haired Raffles of the Hornung stories, cool and serenely unscrupulous, will be disappointed. . . . But, if not the original package, we have Ronald Colman, who can suggest that all sorts of things can happen, though in the end it has turned out to be nothing more thrilling than outwitting an unusually stupid gentleman from Scotland Yard. Colman keeps the interest up more than would seem possible, and Kay Francis manages to give the impression that the most entertaining part of the story will come after she and Raffles are safely on the Continent."

In the spring of 1930, after filming was finished, Ronnie took time off for a vacation and found company in Percy Marmont, who was returning to England where his wife was already waiting for him. They took the train to the East Coast and then the boat to Europe.

Marmont: "It was four or five days' journey with a change in Chicago where you spent several hours between trains. Ronnie was so frightened about press and publicity. It was quite genuine, not a pose. He was scared stiff. He said, 'Will you take care of the luggage for me?' I said, 'Don't worry, I'll do everything. Go and hide yourself.' So he put on a pair of dark glasses and pulled down his hat, which made him look like some motion picture thug, and we crawled out of the train. I was doing the luggage when I heard this colored porter say to him, 'Hey, boss, isn't that fella Mr. Percy Marmont?' whereupon Ronnie said to me, 'Jesus, I'm going to take them off!' But of course he didn't.

"We arrived in England, having discussed on the trip what we should do, and one of us suggested going to Holland with my wife, Dorothy, our suitcases, and no plans. We had more fun on that trip. We took the ferry at Harwich and when we got off we realized that the Automobile Association man who had dealt with the car had kept the ignition key, so we got towed off to a garage, where there was a wonderful Dutchman with his family. He said it would take quite a long time as he'd have to remove the dashboard to make the new key, and in the meantime, would we come in and have lunch with them? They were awfully nice, and had no idea who we were at all. We had lunch, went out for a walk, came back and had tea with them and everything was finished. Lots of handshakes and thank yous and goodness knows what. Ten days later, on our return, we thought we'd go and say goodbye to our pals. By this time, of course, photos had been published in the press and their attitude was entirely different. They treated us like royalty, instead of two rather nice fellows and a pretty girl who had been landed in an awkward position.

"As Ronnie and I got to know each other better, he revealed to me a tremendous lot of his wonderful imagination and his rather deep thoughts about life. How we and Hollywood were living on the crest of something that nobody seemed quite to understand; how there was a sense of impermanence about it. But then he would check himself. I remember one of his slogans was, 'Come on, let's have a drink. Back to normalcy!'

"He was one of the most idealistic men I have ever met. Insofar as women were concerned, he didn't regard them as inferior creatures, but he was scared of them. When friends started to match-make during the course of a conversation, he would just clam up. He expanded on most things. I don't know of any other subject where he would clam up."

Ronnie stayed briefly with the Marmonts upon their return to England, hiding inside their house to avoid the more determined newspapermen, while Percy Marmont stated obstinately that he was definitely not there. He visited Gladys and Edith, each living outside London, the only members of his family still in England, and with an old friend of his from English stage days passed through Bramlin's Theatrical Agency to ask nostalgically, "Anything today?" They didn't bat an eyelid! He left for Paris in the early summer to meet Bill Powell and the Torrences.

Bill and he sailed back to America together, arriving in time for Ronnie to emphatically deny rumors of an engagement to his leading lady, Kay Francis. The most significant events during his absence were Warner Baxter's Oscar for Best Actor (*In Old Arizona*) and the Academy's new contract following Equity's war between actors and their employers. The main innovations were the clause allowing players at least twelve hours' rest between leaving the studio at night and resuming work in the morning, and the provision that actors would be paid overtime after eight continuous hours—a more than welcome relief to every overworked actor in the business.

When Ronnie and Bill returned in the summer of 1930, Ivor Novello was scoring a great Broadway success in his own play, *Symphony in Two Flats*. His leading lady was a sparkling young (twenty-six-year-old) British actress, Benita Hume, already a big name in English films. American producers, who had seen her first talkie, *High Treason*, and the thundering Light Brigade production of *Balaclava*, were besieging her with contracts, one of which (RKO) she eventually signed for £50,000. As the weeks went by in the sweltering summer of New York City, she became increasingly homesick and finally reneged on the contract. The reason was that she simply did not want to be away that long from London *and* her husband-to-be. So, at the end of the play's run she returned with Ivor to London and to her man.

In an interview six months earlier, discussing filmgoers' motives with London's *Film Weekly*, she had digressed somewhat when the interviewer expressed his sadness as to audiences being able to buy their romance at so much an hour and the actors having to manufacture it. He felt this must be the reverse of romantic, that the happy picturegoers are able to fall in love with the film star, while she, on the other side of the screen, must find it difficult ever to take the same stars seriously. "Think so?" she said with a sort of pitying twinkle. "I'll tell you a story that will knock your theories endways. A year or two ago I was eating at a West End restaurant. There was a good-looking man at a neighboring table. I felt his eyes on me—dark, compassionate, exciting eyes they were. We kept looking at each other all through lunch. . . . I got so interested I forgot to eat. I told my companion that I must at all cost meet that man. 'Impossible,' she said. 'That's Ronald Colman.' I've seen every Colman film since. How's that for appreciation of what you call glamour?" *

* December 9, 1929.

By Christmas Benita was back in London again and continuing her success in English films. She also married her fiancé, a young English-German writer.

Cashing in quickly on the success of *Raffles,* Goldwyn made certain the next film was in the same vein. English actor Frederick Kerr, already in his seventies, had made such a personal hit with the public as Lord Melrose that Sam brought him back from England for his next venture. It was playwright Frederick Lonsdale's first screenplay and one written especially for Ronnie. The film started production with the familiar Goldwyn traumas and changes.

Irving Cummings, once an actor himself, was to direct, and after the usual endless auditions for the leading lady, a young stage actress from the East was chosen, Constance Cummings (no relation to the director):

Constance Cummings: "The only other film I had done was one of Ripley's *Believe It or Not* shorts, where Ripley would stand in front of a baronial mantlepiece and tell a group of assembled weekend guests these astounding facts. I was one of the guests. . . .

"I was thrilled about the idea of Hollywood, Colman and the lead in his film. I could hardly contain myself about the idea of playing opposite him. He was one's charming, romantic ideal, and I already had a strong image of him—everybody did. He was a very big star in a way that is very rare. Really every girl's idea of what her future husband should be if she were lucky. Once we'd met, I did not stay in awe of him for long, because he was so unaffected. Very warm and real with no chichi or starry nonsense. He was shy about people making compliments to him or making a fuss over him, but he was a very cozy person in a way a lot of Hollywood people were not.

"Filming had been going on with Irving Cummings di-

Marjory Colman

Charles Colman

As the patient in *Damaged Goods,* Fisher White as the doctor, earliest photo of RC on stage, spring, 1917

RC, 1917

Thelma Raye in her biggest
stage hit, *The Joy-Ride Lady*,
1914 (from the Mander and
Mitchenson Theatre Collection)

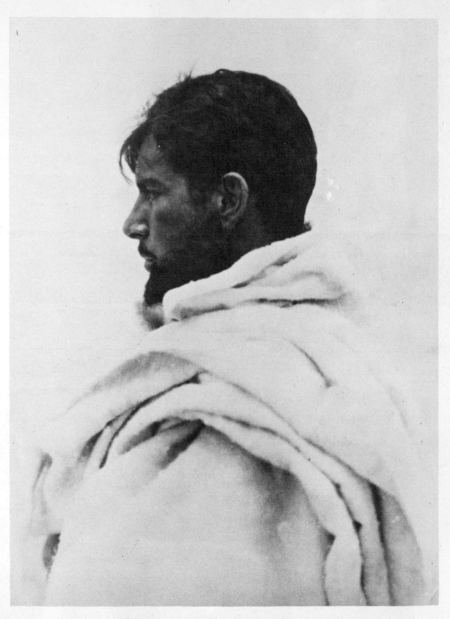

RC during the filming of *The White Sister*

With Lillian Gish in
The White Sister

From *The Dark Angel*,
first film with Vilma Banky

With May McAvoy in *Lady Windermere's Fan*

In this close-up from *Lady Windermere's Fan*, with RC and Bert Lytell, May is obviously standing on a ramp of some sort

With Vilma Banky in *The Night of Love*

With Vilma Banky in their last film together, *Two Lovers*

On board ship with Philip
Strange and Dorothy Feiner
(now Mrs. Richard Rodgers)

With Helen Hayes in *Arrowsmith*

With Richard Barthelmess
(kneeling) and William Powell
(standing) on aquaplane (1930).
On the Sahara Desert with Al
Weingand (1932). Amid the
Temples of Bali (below)

With Donald Woods
in *A Tale of Two Cities*

With Loretta Young
in *Clive of India*

Filming *Lost Horizon*,
underneath the waterfall

With Claudette Colbert
in *Under Two Flags*

Lost Horizon with, l. to r., Thomas Mitchell, Edward Everett Horton, John Howard, unidentified actor, and H. B. Warner

On the set of *The Prisoner of Zenda* with Mary Astor

Rehearsing the coronation scene with Madeleine Carroll
while filming *The Prisoner of Zenda*

With Ida Lupino in *The Light That Failed*

With Benita in Summit Drive garden

On board the *Dragoon* with Benita and Pat Boyer, and with Robert Montgomery

With Basil Rathbone in *If I Were King*

Wedding photo on veranda of San Ysidro house with Tim McCoy (best man) and Heather Thatcher (matron of honor), taken by Al Weingand

After christening of
Juliet Benita Colman

On *Lucky Partners* set
with Ginger Rogers

With Ingrid Bergman and Marlene Dietrich on the set of *Kismet*

RC and JBC

RC and Loretta Young

In *A Double Life*

With Benita in *The Halls of Ivy*

recting Ronnie, Frederick Kerr and me for ten days or so, when there was a pause. An ominous silence when I was not called to the studio. Every time I telephoned, they would say, 'We'll let you know.' Finally, I was called back and into Arthur Hornblow's office. I thought this was bad, since when I had first arrived, it was Goldwyn who had welcomed me into *his* office with open arms and a lot of 'I'm so pleased to meet you and I'm going to make you a star,' etc. Then, later on, during the filming, Sam used to tell me I smoked too much, and that I mustn't and the whole company was onto this. So when Arthur Hornblow called me in and said, 'Sit down and will you have a cigarette?' I knew it was disaster. He told me very nicely that I wasn't going on with the film.

"I was devastated! It was a big film, and I was going to be a big star and suddenly it was all over, and I felt it was the end of everything, that I would have to go back to New York without ever having done a film in Hollywood, and of course I was head over heels and agog about Ronnie. When this happened at the studio, he must have known how bad I felt. He rang me up and said he wanted me to meet a great friend of his, Noll Gurney, who was in the agency business. 'I've asked him to get you a film so that, at least, if you want to go back to New York later, you will have made one film.' It just hit the spot. And Noll Gurney got me a part in a film called *The Criminal Code*. So what would have been an absolutely devastating experience turned out to be very nice because of Ronnie. As a result of his help came my first film and my staying in Hollywood and really The Beginning.

"When I saw the finished film, I realized what they had wanted. The girl was supposed to be English and I had a very strong American accent then, and a peculiar strong 'r' which was practically my own invention. They had wanted me to bleach my hair blonde, and I'd said No, so they'd put me in a blonde wig which didn't help. They thought I was chubby and sent me off to Sylvia, a tiny Swedish ball of fire, who slapped it off you, which was rather painful. So I would arrive on the set rather self-conscious, feeling I was too fat, and unhappy in my wig.

"Irving Cummings (discharged from the film soon afterward) perhaps wasn't 'svelte' enough either, because they wanted a smooth, polished English comedy sort of thing, which of course is what Freddie Lonsdale had written. Freddie complimented me on my test, for which I'd read a scene from *Doctor's Dilemma,* and said, 'When I get back to England, I'll tell Shaw that I heard this speech read as well as I've ever heard it,' And then later on he said to me, 'Now, my dear, I'll tell you a word of warning about Hollywood: They will try to change you. They will try to change you completely. Don't let them!' And then he went back to England and that was the last I saw of him. And of course, they did try. They sent me off to get thinner, and tried to change my hair, and finally changed me for Loretta Young!"

The story of *The Devil to Pay* spans a few weeks in the eventful life of the affectionate, carefree son of a wealthy English family. Frederick Kerr plays the harrumphing father with whom the son stays in between his foreign escapades. The son's world has always been his beloved oyster. Life, loves, and money are regarded with equally joyous impermanence. He is secretly envied by the men and less secretly adored by the women (including Myrna Loy and Loretta Young), about whom he thoughtfully asks advice from George, his terrier. He remains in the good graces of all, however, for in one way or another he unfailingly manages to make the lives of everyone with whom he comes in contact happier.

Ronnie bounces through the film, followed in sprightly fashion by George and the rest of the cast, whose good humor is infectious. Swinging round an old woman one sunny morning upon his return home, he grasps her elbows and smiles, "Have no fear for the day, you look divine!"

The critics caught the spirit: "Six reels of Mr. Colman being charming, but since it happens that Mr. Colman can be charming without offense, ostentation or self-consciousness, and that Frederick Lonsdale is an expert at making something out of nothing, the result is a polished, tasteful and entirely likable screen comedy." *

It was Loretta Young's first film with Ronnie and her first with Goldwyn. She was only sixteen years old when she replaced Constance Cummings, yet she was already a proven professional and indeed came across on the screen as a very sophisticated young woman.

Loretta Young: "I was already in the movies when I was four, playing an Arab kid in *The Sheik* with Valentino. When I was about eight, we had a game in our house. (There were my two sisters at that time and three cousins—my mother ran a boardinghouse and she preferred families with children, so there were always lots around.) The game was called 'Dibbies.' You would have to get up early in the morning to dib the movie star you wanted for your boyfriend that day. We had a blackboard and I would always put dibbies on Ronald Colman, which meant that he was mine, all mine, for a whole day. I was eight and I'd get up at four in the morning to put dibbies on him, then go back to sleep again. I'd already seen him in *The White Sister* and to me he was the White Knight, the epitome of romance. Even for an eight-year-old.

"By the time I was nine, I hadn't varied and gone off to being a Valentino fan—I still preferred Colman. One Saturday afternoon, I was going off to a matinee alone. I was standing on a corner waiting for the signal to change and daydreaming about you know who, when all of a sudden this

---

* New York *Herald Tribune,* December 20, 1930.

roadster drove up and stopped and there He was driving it. For a minute, I didn't know whether it was part of my day-dream, and I just stood with my mouth hanging open. He must have felt me staring at him because he looked at me and then he smiled. I was thunderstruck. The signal changed and off he went, and I just stood there for about five minutes. I remember thinking after he drove off that when I was a Big Star (and I was always sure that I was going to be a Big Star, not just an actress), I was going to smile at everybody who looked at me. And my instinct with everybody whether I know them or not has always been to smile. I've gotten myself into a lot of trouble that way, actually, and it's lucky that smile was all he did that afternoon! I'll be in a car and some-body will drive up next to me and stare and smile and I smile right back and he'll say something like, 'Do you think we'd be compatible?' I've learned to just smile back and drive on!

"I became very sophisticated around fifteen or sixteen when I was under contract to a studio, and my crush on him grew with the years, as he grew in his stature and attractive-ness and ability. I watched his career, what he was doing and who he was doing it with and wishing it could be me. A very good actress called Constance Cummings was going to be his next leading lady. Then I got a call from Goldwyn's studio saying, 'Come over, we want you to make a test for the lead with Colman.' Goldwyn had decided to change Constance Cummings. It seemed he wanted someone skinnyish, since he thought an English lady should be skinny and tall. That was the only recommendation I had!

"I sneaked up to the projection room, which was not al-lowed, to see her in a rough cut they were running. She was so marvelous that I got this terrible inferiority complex. It is possible that I looked more the part, but I didn't have her talent. I panicked. (I hadn't met Ronnie yet.) So there I am doing my test and all of a sudden I see him and my mouth went dry and I couldn't swallow and it was sad! I was too embarrassed to tell anyone how I felt about him. Anyhow, I got the part.

"I only went up to the eighth grade at school, and in those days I'd say 'Dinin' ' and 'Dancin',' hardly the way an English lady speaks, so they gave me a coach. He was a very fine English actor who used to work with George Arliss, and he worked with me for about three weeks to give me some kind of an English accent. I would be fine in rehearsals, then I'd get with Ronnie and I'd forget everything except him— my dreamboat! Finally, Fitz (who had replaced Irving Cummings) said to the coach, 'What's the matter with her? She's OK until we turn the camera and then nothing comes out.' So the coach called me into the dressing room and I burst into tears and said, 'Well, I'm just so crazy about him. I think I'm bad in the part and he knows I'm bad.' He said, 'Oh, that's all right, dear, you'll get over it in a day or two!'

"Well, he must have said something to Ronnie, and he explained it to Fitz. Ronnie was almost a psychiatrist in the way he handled the situation because he wooed me enough to fulfill all my romantic dreams about him (being a sixteen-year-old in those days of purity, a touch on the hand was ecstasy!), and still not enough to encourage me beyond our eight hours on the set. He was so darling, such a mature man and always so tender with women. I really fell head over heels in love with him on that picture.

"He'd rehearse each whole scene with me. Usually the star's close-up is the first to be done, then the leading lady's, and male stars would walk off and let somebody else read their dialogue for them. But Ronnie never did that. He was always there, even if it was reading his lines for the bit player. He always gave everybody full advantage of himself, as well as his talent and his efficient timing.

"He knew his dialogue before anyone else did, and very seldom improvised. He never listened for cues, he listened for thoughts. When your thought was finished, he would answer that thought. (It was what they later learned and called method acting). He listened and thought and answered in his own terms. There wasn't a false move. He was a delicate perfectionist, where other stars I've worked with tend to be trying perfectionists. Before going into a scene, for instance, they'll say something like 'Just a minute, if it's hot inside this room and frosty outside, why is there no frost on the windows?' And it would throw me completely; I would go into the scene wondering why there was no frost on the windows, instead of about the contents of the scene itself. If Ronnie had anything to say like this, he would do it alone with the director and never disturb anybody else's concentration.

"He was the first actor to have humor on screen. There was no humor in acting in those days, naturally excluding comedians. Valentino and all of them were dead serious. He had a charm and a twinkle. In those days, you didn't have fun on the set. You had 'fun' if you did your work well. There was no such thing as kidding around or joking, it was a dead serious business. That's probably why Ronnie's gentle, humorous touch impressed me so, because nobody else had it or ever thought that way. I tried to learn a little of it from him. I hope I have, even to this day!

"His attitude toward women was always a little aloof, which of course made them all flock after him. He used to give charming parties, and after *The Devil to Pay* he used to invite me to them. I was always disappointed that *he* didn't come and pick me up and take me home, but I never presumed that he would because he didn't give you that feeling. Yet, when you got there, you thought that he was giving the party just for you. This is a marvelous quality, and I think he made everybody feel this way. His person-to-person attitude is rare even today."

Another friend, hotel manager Al Weingand, shares similar memories:

"Some of the most remarkable parties were given at Mound Street. He was a great host and entertainer and very warm to all his guests. He had a knack of encompassing any stranger and bringing him into the group. Always good food, good booze, but more important, all kinds of activity. More damn games and things, as well as all kinds of singing. The old drinking songs, 'Old Heidelberg,' and one that Ronnie, Tim, and Adolphe Menjou used to sing that went something like:

I don't want to march with the infantry,
Ride with the cavalry,
Shoot with the artillery,
For I am with the King's NAIVEE!

Also one that ended up, 'Once between a horse's mane and tail, a fixture!' "

"All the other parties that I was ever invited to never attained the warmth of his, and he liked giving them. Usually fifteen or twenty people. For little dinner parties of six people or so, he liked showing movies—not his own, just other good movies. He had a projector and screen, and he hired a projectionist."

Another frequent guest was actress Bessie Love, whom he squired round prior to her marriage, and it was through her that Ronnie met William Hawks (brother of director Howard). Bill became his friend, tennis partner, and business manager, as well as Bessie's husband. His first and most important client, Ronnie told Bill early in their business relationship, "Go in and do what you can for me. Before God, I'm probably worth thirty-five dollars a week. Before the motion picture industry, I'm worth anything you can get!"

It was Bill and Bessie who introduced him to Mary Astor, then the widow of the third Hawks brother, Kenneth. This dark, beautiful, fine actress gave Ronnie his first serious thoughts about pushing through his divorce. A brief romance ensued. "Ronnie asked me to marry him. Unfortunately, I was all entangled with a man who didn't want to marry me, and whom, also unfortunately, I later married. I was certainly attracted to Ronnie. He had wit and charm in abundance. But I wasn't using my intelligence about relationships in those days. It was a brief encounter—and a lovely one!" They continued to see each other as an occasional foursome prior to Mary's engagement, but Ronnie's proposal remained secret even to Bill and Bessie. Most important, the seed of freedom from Thelma was sown!

Having completed *The Devil to Pay,* one of his favorites, Ronnie launched into the film he later regarded as his poorest. *The Unholy Garden* was a misfortune before the cameras even started rolling.

Goldwyn and Hornblow, in New York searching for the next Colman vehicle, were joined one night at the Pierre Hotel by playwrights Ben Hecht and Charles MacArthur (ex-journalists and by then well-established writers), who proceeded to narrate their idea for a possible movie. The story revolved around a crooks' hideaway in the Sahara, with some hidden loot and love interest thrown in. Hecht and MacArthur were wizards with words; the evening was most enjoyable and resulted in their idea being sold to Goldwyn, who brought them back to Hollywood and clinched the deal. Unfortunately, they surreptitiously started work for Howard Hughes—and more money—on *Scarface,* putting *The Unholy Garden* job into the incapable hands of some lesser writers. When Goldwyn finally received the script, it was only to realize that although he had the basic story that had been gaily recited at the Pierre, he had been completely cheated out of the writing talents of Hecht and MacArthur. It was a story that needed *all* their talents to make it credible or at least amusing. Without them it was neither. But Goldwyn was committed. The script was late coming in. The production was already set up. Ronnie, obliged to fulfill his contract, felt ill-used in a role hardly worthy of his status as an actor, let alone as the biggest box-office draw in the Goldwyn studio. Goldwyn retaliated by letting it be known that Ronnie was being ungrateful for all he had done for him.

Hornblow said, "I don't think he was ungrateful, but their bust-up was a long time pending, even from the time I first arrived." Goldwyn's brash, uncouth manner had long grated upon Colman's natural reserve, despite the valuable intervention of "buffer" Hornblow. Although their business partnership was of unaccountable mutual value over seven years, maintaining a balanced accord throughout required effort and self-control, neither of which Goldwyn supplied in quantity. The relationship was precarious, and certainly not abetted by the atmosphere surrounding *The Unholy Garden*. Fitz, diplomatic, careful to avoid taking sides, directed the film (his last with Colman) detached to the point of disinterest. This badly written and miscast production, after their lists of triumphs, can hardly have been a welcoming challenge.

Colman, though more remote than usual, entered into the filming in his precise, organized manner—always on time at the studio, always in command of the entire script on the first day. He continued to look casually immaculate and was never anything but polite to cast and crew. Inside, however, he was fuming. During the winter a stronger than usual earthquake rocked Hollywood (the only entertaining outcome being the reactions of well-known people, quickly garnered by the press). Ronnie, on the set at the time, had calmly remarked amid the cries of alarm, "That's no earthquake, it's merely Mr. Goldwyn seeing yesterday's rushes."

Shortly to become *King Kong*'s leading lady, Fay Wray was *The Unholy Garden*'s romantic interest:

"It was the talk of the studio that Ronnie was not speaking to Goldwyn, and there was something rather admirable in the air he had, the fact that he could be doing pictures for

Sam and still not tolerate any communication. You had to say, 'Well, hooray for you, for the strength you have to be that way!'

"He made no overt objection to the film, but there was an air of discomfort about the whole thing. I wasn't comfortable in it either. I felt an uneasiness in playing scenes against so grubby a background, wearing pastel chiffon with Alençon lace and having a hairdresser standing by. I was a brunette then but because all the women that had played opposite him had been blonde, I was made a blonde.

"Ronnie really was a teacher; every Aquarian I have ever known is that. I think this made him objective about himself, gave him a self-awareness. I felt that while we were running through the dialogue, while he made suggestions, that he was not in his part, that he was directing to some degree. Fitz was the director, but I remember much more keenly rehearsing with Ronnie. He was both *in* the scene and watchfully outside, making significant observations about how, for instance, I reacted to a poem he was reading: 'Hark! Hark! The lark at Heaven's gate. . . .'

"Fitz knew how to put a film together smoothly, but his speciality was drawing-room drama. What this particular piece needed was all the realism you could get into it. It was very frustrating for me, because though I was happy to be working with Ronald Colman, the part didn't blossom at all.

"One evening, when we were going to do night shots, I had come home for dinner and done something that was very rare for me. I had a glass of champagne with dinner, and when I went back to the set, I was just a little sparkling. Again he was my 'teacher.' He said, 'That's wonderful, you should do that more often!' And I was just so pleased; one might have expected something different from this very proper man. He enjoyed his Scotch and soda a lot too, but I never saw him the slightest bit tipsy."

Ronnie was very dissatisfied with the entire affair, and most of the critics agreed with him as far as the film's merits were concerned, except—surprisingly—*The New York Times,* which found it most "enjoyable and gripping an adventure." *The Unholy Garden* was an example of the disadvantages of being under contract to a studio: A star had occasionally to do films that were not up to his standards and that he did not want to do. This was the first film that fell into that category for Ronnie.

When Arthur Hornblow first suggested buying the rights to *Arrowsmith* from Nobel Prize-winner Sinclair Lewis, Goldwyn demurred. The wife dies in the story, and a dying heroine was unpopular as far as film audiences were concerned. And this would be a big production, a large investment not to be gambled with. Ronnie heard the rights were in the offing, and stepped into the fray. He was an admirer of all Lewis's work and as eager to see *Arrowsmith* filmed as he was to play the role of the doctor. Sidney Howard soon heard the news and let it be known that he was equally eager to write the screen adaptation, and Sam was faced with two strong arguments for making the film, as well as perhaps a twinge of conscience over his last picture with Ronnie. Finally he was sold on the idea.

Helen Hayes was brought from the theater to play Leora in this, her second film. (She had already won an Oscar for her first, *The Sin of Madelon Claudet.*) Richard Bennett (father of Joan and Constance) and A. E. Anson (who later auditioned for the role of the High Lama in *Lost Horizon*) added further status to the cast. Myrna Loy slinks seductively about the tropics as "the other woman," and Goldwyn brought John Ford over from 20th Century to direct.

Lewis's story is of a stubborn young doctor who, impelled by his feelings of duty to his profession and mankind, leaves his cozy practice to search for a cure for the plague in the West Indies. Leora, his wife, accompanies him much against his will, and dies during an epidemic, leaving him to continue the search alone. Hayes and Colman play off each other with natural ease, most delightfully in their first meeting, when young Doctor Arrowsmith trips over the attractive, outspoken new nurse, floor-scrubbing as punishment for having been caught smoking. He is annoyed by her lack of the respect that he feels to be his due as a doctor—albeit an extremely recent one. Snapping back at him from her floor level, she realizes she's getting herself into deeper trouble. Then, almost catching themselves off-guard, he has invited her to dinner and she has accepted, and the whole tone of their no-nonsense relationship is set. Rarely is an entente as deftly outlined in so short a scene.

Though Ford buffs do not regard this as one of his best, it was a success with the public, certainly one of Colman's favorites, and indeed Sinclair Lewis's, who inscribed the copy of his book, "To Ronald Colman, who to me *is* Martin Arrowsmith," and who wrote to Goldwyn, "I want to thank you and Sidney Howard and Ronald Colman and Helen Hayes and A. E. Anson and Richard Bennett for a film which has completely carried out everything I tried to do in *Arrowsmith*."

Goldwyn had one bad moment mid-production when his director disappeared for personal reasons, and Sam was concerned that he would have to start looking elsewhere. Much to everyone's relief, however, Ford returned a week later at peace with the world. This was his first major sound film:

John Ford: "*Arrowsmith* was already cast when I went over to Goldwyn. Ronnie and I were friends, so I was delighted. Though he was the leading star of the business then, nobody ever acknowledged what a superb actor he was. They just accepted him as Ronald Colman. He did everything so easily. He never played drunken scenes or grew a beard or did any of those things which get Academy Awards, but he was the greatest actor I have ever known.

"When you work with Sam, there are always problems, if you allow them to worry you. He would come onto the set after I had started work, and I would sit down and order tea or something. He'd say, 'Why aren't you shooting?' And I'd say, 'Well, if I came into your office while you were working and watched you work, you'd be very much annoyed. This is my office, I am working here, and I am not going to be rude and work while you, the president of a company, are here, sir. Very bad manners!' He couldn't understand that, so we'd wait until he'd left, then we would resume shooting.

"You didn't have to *work* with Ronnie—it was that simple. He knew exactly what to do and was letter-perfect when he did it. We didn't rehearse on the set. We had a little room where we'd sit down and go through the lines. I would give what suggestions I could, and they'd all listen and then we went out and shot the scene."

Goldwyn, despite his preliminary worries, enjoyed a success both in his choice of book and his treatment of it. This was a "status" film, and an intense relief to him after its predecessor. It was admired by the critics, listed among *Photoplay*'s and *The New York Times'* Best Films of the Year, winner of London's *Film Weekly* Gold Medal for Ronnie himself, and nominated by the Academy for Best Picture— to be beaten by *Grand Hotel*. Arthur Hornblow, whose idea it had been to buy the rights, had another kind of success; he later married that "other woman" of the plot, Myrna Loy.

Changes were occurring among Ronnie's friends. Tim McCoy had finally separated from his first wife in the spring of 1931. In the fall Bill Powell married Carole Lombard (his second marriage), climaxing a two-year romance. The Clive Brooks, Torrences, and Dick Barthelmess and his second wife were at Bill's house for the occasion. Ronnie, in Santa Barbara at the time, congratulated them from afar. He had now become known to the press as "the last of the three famous bachelors." Having witnessed their marital merry-go-rounds, he was understandably content with his title!

Several months earlier Charlie Lane had taken off on a traveling spree and finally retired to live at the Del Monte Hotel in Carmel. The hotel manager, Al Weingand, who had gotten to know Ronnie on his visits to Lane, was a down-to-earth, gregarious, humorous man with absolutely no interest in the film business. "Ronnie used to come to visit Charlie at the hotel, and because I played tennis and enjoyed Scotch, I was brought into the act. We hit it off at once. I'd spoken to him of my two ambitions: to visit Europe and to eventually have a small but beautiful inn somewhere which would attract interesting, congenial guests, and where I could wear tweeds, smoke my pipe and carry a stick! Ronnie, who was then footloose, said he'd always wanted an anchorage, a place to leave his trunk, and that such an inn would be ideal for his purpose—and so began our quest for a hotel."

Goldwyn's idea at this time was to cut down Ronnie's films to one a year, thereby setting him apart as a superstar and putting him in the secure position of being seldom seen but always sure of a welcome. This was a natural procedure when a star reached a certain stage of popularity. In short, Goldwyn was making his exclusive star even more exclusive. This allowed for further freedom in Ronnie's life, and he profited by taking a prolonged trip abroad armed with camera and little baggage. He and Al sailed in the autumn for France, leaving Goldwyn and Hornblow on the perennial lookout for suitable stories.

They sailed from New York to Villefranche, from where the train took them due north. They ate and absorbed Paris until stomachs and eyes were satiated. They rode past Ronnie's battlegrounds of the First World War en route to Berlin, and he touched on the subject briefly to Al. In Berlin he found the German language difficult and he was not a beer-drinker. He mentally waltzed around Vienna, totally captivated by its spirit and charm. Budapest; and then the welcome rediscovery of Italy, where expressions, lilts, and gestures of the language came back to him easily. Venice, truly like every Canaletto he'd ever seen; Rome, where he left few stones unturned; Taormina; Naples and the poignant eloquence of Pompeii; the bustle and push of Genoa. Then they crossed the border into France and the old heart of Marseilles.

From there they sailed to Egypt, and Ronnie pored over a private edition of T. E. Lawrence's *Seven Pillars of Wisdom* before visiting the Nile and the Sahara. There were few tourists and fewer airstrips. The boats, trains, and cars gave them a feeling of time and distance that has inevitably been lost in the jet age. They sailed through the Red Sea, crossed the Tropic of Cancer, touched French Somaliland, rounded Aden's tip into the Arabian Sea, and then straightened toward Ceylon. There they picked up Marco Polo's thirteenth-century trail through the Strait of Malacca, where from the deck at night they first sighted the Southern Cross.

They slipped and churned through the China Sea toward the homelands of Charles Colman's silks. His son's expectations and dreams were not disappointed, meeting the realities thirty years later. Tracing his nostalgia to its source created further dreams, and it was impossible not to succumb to the desire to tread further "globe granite."

> *For my part, I travel not to go anywhere, but to go. I travel for travel's sake. The great affair is to move, to feel the needs and hitches of our life more nearly, to come down off this feather bed of civilization, and find the globe granite under foot and strewn with cutting flints.**

* R. L. Stevenson, *Travels with a Donkey.*

Hong Kong. Wherever they landed they took a guide, driving about in their own time, absorbing, Ronnie taking endless reels of photographs. They sampled the food and the theater and the temples and then continued on to Shanghai.

Al: "We were in Shanghai during the Japanese-Chinese war. We had to lie down on the deck going in because they were shelling Woosung Fortress. We waited outside while the Japanese destroyed the fortress, which protected the waterway that led into Shanghai. Captain Frederick S. Moody (the husband of Helen Wills, the world tennis champion) of the Marines invited us out to watch the fighting from a warehouse in the American sector of Shanghai. They were firing at each other down the streets."

They called on Charles Colman's brother, who lived in Shanghai with his wife and child. A pleasant, courtly gentleman, he was the same uncle who had offered Ronnie the possibility of a consular post shortly after he had been invalided out of World War I. This time he offered Ronnie and Al his hospitality and as much of his city as he could.

Al: "When we left the harbor—on a Japanese ship—we had to lie down again; there were snipers shooting at the ship, so we lay on the deck going down the river until we were past the destroyed fortress and out onto the open sea. One night, the captain, Ronnie and I got drunk and we had to carry the captain to bed. Imagine this big ocean liner and the skipper happily potted. We came back via Honolulu and finally landed in San Francisco six months after we had left."

It had been a broadening six months. Revived, renewed, reinterested, Ronnie arrived back in Hollywood during the spring of 1932. He found the city avidly guarding its children with dogs and hired men, in the wake of the Lindbergh kidnapping. Bill and Bessie Hawks had had a baby, though not a "Kenneth Ronald"—it was a daughter. Dick Barthelmess, now remarried and happy, was scoring a personal success in *Alias the Doctor,* before semiretiring, as was Clive Brook in *Shanghai Express.* Swimming champion Johnny Weissmuller was being hailed as the new and best of the screen Tarzans.

Lengthy discussions had been going on about Goldwyn's next production for his star. He had signed a young Russian actress, Anna Sten, with the idea of using her with Ronnie in a screen version of *The Brothers Karamazov.* Then problems arose in obtaining the rights and Goldwyn began to feel that it might conflict with the German talkie version (in which he had discovered the beautiful Sten), and that perhaps it was too "heavy" a piece anyway.

Hornblow had been combing London. "Ronnie was not more difficult to cater for than other big stars, but they had to be romantic, attractive roles to suit his image. It was easier finding female roles!" He saw the stage production of *Cynara* with Gerald du Maurier and pushed the idea of filming it to Sam and Ronnie, neither of whom were keen. Both thought it would be unpopular to have Colman playing an adulterer, the idea of which did not appeal to Ronnie personally anyway. Hornblow: "I made a nuisance of myself about *Cynara,* but I won! I was in the doghouse, though, because they were right! Years after, Ronnie would still say! . . ."

Though Colman fans were able to accept his wife dying in *Arrowsmith,* they were simply not ready for their handsome hero to be an adulterer. They were not willing to accept him as an actor if it detracted from his personality as a star. It was a great shame, because this untimely film contains one of Ronnie's most subtle performances in a perceptive (though now forcibly dated) story. The reception of the film, however, has improved with time, and it has become, belatedly, well-appreciated.

The story revolves around the happily married barrister James Warlock ("There are two things in the world you can trust, the Church of England and Jim Warlock!"), separated from his wife Clemency (Kay Francis) for the first time in their seven-year marriage, when she accompanies her younger sister on a trip to Italy. During her absence Jim meets a young shopgirl, Doris (Phyllis Barry), through the wandering eye of his elder law partner (Henry Stephenson). Doris, not physically unlike Clemmy, falls for James, and with the good-humored help of the partner (who regards his friend with tender irony as being a bit too straitlaced) arranges a second "chance" meeting. With some conniving, she gets him into her flat and entices him into an affair, promising to release him of all obligation when his wife returns. Endearing and gay, she is a young woman to whom any man would be attracted, and James is no exception. By the time Clemmy does return, however, the young, rather emotionally immature Doris is so infatuated with Jim she is unable to face the thought of calling an end to their brief affair. She kills herself. At the inquest Jim does the gentlemanly thing, refusing to admit he was not her first lover. ("That was *her* secret," he later tells his wife). Judge, jury, and his associates all wrongly conclude that he forcibly seduced, then deserted the girl. His career is ruined, and his wife's trust is destroyed.

Clemmy had been happily untroubled during their seven years of marriage, during which time they had been the ideal couple who loved each other very much—but who had never had any reason not to. Those years of dependability ("Sometimes I wonder, ought one to be so sure?" Clemmy said upon her return from abroad) suddenly culminated in the real possibility of their losing one another. As Jim is about to sail for a new future in South Africa, the law partner arrives to talk to the desolate wife alone. He wisely advises her to imagine "if you were never to see him again, if he never got to South Africa." The realization that he might end his life en route jolts her into seeing the narrowness and finality of her decision. She had neither made an effort to restore their marriage nor handled the situation with maturity, and James was worth all this. She just manages to catch the boat. . . .

Kay Francis had the same wide, generous brown eyes as Ronnie, and was equally adept in projecting her thoughts in such a manner that each member of the audience felt he alone really knew what the character on screen was going through. Director King Vidor's carefully assembled interiors—the living room, bedroom, etc., of their London house—are extensions of the characters involved. One feels Kay Francis herself *must* have chosen the Dresden figure lamps, the perfume flasks and silver-backed brushes on her dressing table, the four-poster with enormous pillows and delicately embroidered linen sheets. Ronnie's interpretation of Warlock—tender, fallible, mature, infinitely human—is down-to-earth and believable. His initial reluctance, and continuing concern about being an adulterer, the secure marriage in which he is involved, and the protection of the dead girl's honor all define different elements of his own ideals.

The Los Angeles *Times* picked up what the public missed: "One of the most distinguished features of this or any other year . . . presented here recently to no great popular acclaim. Except for a few details of the action where condensation took place, it has all the values of the original piece written by H. M. Harwood and R. G. Brown, and has added numerous others which should find audiences more responsive to its elements and entertainment. Entertainment does not, however, enter into a discussion here, as does the fact that a fine, serious and absorbing study is projected with Ronald Colman at his very best. Here is something that is well-nigh a microscopic study of psychology and emotion with characters well-nigh perfectly drawn and situations that rise to rare reality and touch deep poignancy. The picture sets almost a new standard for its director, King Vidor [who was already one of Hollywood's finest]. And a word too for Henry Stephenson as the friend. . . ." *

Cynara was a prime example of the price often paid when a star contradicted any part of the image his public treasured—

* The Los Angeles *Times*, October 27, 1932.

and, indeed, paid for. It was a finely executed film from every point of view. However, simply because his millions of fans felt they could not have misplaced their faith in him as a true gentleman of integrity and honor, and because of this were certain that Ronald Colman could not possibly be an adulterer, *Cynara* did not stand a chance. In the public's opinion it had been cheated of its money's worth of Ronald Colman. The established image was needed and loved; divarication was difficult.

By the time Ronnie entered into his next production, *The Masquerader,* Arthur Hornblow had left Goldwyn to become an independent producer for Paramount. The buffer was no longer there. Goldwyn and Ronnie were once again face to face with the tensions that had built up over the years. When his new leading lady, stage and screen actress Elissa Landi, became ill shortly before shooting commenced, it was thought she would not be able to do the film. Auditions were quickly held, and one of the actresses to run through a scene with Ronnie himself was Benita Hume, laughing to herself about fate and crossing her fingers at the same time. She had just arrived from London under the protective wing of MGM and was excellent as the sophisticated and estranged wife of the drug-addicted M. P., John Chilcote (Colman). However, before Ronnie could figure out why she seemed familiar, Elissa Landi recovered, the production sped into belated action, and Benita charged into a succession of MGM glossies: *Clear All Wires, Service, Only Yesterday* (this on loan-out to Universal), and *The Worst Woman in Paris.* Her name was on its way to becoming as well-known in Hollywood as it was in England.

The Masquerader had already been a Broadway hit and a silent film (1922), both of which starred Guy Bates Post. It was Colman's second dual role, this time as the journalist John Loder who replaces his cousin and physical twin, a shattered M. P. at the time of a national crisis in England. The trick photography is superbly carried out, and Ronnie talks with "himselves" convincingly. In the suitably shorter of the two roles, he is debauched and as unlikable as possible playing the doomed politician and, much to the public's relief and delight, he is his own debonair and gentlemanly self as the literary cousin for most of the film's footage. It is an impossible story made as believable as possible, with delightful Moss Hart humor added to the script.

It was during the filming of the Chilcote sequences of *The Masquerader* that Goldwyn fabricated a publicity release claiming Ronnie played an addict better after several drinks, which was how he was coping with that particular half of his dual role. There was no diplomat like Hornblow to rephrase the remark, and Ronnie had always been a stickler in his struggle for correct publicity releases. He strode into Goldwyn's office to determine whether this false information had in fact been passed by him. Sam, wavering under the stern gaze, admitted that he had been responsible. Outraged that his own producer should invent such outlandish and unnecessary stories for the benefit of publicity, Ronnie stated he would never work for Sam again. Goldwyn retaliated with the fact that he could not work for anyone else until his contract expired two years hence. Colman asserted that, in that case, he would simply not work.

Ronnie responded to Al Weingand's note of sympathy on the proceedings (plans for a second world trip were already in the air): "A dirty business, as you say, but if you knew the details, you would agree it had to be done. I tried every other way to try and stop them supplying such material to the press. We [the publicity department and Ronnie] squawked often, but they persisted. Crazy and incredible I know. Other things behind it of course. I am confident it will come out all right, however, and pretty soon, and I believe with honour to myself. It all makes Bali, Java and even Djibouti seem pretty good spots though! Keep your eye on next Jan! And thanks again, old lad, for your 'swell' letter. Ever and aye. R' "

It was a lone, gutsy, and unique action—a top star slamming the door on his studio for a point of honor. The fact that his career was at stake was secondary to Ronnie. As far as he was concerned, his retort of a two-million-dollar libel suit balanced the enormity of Sam's slander. Naturally Bessie and Bill Hawks were involved, both as friends and from the business angle, for Bill was still Ronnie's manager.

Bessie: "I would hear people say to Bill, 'What on earth is Ronnie doing?' but Bill would never let him down. I used to think to myself I'd like to get Ronnie by the heels and shake him because this was a tremendous thing to do. I don't care what Goldwyn had done to him. Two million dollars then! It doesn't sound so much now, but then it was a tremendous amount of money. Ronnie said he didn't care about the money, he would give it to charity. It was a punitive thing. The whole business had nothing whatever to do with Bill; it was never his idea. He would not have had that kind of courage. With all due credit to Ronnie, if somebody had said, 'Well, this will ruin your career,' he'd have replied, 'So, it will ruin my career!' And then he left Hollywood and went around the world. Imagine a Hollywood star saying, 'Well, I'm going to stay out of work for two years, good-bye!' And that is exactly what he expected to do."

Ronnie made his side of the situation quite clear in one of his infrequent interviews, feeling facts needed stating:

"I realize that nobody can be in a public business like making motion pictures without arousing a certain amount of public interest in one's affairs. I realize that there must be publicity, but it is only the kind of publicity to which I object. When certain policies of a corporation damage me as an individual, I must try to right the matter in some way. This matter has not been the only incident. It is a matter of weeks and months, perhaps years of similar things. I have tried in every way pleasantly to put an end to it, but it is useless. Finally, with this last incident, I realized that something must be done.

While bringing the suit was really quite drastic, I was at a loss to know what other weapon to use. I was certainly not seeking publicity for the statements I believe damaging. I only wish to put my objections on record in a forceful manner. By suing, I'm trying to state my side clearly, simply and honestly. . . . There are times when principle must come before policy. . . . Frequently I have suggested that I be allowed to look over the routine publicity sent out about me. Of course, I don't wish to be a prig, or to set myself up smugly to the public as a model character. I have never asked to censor interviews, but merely data sent out by the company. This was refused. After my original objections to the material given a New York columnist (and for which he was in no way to blame), this same material was given out to a newspaperwoman, a friend of mine, who came to me and expressed her indignation over this material given her for use in writing a biography of me. She too felt that I was being damaged, then I took action. . . . I do object to being victimized. It concerns me personally as well as my value as a business investment." *

Goldwyn had definitely stepped out of bounds and Ronnie's decision was irrevocable. It seemed an opportune moment to go away and explore the exotic places he and Al had missed on their first trip.

They sailed south from Los Angeles this time—through Panama to Havana and from there boarded another boat across the Atlantic to Vigo in Spain. Sea travel was part of feeling the "globe granite" to Ronnie. The freedom from studio, household, telephones, business, and Thelma enhanced the expanses through which they passed. They spent a couple of months in Spain where—with a car and driver—Al's bit of Spanish and Ronnie's Italian triumphed over any language difficulties.

And then to Paris, where Ronnie bought a Cadillac so

* *Motion Picture,* December, 1932.

they could cover the rest of Europe and be their own chauffeurs.

Al: "In Paris, I used to cut off at night. I was thirteen years younger than he and had not traveled extensively, so I'd go round to the night spots and he'd be very happy in the hotel after dinner, just settling down to read. Every now and then, I'd find something that looked pretty good, and if there were two of them, I'd invite them home, knock on his door and say, 'Got somebody here, put your robe on and come in.' And every now and then, they would stay the night. It wasn't very often, but if it was someone pretty and nice, he joined in. He was never promiscuous; it was not in his nature, only when something tickled his fancy."

Ronnie, ever Thelma-wary, was not about to include England on this trip; she was there, and he knew that meant the possibility of a physical confrontation and doubtless some form of publicity. Their legal arrangement of ten years earlier had expired, and both his lawyer and he had agreed that they should now repeat his request for a divorce, this time supplying the necessary basis and offering a substantial alimony as the carrot. It worked; Thelma chomped on the juicy offering, swallowed her pride, and quietly counted the cash.

The actual mechanics were set up by a mutual American friend of Al and Ronnie now based in Paris, from where he kept them up to date on the latest restaurants, shows, and current activities. He set up the girls and the hotel, where the English lawyer would appear to check on all the details for the divorce petition.

Al: "We had to register in an obscure little French hotel for two days with two women. I think we had to stick it out for thirty-six hours. It was pretty grisly and several times Ronnie said, 'I can't go through with this.' And I said, 'You've got to go through with it, we've gone this far!' He hadn't decided to marry anyone else; it was just that it had to be done, to get out from under the burden of Thelma, to get it over with rather than having her accuse him of adultery, sincerely and honestly. Then a solicitor came over from England and interrogated the hotel owners: 'Do you know about this Englishman and another woman?' etc. And it was all legally dealt with.

"I had first met Thelma when I was working at the Samarkand Hotel in Santa Barbara, before we took our first trip. Somehow, she had discovered that I had become a friend of Ronnie's, so she had come up as a guest, and told me that she was his wife. Hoping for something I could tell her about him. But I had heard all about her, and had nothing to say. She was a very evil woman. She just 'took' him. All the time I knew him, until he got the divorce in '33, she and her lawyers were always hounding him for more money. Not only that, she would write him nasty letters."

They left Paris light-hearted with freedom and drove around Germany and Switzerland.

Al: "It was never 'spotlight' traveling. It was during the Depression, and there were very few people out then, and except for really warm friends, he didn't make his presence felt. Otherwise, there would have been elaborate dinner parties all over the place. If things began to get a little hot, we'd pull out and leave. I don't think more than once or twice did we ever share a room on ship, train or in a hotel. If it were possible, we would always have a living room and two bedrooms, and first-class restaurants. We always had the best available. He was absolutely 'first-class,' but he never spent money idly. We traveled within our suitcases, never a lot of clothes. Clothes were of no interest to him on these trips.

"It was just the two of us and I got to know him pretty well. Once in a while people joined us, but generally we had lunch and dinner together, and on rare occasions only were there violent disagreements. There would be the usual huff over a nightcap and the next morning it would all be forgiven. He never held a grudge. His friendships were with people who meant a great deal to him and who had something to contribute, because he in turn was not given to small talk and prattle. He wanted someone that he could try out ideas on or whose ideas he could listen to. He would have no truck with people he didn't like."

With maps, French dictionary, baguettes, Brie, and Beaujolais, they drove through the Haute Loire and the Dordogne down to Guéthary near Bayonne on the Basque coast, where they rented a villa for a month in order to have a mutual friend and her daughter down.

Al: "The mother was not in the arts. I've forgotten how they became friends, but I think it was from childhood. His love life was very well concealed. He never boasted of conquests. I think that at one time he had a little heart interest with the mother, but when she brought her daughter down, Ronnie was kind of fumbling around with the daughter, whom I thought was sort of for me. I ended up with the maid!

"There was another very pretty girl from England whom he was interested in, but I never really knew how close they were. Certainly, he didn't have any of these women shacking up with him in the hotel suites that we occupied during the trip. I think if he had, I would have known. . . . I would have asked him why he didn't cut me in!"

At the end of the month the four of them disbanded and Al and Ronnie drove off to Genoa, from where they sailed through Suez once again. This time it was to Sumatra on a Dutch ship, the Stommvart *Johan von Oldenbarnevelt*—a gag name with Ronnie for years afterward.

Al: "His name could never be seen on the passenger list of a ship, to avoid any advance publicity, and I would register in the hotels as 'R. C. Colman,' never 'Ronald,' because he would have been instantly detected. He was at the peak of his popularity then, the ideal of the Philippines and the Orient as well as everywhere else. Anyway, when he did get trapped by the press, he could turn on such charm—give them the drinks!"

This time they motored across Java and shortly afterward lost their hearts to Bali: the wide white beaches, dense tropical vegetation, golden-dark girls, and the tiny flutes on the legs of the birds that whistled in the blue air. Ronnie was not yet familiar with Hilton's Shangri-La, but this scene, the scent and the feel of the island, all came back to him when he read *Lost Horizon* later in his career.

A Dutch ship took them through the Macassar Strait and the Celebes and Sulu Seas to Manila, where they changed to a larger American ship; the *President Jackson* sailed them across the Pacific to Seattle, and from there they took a train down the coast of California.

They returned to Hollywood ten months after they had left it, tanned, traveled and relaxed with reels of Ronnie's photographs to be developed. He was free from his marriage with a minimum of publicity, and Thelma was settled with an annuity until her death (which was after his).

The impasse in his filmmaking had been unexpectedly overcome. Once it was known that Colman had left Goldwyn, there had been heavy bidding for his services by every Hollywood producer. However, United Artists Corporation, through which Goldwyn's pictures were released, had decided to keep Colman in the family. He was sought out by Zanuck, who had boldly resigned as production head of Warner Brothers (when they refused to reinstate pay cuts at the time the banks reopened after Roosevelt's moratorium) and joined with Joe Schenck to form 20th Century Pictures, the youngest group of companies operating under the United Artists banner. Sam released Ronnie, each of them relieved to have the matter quietly settled out of court, and no further brouhaha in the press. Certainly Ronnie had made his point and won his freedom honorably.

The sole unfortunate aspect of the trip had been missing the opportunity of working with Garbo in *Queen Christina,* for which MGM endeavored to find him during his absence.

There had been changes in Hollywood as well as within Ronnie's own circle of friends. Not long after he had left, in the spring of '33, Hollywood had begun to feel the weight of the Depression that had already been affecting the rest of the country for some time. It had also felt another hearty earthquake. Suddenly the soaring salaries, the excess of personnel paid an excess of wages, and the extravagance spent upon lavish productions caught up with the state of the country. The crisis was such that, had not every person within the industry helped, the studios would no doubt have gone under. It was quickly decided that the only way they could remain open would be if everyone concerned would work at half salary for a period of eight weeks, this to include the stars as well as the stenographers. This period would give the studios the necessary chance to breathe and recuperate. There was no letdown of activity; in fact, work was speeded up in order to get everything done that needed to be done.

Perhaps in the long run this close shave with disaster was good for both the industry and its workers, reminding them for a while of the value of money as well as the better ways of spending it. As *Photoplay* noted, in words strikingly reminiscent of the Hollywood of the seventies: ". . . In the final analysis, after reorganization shall have been effected, Hollywood may again resemble the Hollywood of the old days, the days when the film pioneers as independents, stood upon their own convictions, fought their own battles, and made their own pictures. And good pictures." *

There were further events: stars, writers, and directors

* June, 1933.

resigned from the Academy of Motion Picture Arts and Sciences to form their own guilds. At last each group had its own spokesman and protection, a far cry from the old days when Ronnie had just arrived in Hollywood under Goldwyn's wing. Colman's first major film, *The White Sister,* had been remade, starring Helen Hayes and Clark Gable, but its success was overshadowed by its famous predecessor. Cooper (whose first film had been one in which Ronnie had starred), Gable, Shearer, Mae West, Dietrich, and Garbo were the most talked about and the most popular stars.

Bill Powell and Carole Lombard had separated, though they remained friends. Hollywood's most famous couple, Mary Pickford and Doug Fairbanks, Sr., had, after many months of rumor, finally divorced. One of Ronnie's earliest friends in Hollywood, though not a contemporary, Ernest Torrence, had died in New York en route to England. It was on the whole a more sober atmosphere than the intoxicating Hollywood of old to which he returned.

Also during his absence a young English actress, a divorcee, of dark beauty and perfect profile as well as considerable talent as a witty comedienne, had been making a name for herself under contract for MGM. Ronnie was familiar with her name and remembered her face from their brief meeting on the set of the ill-fated *Masquerader.* Benita Hume had greatly enjoyed her active ten months' stay in Hollywood, but refused a profitable contract renewal in order to return to London and her fiancé. When it was a choice between her career and her heart, she was guided by the latter. She'd left for home shortly before Ronnie returned to Hollywood.

The editors of London's *Film Weekly,* who knew they could rely on her for some intelligent dazzle, had asked Benita before she'd left for Hollywood to contribute to their series on Love and Marriage by the Stars: "There are a few stars who should never marry, because if they did, I think it would affect their screen personalities. What would become of that romantic incompleteness, that hurt, frustrated romanticism of Ronald Colman if he were happily married? That celebrated twisted smile, that hurt uncomplaining yet revealing look in his eyes. They would be lost forever to the screen and twenty million women would no longer feel convinced that they could cure the Colman melancholy." *

Ronnie never read *Film Weekly.*

Also during his absence his last film for Goldwyn, *The Masquerader,* had been released. Though the picture had been made shortly after *Cynara,* Sam had not wanted it to follow too closely upon the heels of his star's previous film. A keen businessman to the end, Sam thought *The Masquerader* would be Colman's last film for the studio. For those who had already seen the Guy Bates Post performances, the reaction was lukewarm to the 1934 version, whereas the critics who were new to it showed more appreciation. And with that, his eighteenth film for Sam, ended the era during which Colman had developed and prospered in the Goldwyn studios. The Colman "image," the impeccably mannered gentleman of integrity and honor, ever in control of himself and the situation, had been nurtured and firmly established. There were more frequent departures from this image to come, although he could never step completely clear of it, any more than he could step completely clear of himself. However, it was after leaving Goldwyn that he grew as an actor in roles that did not depend for their interest on the Colman personality; films that allowed interpretation rather than simply stamping the image, like *Clive of India, A Tale of Two Cities, The Light That Failed, Talk of the Town, Kismet, The Late George Apley, A Double Life.*

There never was another Goldwyn star as exclusive as Ronnie, though Sam continued to make films for some time in which Colman would have been the ideal lead, imper-

* *Film Weekly,* March 22, 1922.

sonated by a variety of stars: March, Cooper, McCrea, Niven. Sam even tried to repeat Colman hits: *Raffles* and *The Dark Angel.*

Ronnie had learned virtually everything he knew about the film business during these seven years with Sam. It had been an invaluable experience and one from which he was to profit in the years ahead. There was a wealth of shining engagements to come.

7 ❧
The Shining Thirties

The changeover of studios was hardly as dramatic geograph-
ically as it had been emotionally; still on the United Artists
lot, Ronnie simply had to move into another dressing room.
He had been emotionally prepared not to work in films for
the remainder of his contract, and it is more than likely that
if the problem had not been resolved by the intervention
of Zanuck and United Artists, Ronnie would have prof-
itably filled his time with traveling—and theater. He even
mentioned it to Al, asking him to join him in a repertory
company as the manager. Al was not theatrically inclined,
however, and at the end of their travels Hollywood once again
put an end to thoughts of theater.

The first film after the Goldwyn divorce continued warily
and wisely within the familiar image. Since Ronnie had left,
time had engulfed publicity on the subject, and he slipped
once again into the character of Bulldog Drummond with
few people outside the business any the wiser for or interested
in the change of producers.

Zanuck supplied the finest framework to *Bulldog Drummond Strikes Back,* which was not a sequel to Colman's first
sound film but a most enjoyable escapade with the same char-

acter. Nunnally Johnson wrote a good-humored script, and Roy Del Ruth directed Loretta Young (as Drummond's love), Charles Butterworth (his sidekick, Algy), Una Merkel (Algy's bride, Gwen), C. Aubrey Smith (a harassed Scotland Yard inspector), and Warner Oland (the Oriental "baddie").

Much of the comedy is supplied by Butterworth and Merkel. Departing for his honeymoon at the beginning of the film, the blissfully vague Algy takes leave of Best Man Drummond: "Don't forget to telephone, even if it's just a postcard!" Algy and Gwen's marriage is doomed to remain unconsummated due to the interfering adventures of Drummond, who is forever in need of his friend's assistance. Having been called from Gwen's arms for the umpteenth time, Algy (played very à la Stan Laurel) wistfully sighs, "We might be very happy in our quiet, platonic way. . . ."

Dash and glamour are lavishly supplied by Ronnie and Loretta, and the entire picture, as well as all its characters, is washed with humor. "A jolly potpourri which is not intended to be taken seriously for a moment. The picture is full of quite effortless nonsense and is highly entertaining throughout." *

Through the marriages, divorces, and comings and goings of partners and opponents, the tennis "club" of Mound Street carried on. A new addition was a young English actor recently arrived in Hollywood.

David Niven: "When I first arrived in California, broke and twenty-two years old, I had no training as an actor except what I had picked up as a professional soldier during the previous six years in Sandhurst and the Highland Brigade.

"I was working as an extra in Hollywood and also as a deckhand on a swordfish boat in Balboa. Al Weingand was then the reception clerk at the Hollywood Roosevelt Hotel. I met him and he gave me a room in the servants' quarters for

---

* New York *World-Telegram,* August 16, 1934.

a nominal sum. He also played tennis with me and beat me consistently. One day he said, 'Ronald Colman is a friend of mine, and he's looking for a fourth for tennis on Sunday. Would you like to come?' Ronnie was at that time the king of Hollywood and famous as a recluse, living on the top of Mound Street. On Sunday, I met the great man, and was there all day with his chums Bill Powell, Dick Barthelmess, Warner Baxter and Clive Brook. He was marvelous to me, and an odd link was formed because of our joint efforts in the Scottish Regionals.

"A few months went by, and I became a constant member of the tennis group. I don't remember any extra ladies around at that time. He was quite a hermit from all I could gather, though I doubt if I pried very much, being far too flattered and happy to be part—at least—of the tennis group!

"Luckily, my career prospered quickly, and Ronnie was full of advice, but horrified when I told him I had just been offered a small contract by Goldwyn. 'The best producer by far, but watch it, he can be a real bastard!' As we became good friends, I graduated from the tennis to the 'supper group,' not much of a change of cast, I must say! Goldwyn meanwhile saw me as a possible replacement for Ronnie, whom he obviously missed hugely. When I say replacement, I mean he simply saw me as being British and moustached and that's about all!"

Darryl Zanuck, having taken over the hunt for the next Colman film, had made a discovery in London. He'd seen the successful West End production of *Clive* by R. J. Minney and W. P. Lipscomb, a biography of Robert Clive "of India." Excited by its prospects, he bought the film rights and brought its two authors back to Hollywood with him to write the screenplay themselves.

Ronnie was pleased with Zanuck's choice and with the opportunity of getting to know such an interesting historical character. He read virtually every relevant book that was available to him, and during the course of his research, found basic similarities between Clive and himself. They had both been clerks in their youth (Clive at £5 a year!), and having later achieved fame and fortune, had each remained quiet men, not given to bragging about their feats.

When he met biographer Minney, he plied him with questions about costumes, settings, and Hindustani pronunciations, determined to be historically accurate.

Minney: "Ronnie analyzed the character of Clive, which was very important. He wanted me to interpret the character for him, so that he could get inside it. He had read the biography and of course knew that my research had created it, so that I would know a lot about the character, and he went into it very thoroughly; Clive's reactions to certain situations, what his real feelings were when he had to go back to India and his wife wouldn't go with him, and that sort of thing. He was very thorough. He had a sense of history. He didn't suggest any alterations in the script; all he wanted to know was how to best interpret it and be correct. I don't think I ever wanted anyone else for the part but him, because he was so exactly right."

Clive of India, directed by Russian director Richard "Boley" Boleslawski (who the same year made *Les Miserables* for 20th), was Colman's last film with Loretta Young:

"They used me for Lady Clive because I was under contract to Twentieth Century. Ronnie was far too big a star to 'need' any leading lady. I just fitted the part, I looked it, and I was under contract. When you are under contract, you work!

"I had to wear hoop skirts for the role and there was an enormous staircase in Clive's house. In one scene, she tells Clive she's pregnant, and he scoops her up in his arms and dashes up the stairs carrying her. Well, Ronnie was no six foot two, he was an average size man, and although I'm thin, when you put fifty pounds of hoop skirts on me, and velvet and I'm quite tall. . . . When we started the rehearsals, I said to Ronnie, 'You just can't do all this in one shot.' He said, 'Oh, don't be silly,' but by the time he got all the way up the stairs, I could feel that his arms were weakening. I went down and said to Boley, 'Cut that, there is no reason for it. At least cut it in a long shot and let me take the hoops off, because once he has me in his arms, the dress falls all over anyway. That steel hoop alone weighs thirty pounds.' (I wore pads on the hips to keep it from cutting me.) Well, we did this and Boley said 'Cut it' and Ronnie was furious. He said it was going to spoil the sweep of the shot. So finally just before we shot it, I slipped the hoop off. Afterward Ronnie said, 'Well thank you very much, Loretta, but I think I could have done it.' I said, 'Yes, you could have, but why?' He said, 'Because it makes it more real.' Now—he didn't mean 'phoney' real, he meant it for what it was.

"It was the same in *Clive* as in the other films we did together—I always felt he enjoyed everything he did."

With the exception of the thundering, elephant-crowded Battle of Plassey, *Clive* is a relatively quiet biography of one of history's most dramatic and interesting characters. It goes into the mind of the man who knew his destiny to be that of securing British rule in India, for which he sacrificed all: his child's life, his wife's love, his own wealth and reputation. In its historical accuracy, combined with both Minney's and Colman's assiduousness, it succeeds in giving an insight into Clive's thoughts about his life, if not all the glamour of the life itself. "It is a good lecture about the valors of imperialism, combined with a sentimental domestic drama about love and duty." *

* New York *Herald Tribune,* January 18, 1935.

The role certainly offered Ronnie more depth than any of his other films since *Cynara*. Looking back on this part of his career, he admitted in an interview for *Photoplay:* "No film star alone can ensure the success of a picture, but he can, and sometimes does, take most of the blame for an unsuccessful film in which he may appear. Two or three bad films in succession have been known to dethrone some of the public's greatest screen idols. Can you wonder that the most established stars prefer to play for safety?" * He never lost his awareness of the precarious tightrope called success upon which he walked.

The year 1935 saw the first American film to be shot in three-color technicolor, *Becky Sharp,* and was a vintage year for filming classics. *Clive* (soon followed by *A Tale of Two Cities*) was in the excellent company of *Mutiny on the Bounty, Anna Karenina, David Copperfield, Les Miserables,* and *A Midsummer Night's Dream,* all of which were good box-office as well as first-rate productions.

Ronnie disappeared for a desert Christmas at La Quinta; the dry, clear, sunny air was welcome after the weeks of studio work on *Clive*. It was hot enough to swim, and he golfed and played tennis as usual. It was upon his return to Hollywood that he headed simultaneously into two joyous involvements. One was the long-cherished role of Sydney Carton in Selznick's production of *A Tale of Two Cities,* MGM's followup to their highly successful production of *David Copperfield*. His leading lady was to be English actress Elizabeth Allan, whose old chum, Benita Hume (freshly arrived to do MGM's next Tarzan film with Johnny Weissmuller and Maureen O'Sullivan) was staying at her Hollywood house. It was there Benita and Ronnie renewed their acquaintance of three years earlier, when the only conversation had been written in the script of *The Masquerader*.

Benita was fifteen years younger than he, with dark-brown eyes and hair and almost chiseled features. Much pur-

* January 25, 1935.

sued and in demand both socially and professionally, she had already been financially independent for two years as a successful actress in London before marrying at the age of nineteen. He was an intellectual Anglo-German writer, who would have been happiest had she spent her life inside the house. The marriage did not last long (as she said to me years later, "The young have a lot of sense—very little of it common"), but it had given her close insight into coping with the male ego. She had made her exit with a healthy sense of perspective due to her good friend, Ivor Novello. Benita had interrupted Ivor's breakfast-in-bed very shortly after her husband had tried to kill her in an unlucid fit of jealousy. She had escaped him and run all the way to Ivor's house, where he took in her state of angry disarray, listened to her melodrama, and, quite contrary to what she had expected, promptly burst into gales of laughter. She never looked back; perspective and laughter became two of her foundation stones.

Benita enjoyed people with whom to sparkle. Glowing with vitality and exuberance, she was not happy on her own for great lengths of time. Her personality never allowed her to become a loner at any stage of her life, and perhaps because of this she had a remarkable lack of selfishness in her attitude toward people.

Ronnie quickly discovered that she had one of the merriest laughs on either side of the Atlantic, as well as a quick wit and boundless good humor. She was the *coup de foudre* for him more immediately than he was for her. This was the first time that he had encountered a woman whom he found not only extremely attractive and down-to-earth but who stood in no awe of him whatsoever and who could verbally tickle him and get away with it. Cynicism played no part in her humor, and her natural warmth must have been reassuring to Ronnie.

She found him as devastatingly attractive off screen as

he was on, but hardly as exuberant or immediately witty as her own crowd of friends, many of whom were a reflection of her own musical interests—in London, Ivor Novello, Noel Coward; in the States, the Gershwins, Cole Porter, Oscar Levant. An exceptionally good pianist, Benita had studied for several years at the Academy in London and had very nearly taken it up professionally. Music remained a central and active part of her life, with few days away from her piano.

Their mutual attraction soon led them to discover common interests. They found they were surprisingly widely read on a similar variety of subjects, an intellectual par that allowed for much verbal jousting. Though Benita had a cluster of admirers on either side of the ocean (as well as a fiancé of several years in England), she was drawn more and more to Ronnie. During the ensuing weeks they met at Elizabeth Allan's (also a keen tennis player) and the MGM studio. His very difference from her "type" was a magnet. He was a challenge, and a man to discover ad infinitum. Ronnie had a diffident nature, so it was a slow process. The night he eventually invited her over to the seductive candlelit dinner at his house, all he was able to talk of throughout was his good friend Tim McCoy. Benita, who had not as yet met Tim, was ready to hate him by dessert. The evening ended happily, however, as did the *Tarzan* films: there were unusually lengthy holdups. Benita was obliged to remain in Hollywood. In fact, she made some other films for MGM in the interim period, all the while being paid weekly for *Tarzan*.

As Ronnie knew her better, his defenses melted along with the instinctive wariness with which he regarded all women. Her openness, intelligence, and vitality sparked him. He was able to laugh easily, even at himself, and to share his thoughts with her more readily, as he discerned the depth beyond her effervescence. He was, however, the confirmed bachelor who had lived according to his own desires for many years, responsible only to himself. His self-sufficiency had led easily into selfishness. There was no way of remolding his character. Not wishing to base the relationship upon any misunderstandings, he told her he had no wish to remarry.

The time with his pals continued, along with their tennis and poker, as did Benita's own social life, but she was more and more at his home, both privately and as hostess to his dinner parties. Never a member of the illustrious tennis group, she was at the piano most of the times they occupied the court, but there were a good many sailing trips together in the company of other friends. (The antirumor campaign was ever present. In fact, I came across only two photographs of them together during this period, one of which included the Adolphe Menjous.)

And as Benita knew Ronnie better, she became fascinated. He had a serious no-nonsense streak, yet inherent humor, and an intelligence for which she had great respect. Though she was able to make him laugh by her unfailing ability to throw things into perspective, revealing the amusing side, he was equally adept at switching a conversation when he wasn't in the mood. Their personalities complemented one another. He was inclined to be moody; she was not. Whereas he was cautious about caring and expressing the fact, she was far more emotionally extrovert and . . . secure. Where he was liable to understatement, she enthused. Though clearly mad about this "blithe spirit," he hardly manifested his feelings as patently as her other suitors, past or present.

Benita accepted the fact that he did not want to remarry simply because she already knew that she was besotted about him. She remained unwaveringly so for twenty-three years.

Twentieth Century merged at this time with Fox Film Corp. of which Joe Schenck became chairman and Zanuck production head. Colman's first picture with them was a gay trifle, *The Man Who Broke the Bank at Monte Carlo.*

Though it was the longest title, it is the shortest film he ever made (sixty-six minutes) and cannot actually be called boring! Zanuck worked on the script, as he did with all his films in those days, in this case with Nunnally Johnson and Howard Smith. The story was taken from the play *Monsieur Alexandre,* about a Russian who broke the bank . . . . with money raised by his fellow emigrés. Looking at this period of Ronnie's career in retrospect, this little film is positively lost amid the splendid productions with which he was involved around the same time.

The same year, Ronnie's tenth in Hollywood, he was voted the handsomest screen actor by fifty-one actresses, receiving twenty-two votes to Clark Gable's eight and Fredric March's seven. There was only one vote out of the fifty-one that he really cared about, though.

In the mid-thirties Bill Hawks separated from his wife, Bessie Love. Ronnie, by this time a close friend of each, was determined to remain so.

Bessie: "Ronnie went to Bill and said, 'Remember I knew her before I knew you, so I'm going to see her when she comes out here. She is a friend of mine!' Bill said, 'Of course, that's fine.' That was typical of Ronnie. When you get a divorce from anyone, whether man or woman, the minute you are free, everybody invites you out. But Ronnie was a friend of the family (if our daughter had been a son, it would have been Kenneth Ronald), and he came to call on me because I was a friend who needed help, and he was going to give it."

He continued to see Bessie until she moved to London, and found it most civilized that two people could have a divorce and remain on sensibly friendly terms. Bill remained his business manager, agent, and friend, and it was with his help around this time that Ronnie made three major investments.

The smallest investment was the biggest luxury—the *Dragoon*. He had been spending more and more time sailing —with Bill, Dick, Benita, and others—and had been keeping his eye peeled for a boat of his own that would be both a reasonable size and buy. The result was a sixty-seven-foot ketch, which he went up to investigate with Bill and Al in San Francisco. She was sturdy and seaworthy but sadly lacking in comfort. Ronnie bought her and had her sent immediately to her home port, Wilmington, where she was transformed, according to Al, into "one of southland's most beautiful yachts."

A Norwegian skipper and cook made up the crew, with additions for lengthy cruises. The press lost no time in starting rumors that he and Benita had been married by the *Dragoon*'s captain.

Second, a well-located property in Beverly Hills came on the market at a good price. It offered more acreage than Mound Street, as well as a tennis court and swimming pool. The house itself was mock Tudor, with two main bedroom suites and three reception rooms—one the perfect library and one ideal for screenings. The staff quarters were completely separate and self-contained. Mound Street was a quick sale as was the profitable little Malibu beach house, and he moved into Summit Drive along with his butler and English gardener (the two Harrys) and the gardener's vast poodle, Coco. Tommy Turner remained as "day man" and coped with hiring the other staff, as well as everything else, from his own downstairs office. The house managed to retain the same privacy as Mound Street, though on a larger scale. The grounds and high wall shielded it from the road, along which he had the excellent company of (in order): Charlie Chaplin, William Wyler, Fred Astaire, and Mary Pickford's *Pickfair* (the sole big property that remains intact today).

The tennis group continued at Summit Drive, as did the dinners, with Benita usually at the other end of the table.

She got on more immediately with Ronnie's friends than he with hers, being by nature a far more social, extrovert, and flexible character. The parties were sparkling and yet cozy, dinners of eight to fourteen people.

Charles Boyer: "They were delightful parties because he really didn't like big groups. He'd have great fun with Benita arranging a different corner of the downstairs for us all to sit comfortably in before dinner. They would practice and giggle, making certain the chairs were the right distance from the drinks and the ashtrays! He would always comment on a guest's new dress, or its color if it suited her, or a new hairdo. And Benita always made certain there were lovely girls around because she knew he liked that. Then if he knew a friend was involved with something important to him or her, Ronnie would always remember to ask about it. A marvelous host, and also a marvelous guest, when he came to our house or other people's houses. If ever any gossip writers appeared, he would find some excuse to leave without any fuss and without being rude.

"Occasionally, the parties were dressy and we put on our black ties, of course at Christmas and New Year's, but not all the time. He would run films at his house after dinner, sometimes old silent ones and sometimes one of the latest. Benita would always sit next to him for the film, and they would hold hands. He loved watching Fred Astaire (and Fred was also at the house quite often), and he loved comedies."

Cedric Hardwicke, another guest at the Colman Summit, said in his autobiography: "I found a friend in Ronald Colman, who after scoring no memorable success as an actor in Britain, was now a full-blown star, complete with mansion, butler and chauffeur. 'God, how I love the theater!' Ronnie was given to exclaim at least once a week. 'Oh, for the good old days!' " *

* *A Victorian in Orbit* (Garden City: Doubleday), pp. 211-212.

His last and largest investment was the least profitable financially and yet brought him the greatest happiness: he bought—with Al Weingand—San Ysidro Ranch, a 525-acre property south of Santa Barbara, which nestled against the coastal mountain range and had its own beach facilities a few miles away.

Al: "When we had decided seriously to go into the hotel business, we'd settled on California after investigating other parts. The Beverly Hills Hotel was for sale then, and a ranch in Palm Springs. We could have picked up the Beverly Hills for $80,000—not the property, but a long lease and the furnishings. We thought about it, but what we really wanted was a resort, so then it became a question of the one in Palm Springs or San Ysidro. We were both more taken with Santa Barbara than with the desert and Palm Springs."

San Ysidro Ranch had been run as a resort since 1893 (it was two years younger than Ronnie), and all the cottages were already there. No building was necessary, just a little rehabilitation here and there, and the guests flowed in from all parts of the states as well as California.

Al: "From time to time he loved getting involved with the guests, which was half the purpose and pleasure. When Bertrand Russell and Aldous Huxley were there, they all had a great time together. Then the John Kennedys were there for their honeymoon, sent by Robert and Ethel who were frequent guests. Nixon chose to run for Congress and the Senate in Eucalyptus Cottage. Stevenson and Humphrey also 'did time.' John Galsworthy revised *The Forsyte Saga* in Outlook Cottage.

"In those days, not only were the movie, theatrical and radio people at the Ranch, but also a lot of other so-called high-powered industrialists and socialites; people of great importance in America gravitated there. If there were somebody of particular note, I would always invite Ronnie and them over for cocktails. He loved that. I got him away from his own professional set.

"Outside of doing well with the original investment, the Ranch never actually made money, but he always told friends that it was his happiest investment."

Eucalyptus, sage, and citrus filled the air. The cottages sprawled between purple bougainvillea, oaks and oleanders, gardens, tennis court, and swimming pool. On one extremity ran a creek next to which the horses were stabled. On the other was a house, set apart from the cottages, accessible by its own driveway, which Ronnie chose for his own. Higher up the drive, overlooking the house, was a barn with adjacent garage, an offshoot of which became his much-used painting studio. A large lemon orchard separated his private corner from Al's house, slightly higher up the hill. Behind them stretched hundreds of acres of purple mountains from which the distant cry of a mountain lion would occasionally be heard. Ahead, to the west, lay the technicolored Pacific sunsets, and most of the year it was virtually clear enough to see the sheep of the Channel Islands, on one of which Ronnie had struggled several years before with rain, goats, and tents while filming *The Rescue*.

Galsworthy wrote of his stay at San Ysidro Ranch: "How beautiful! when the wood smoke goes up straight and the pepper trees stand unstirring, and behind the screen of tall Eucalyptus trees, the fallen sun glows, a long slow fire over the sea, and the lavender color mist rises between. How beautiful the mountains, behind us, remote in that late light, a little unearthly! The loveliness of these evenings moves the heart; and of the mornings, shining, cool, fragrant. There is something in it all of that dream as of Paradise, which stirred the Italian painters in old days. Well may it be sainted —San Ysidro, Santa Barbara!"

Ronnie used the Ranch, as he had Malibu, on weekends and in between films, often driving or sailing up with Benita and other friends, who could be put up in the self-contained cottages, all within strolling distance of his own house. His most permanent roots were laid in this, his own domain, most beautiful and most loved. As San Ysidro was Ronnie's home for the second half of his life, it became my home for the beginning of mine. My most vivid memories of my father originate there—where I grew up and he grew old, each with the same degree of happiness, for we both loved San Ysidro deeply in our own ways.

The 1936 U.S. poll, representing twenty million votes, placed Ronnie firmly amongst the top ten male stars—it was over thirteen years since *The White Sister* had been made. While things were booming for him, his friend, Tim McCoy —riding, roping, and straight-shooting across the States—was being hit by one of his worst years.

Tim: "I wasn't satisfied with being the star of the Ringling Brothers Barnum and Bailey Circus. I was the Buffalo Bill of my day and for years I'd planned on taking out my own show, much bigger than Buffalo Bill's. I finally did, having decided I'd never make another picture, that I really had it all made.

"There was a lot of money in my show besides mine, but I had plenty in there. I brought people from all over the world: I had cossacks and English lancers and Bengal lancers with their turbans. I brought out the finest trick riders from the U.S. Cavalry. I had gauchos from South America, and my ropers came from Mexico City. I had about seventy-five Indians and cowboys, and it was a terrific gathering.

"I hit the *one* year that every circus on the road went broke. Suddenly the bottom dropped out when we were in Washington. Any other year, it would have been terrific, but

I had to pick that year. Even Ringling Brothers folded up and went back to their winter quarters. So I thought, 'Well, I'll have to get up and go back to work in films again.'

"Eventually, I went back to Hollywood, and soon afterward had dinner with Ronnie. In that shy way of his, he wanted to say something, he wanted to commiserate with me, but he couldn't figure out any way to do it. Finally, he said, 'This may be a painful subject, but you got bitten pretty badly didn't you?' and I said I had. 'Have you still got Garden Court?' (Garden Court was an apartment I had kept for seventeen years.) 'Yes.' 'Is the ranch in Wyoming still there?' 'Yes it is.' And he thought for a minute and said, 'Well, I just wanted to inquire, because if there isn't Garden Court and there isn't the ranch in Wyoming, there is always Mound Street, and if Mound Street ever goes, you and I can put our little bundles on a stick, throw it over our shoulder and walk down the road together.'

"I think that was one of the most touching things that ever happened to me. That is what friendship is, and it's something that is known very little in Hollywood. His terrific success never bothered him; if anything, it made him a little more shy than before. He took it completely in his stride and never lost his balance. He lived a little better, he had a bigger house, but he lived according to his means, and he never did anything that was ostentatious."

The pals joined up for New Year's Day and helped Tim pull the pieces together again. ("I have a great faculty, I never look back over my shoulder, no matter what has happened!")

Tim: "Ronnie picked me up and we went over to Dick's for lunch with a whole group that were going to see a football match afterward. Ronnie refused to 'sit around watching a ball being kicked about all afternoon,' so he left us after lunch, telling me to drop in when we'd finished with the football business, which I did. Al Weingand was then working in downtown Los Angeles at the Roosevelt Hotel, and Ronnie had said we'd drop in for a snifter and a bite to eat. We drove into the back parking lot after dark. After he had stopped the car, I said, 'Ronnie there are Indians around here somewhere, there is an Indian drum going!' He said, 'I can't hear anything' in a rather skeptical voice. 'I can't hear it either, but I can feel it.' This was in the middle of downtown Los Angeles. He said, 'Now Tim, I know we've had a lot of parties over Christmas and New Year's, and it's been rough, and I understand perfectly. Now come along and we'll go in to see Al.' And I said, 'Ronnie, there *are* Indians!' Well, I started scurrying around the parking lot, and sure enough, three or four doors from the corner, there was an Indian curio shop, run by an Indian woman called White Bird, and here were all these Indians gathered for a celebration on this New Year's night. They had cleared out this big back room and there the drum was going and they were all dancing. We wound up with Ronnie—of all people!—doing squaw dances in there with White Bird and her friends, all in full regalia. He had the time of his life!"

Another close friend with whom Ronnie first came into contact in Beverly Hills during the late thirties, who was associated neither with film nor theater, was Artur Rubinstein. Having left Europe before the war, he and his family had also made California their home, and met Ronnie through mutual friend Charles Boyer. They had a similar warmth, depth, and twinkle. Colman had in fact long played a part in the pianist's life without knowing it:

Artur Rubinstein: "My best friend was the violinist Paul Kochanski. He was a Pole like myself. We were the same age and were really closer than any brothers could be. We shared each other's money, everything. I lost him much too early, because he died of cancer when he was forty-five, just after I married. Well, he worshipped Ronald Colman. This was the one man he wanted to see on the screen. He was absolutely crazy about him. This was his example of a man. He wanted to *be* like him, he wanted to *look* like him, and he involved me in that. I went with him to see his films whenever I could.

"When I came to Los Angeles, I loved the place because I found all my friends there! There was Charles Boyer, from Paris, and other Frenchmen—Jean Renoir, Jean-Pierre Aumont, I knew quite a few people from Europe and felt much more at home than in New York. So we took a house in Hollywood, and Charles one day brought to the house Ronald Colman, and I almost fainted when I saw him. I looked at him and he was for a moment startled. Then I told him who he was for me and for my friend and of course, that warmed him up.

"I was a different type from anybody he had met before, and yet I must say, he took to me right away. I never felt in him any barrier. I didn't pay him any compliments. I told him how astonished I was to see him in real life and what he had been to me before and that made him smile, and we were right away on friendly terms.

"We often had talks where we got quite close to each other. There were many links between us, and we really understood each other. He was deeper than the average Hollywood crowd; he saw the whole thing from far off.

"Benita was an old friend of mine already. I knew her from London parties. She was very musical. Of all the Hollywood crowd, she was the only one who was ready to go to the concerts at the Philharmonic Auditorium, which was quite an effort! It was a drive of about forty-five minutes downtown, then back again, and an ugly place to go to to begin with! But she came. Even once when she was, I think, in her ninth month pregnant. I'll never forget that. She came backstage and said, 'Oh, I wouldn't have missed it for the world!' I was very touched by that, and she came alone as far as I remember.

"Ronnie was an ideal Englishman. His feeling for England was very deeply rooted; he was much concerned about every move in England, especially when the war started. He showed his reactions. And those were the times when so many things were happening from day to day. I was very concerned seeing how much he took it to heart. He really was a great English patriot. This impressed me, because he made me conscious of my own patriotism for Poland. I was comparing it; I was sometimes ashamed of feeling certain things less than he did. We discussed those matters very much: England, Poland, the attitude toward the world, the future as he saw it. The whole empire was then in the balance. It seemed like the beginning of the end. I think he missed not living in England. It was for him a sort of an exile sometimes. He never felt American. He was not very much on their wavelength. I admired his beautiful English speech, his beautiful accent. It became better and more marked with time instead of becoming Americanized, which was rather characteristic in some other Englishmen in Hollywood.

"He spoke frankly, calmly, but it was the most beautiful English. He never underlined anything, he never exaggerated any role either. He didn't understate, he was just right. He went to the point with his feelings. Englishmen are very discreet, they don't like exaggerations. An actor must convey his feelings from his inner self, as music does.

"In my case, it is not so much the music—they hear that same music sometimes better on a record—but my emotion is what really reaches them much more.

"To get an audience, you must feel more even than what you want to convey. You must have it in you. For instance, I saw Duse. She never went wild at the dramatic moment. On the screen, Ronnie gave me the profound satisfaction of being able to transmit what he felt without having to scream or shout or make eyes or unnecessary gestures.

"I envied him his good looks. I thought that if I looked like him, every woman would fall for me! I knew Valentino, I even went out with him a few times in New York. He was a boy of little intelligence. I remember a luncheon in London where he came with one of his wives, and there were quite a few intellectuals, about ten persons in all. And he took over the conversation and spoke about a tailor who lost a waistcoat he had ordered. He kept us going for about an hour. He was indignant about this and what it all meant to him and how the tailor had treated him. Absolutely adolescent. And he was known as the Don Juan of the century!

"Ronnie was unconscious about his good looks. He was terribly modest. He never liked to be praised for his performances, unlike the rest of the crowd. He hated it. 'Yes, it is a good film,' he would say. He didn't like to speak much about it. He was very serious about his work, always careful about what he undertook to do. He discussed this with his colleagues. 'I wouldn't undertake that, I'm too old for this.' He saw very well what he could do well or not. There are those who take anything for granted. 'If I'm in it, it can't miss!' But not him.

"He loved books as I did. We talked about Trollope, for instance, a man who had a tremendous talent, and Ronnie put me on his trail. He knew that I too had a passion for books. He had a very good library, and he also was shy about that. He was a man who didn't like to reveal himself; you had to discover him. If I had something very grave, very important on my mind, I would rather go to him than to anybody else for advice, and I knew that I would find an echo."

Ronnie had now been familiar for ten years with the extraordinary phenomenon of being a star, an incongruity for such a basically diffident man. The result was a studied avoidance of star fanfare, no public appearances relating to his films, very limited interviews with the press and magazine writers, no lengthy conversations off the set about his performances, whether good or bad; very little shop talk in the house. He never overplayed his professional status any more than he overplayed any of his roles. He was inclined to think of stars as an overrated race, who would probably be unable to exert any attraction without the help of all the other people involved with every film. He believed these people to be underrated, as was the fact that any good film was the result of polished teamwork rather than simply a star performance, whoever the star was.

He enjoyed his work enormously. It interested and stimulated him. The stardom it had brought had expanded his possibilities and responsibilities and had made him both more aware and wary. His privacy was, as it had always been, of the utmost importance to him, and being a public figure made it more difficult to retain. He compensated for these complications by his relatively secluded (from the public, not his friends) way of life, with his "buffers" accompanying him when he ventured to work or travel. His character had certainly evolved with stardom—Ronnie's last picture for Zanuck and 20th Century-Fox was an all-round better venture than its predecessor. *Under Two Flags* was based on Ouida's famous novel of adventure in the Foreign Legion. From the opening shot of a camel train crossing the brow of a sand dune in the desert sunrise, the film sweeps into adventure, romance, and the glamour unique to Hollywood in the thirties. Frank Lloyd (*Cavalcade, Mutiny on the Bounty*) directed this adaptation by Lipscomb and Walter Ferris, which retains both its pace and one's attention even though it is nearly two hours long.

Ronnie is Sergeant Victor, an aristocratic Englishman, hiding in the Foreign Legion for a crime his brother committed and for which he took the blame. European star Simone Simon was originally cast as "Cigarette," the darling of the regiment, who loves Victor but can't have him, and who in saving the life of his company dies a heroic death. Due to ill health, however, Simone was unable to fulfill her contract, and the bright name of Claudette Colbert took her place. Roz Russell is Lady Venetia, who loves and gets Victor. All are well supported by Victor McLaglen, Gregory Ratoff, Nigel Bruce, Herbert Mundin, and John Carradine.

The film took just over eight weeks to make, and in mid-February the whole company moved to camp in the Arizona desert. It was back to tent living, in Ronnie's case for the third time, each equally more trying than his days with the London Scottish's summer camp in the English countryside. However, they were not only more trying, they were a great deal more lucrative!

During the day's filming, lunch was brought out to the cast and served under the shade of umbrellas, but this was far from as enjoyable as it may sound. The smell of camels and horse dung filled the scorched air, millions of flies were ready to attack anyone who remained remotely still, and scorpions and rattlesnakes did a good job keeping all on the alert.

Luckily the group got along well together. The end of the day was the most pleasant, when after cool showers and dining in the mess tent, it was time for cigarettes and pipes, whiskies and sodas; then Ronnie, director Lloyd, "Willie" Bruce—portly and jovial, best known for his Watson to Basil Rathbone's Holmes—and Claudette Colbert would swap stories.

Along with his leading players, Ronnie was insured for $5,000 against camel bite during the production, but since he always made a point of avoiding them anyway, no misfortune occurred. However, he did have an unfortunate experience with a Yaqui Indian knife-thrower.

The plot required Claudette/Cigarette to throw the knife at Ronnie, which narrowly misses him and lands instead in a wooden post. Doubles were never used as this particular knife-thrower (at $250 a throw) had been infallible in all his twenty years in the business. Nobody thought twice about Ronnie doing the scene himself. Even for Yaqui Indians, however, there is a first time for everything. Afterward claiming that his attention had been distracted by a bystander looking at his eyes when he threw, the Yaqui missed the post, and his heavy knife, going at full tilt, struck Ronnie sideways. The mere reminder of the story gave Benita heart failure for years after. Ronnie was none too reassured at the time, with a large black bruise spreading on his chest. Having ascertained that no rib was cracked, they reshot the scene, and much to the relief of all, the knife squarely hit the post. Yaqui Indian knife-throwers, however, went onto Ronnie's "camel list."

With Hollywood at a peak of film production in both quality and quantity, the second half of the thirties produced a wealth of excellent roles for Colman: Sydney Carton in *A Tale of Two Cities,* the mystic Richard Conway in *Lost Horizon,* the poet François Villon in *If I Were King,* the fatalist Richard Heldar in Kipling's *The Light That Failed,* and the dual role in *The Prisoner of Zenda.* He was, as Jean Brodie would say, "in his prime," and indeed looked a good ten years younger than his age (late forties), both on screen and off.

The Prisoner of Zenda, from the novel written by Anthony Hope in the late 1800s, offered his last and certainly most exciting dual role: Rudolf Rassendyll, the Englishman who replaces his double, the abducted King Rudolf of Ruritania, in order to prevent a takeover of the throne. Producer David Selznick, known for the taste and quality he gave to his films, and director John Cromwell (*Of Human Bondage*) lived up to their highest standards with this film: *Zenda* excels in every respect. The cast includes Madeleine Carroll, Raymond Massey, Mary Astor, David Niven, C. Aubrey Smith and Douglas Fairbanks, Jr. John Balderston and Donald Ogden Stewart worked on the script. The cameraman was the brilliant James Wong Howe, and Max Steiner wrote a rousing score. For sheer beauty *Zenda* is also hard to beat, from the cast themselves through the photography to the sumptuous sets and costumes. The whole is as polished and shining as the blades of their swords.

I am particularly fond of the last part of the film, which has Rudolf/Ronnie at his most dashing. After mounting contention between the two, there is a climactic duel between the Englishman Rudolf and the wicked Rupert (Fairbanks), both fencers of the first order. They fence their way around the castle's pillars with agility and wit (*Rupert:* "I cannot get used to fighting with furniture; fighting with chairs and tea tables is a new sport with me. Where did you learn it?" *Rudolf:* "It all goes with the old school tie.") The long duel ends with Rudolf wounded and Rupert leaping from a high windowsill into the moat. The code of honor, as major a part of the Colman image as of the man himself, struggles and triumphs yet again over matters of the heart. Having saved the life of the King as well as reestablishing him upon his throne, Rudolf leaves the Princess he loves to her royal fiancé, who, hopelessly irresponsible at the film's start, has since his kidnapping had the sobering opportunity for improvement.

> Rudolf: *"If ever I can serve you, sire."*
> King: *"You could never serve me better, cousin, you have taught me how to be King."*

It was through Ronnie that another Briton joined the cast as the young Fritz von Tarlenheim, supporter of King Rudolf.

David Niven: "There is no question that he asked Selznick to give me the part. David interviewed me and gave it to me. I was terribly nervous working in such a huge production with such a huge star, but Ronnie took infinite pains to see that his protégé went through the minimum of agony! For one awful day, I was fired and about to be replaced, but the miracle happened: the rushes of my last day's work turned out to be what David really wanted, and I was reinstalled. The part was built up, and no one more delighted and relieved than Ronnie!"

The film reestablished Doug Fairbanks (already firmly established as a producer-actor in England) as a very popular actor in America. Reunited with Ronnie for the first time since playing his son-in-law in *Stella Dallas* twelve years earlier, he looks immaculately at home as the sophisticated, witty villain. Black Michael, would-be usurper of the throne of Ruritania, was played by Raymond Massey:

Massey: "Ronnie had a genuine acting talent which received far too little recognition from the critics. His performances seemed so smooth and effortless that his acting was taken for granted. But this naturalness and ease were the result of meticulous preparation and technical skill. He always reminded me of Gerald du Maurier; both men made acting look so easy. One had only to see untalented imitations of their style to realize how good they were. He was a perfectionist, and there was never a slipshod moment in any of his pictures."

The director is the only person involved with the film to retain anything but happy memories:

John Cromwell: "I was forty-two when I went to Hollywood to direct pictures, had made my own way on the stage without any help, and I'm afraid had pretty stuffy ideas about obligations and what was generally expected from actors.

"I confess I can't remember which actor annoyed me most, Mr. Colman or young Fairbanks (whose father I had directed in the theater). He made no effort in any direction and I tried to make him aware of what seemed to be a potential. It was rumored at the time that Mr. Colman was receiving $200,000 for his work in the picture, and at that figure it seemed to me no more than reasonable that he should come on any given day knowing his lines for the scenes scheduled. Everyone knew that time was the most valuable item in a picture's budget, so that to sit with the other actors who knew their words and go over a three-page scene until it was sufficiently familiar to warrant exposing film, was something of an imposition.

"The great majority of films were so formalized at that time, individual scenes did not lend themselves to any variety of interpretation. Rather, personalities were exploited to the top of their bent. It was impossible to judge just how good an actor he might have been."

The New York Times was quite carried away by the faultless photography of King and cousin together: "The trick photography wherewith the two Rudolfs are shown together is so convincing that this reviewer believed, until he was corrected by someone in the know, that one or the other of the Rudolfs was a double!" *

At the film's first preview the audience found the action rather dull, whereupon Selznick had the beginning drastically cut (a similar situation to *Lost Horizon*). Max Steiner's exciting score was added, and the whole film took on a new shape and snappier movement. It was an enormous success for all concerned, and today remains the outstanding of the four versions of *Zenda* (1913, 1922, 1937, 1952). Selznick was so pleased with the final results that he signed Ronnie to a seven-year contract. As it happened, however, Ronnie never

* September 3, 1937.

did another film for him. *Julius Caesar* (in which he was to play Brutus) was talked about but never got off the ground, which was hardly surprising as he was never keen to do Shakespeare. He turned down *Rebecca* because he just didn't feel suited to the role, something for which Benita never forgave him! There was also talk of *Jane Eyre*, for which, unless heavily made up, he would hardly have been physically suited; it was eventually done with Orson Welles by 20th.

Rebecca was later filmed with Laurence Olivier, who had made a great study of imitating Ronnie when he was a young man. ("I was never ashamed of imitating people or of pinching ideas from them!") Later his studio had encouraged the resemblance between the two for all it was worth.

Olivier: "Ronnie had heard of the supposed resemblance when we first met in 1931 at a party of John McCormack's. We frankly looked at ourselves, side by side, in the mirror in the long study-drawing room. After looking for a few seconds, I sighed with regret, and Ronnie sighed, I am afraid, with some relief, and we both said, 'No . . . I'm afraid not!'

"Over the years we became friends and forgot all about the supposed resemblance. I suppose the truth of it is, we could have been brothers to look at, the younger nothing as handsome or attractive as the elder. And, of course, completely lacking his magic and magnetism!"

Rebecca, directed by Hitchcock, won the Academy Award for Best Picture in 1940, and Olivier—sporting a thin moustache—bears an unquestionable resemblance to his friend.

Though Ronnie was as keen as Selznick to work together again, circumstances led them in different directions, and it was not to happen. Ronnie signed for two pictures with Paramount. The first is a delicious romp in the fifteenth century as Villon in *If I Were King*. Preston Sturges (later to write and direct the much-acclaimed *Sullivan's Travels,* among his many other successes) took a lot of the eloquent dialogue from Justin McCarthy's play and integrated his own sophisticated humor. Frank Lloyd once again directed.

If I Were King is essentially a "fun" film, an unashamedly romantic version of the real thing. The main character appeals to one in much the same way as Robin Hood; though Colman is probably no more like François Villon than Richard Green is like the original Robin Hood, they both fit their characters' images perfectly. Colman seems to be the essence of what every romantic Renaissance poet should look and sound like: moustached and bearded, his thick curly hair under a rakishly peaked hat—complete with feather—rags for clothes, and high leather leggings, all worn with enormous panache. And no one could have sounded more poignantly poetic quoting the lines of McCarthy's Villon; there was a catch in his voice, and the words emerged rich with dreams;

> "If I were king—ah love, if I were king!
> What tributary nations would I bring
> To stoop before your sceptre and to swear
> Allegiance to your lips and eyes and hair.
> Beneath your feet what treasures I would fling;
> The stars should be your pearls upon a string,
> The world a ruby for your finger ring,
> And you should have the sun and moon to wear
> If I were king."

A fine opportunity to appreciate Colman's sense of timing, his fluency of expression and avoidance of overplay comes early in the film during the church scene. Villon has been dragged into church by his foster father (C. V. France) to repent his sins, and as he kneels next to Father Villon, he sees Katherine (Frances Dee), a lady of the Court, for the first time. Father Villon is deep in prayer and oblivious to his son's bouleversement. Katherine does not see Villon at all. He looks at his father to see whether he too has noticed her, longs to ask him who she is, but doesn't dare. Then, staying on his knees, he backs around Father Villon to his other side, straining for a better view of this ethereal, pearled lady. She rises from her prayers to go. He makes a gesture prior to excusing himself to his father, decides against it, and still not having spoken a syllable, steals behind him and dashes down the church steps in pursuit. Outside her carriage, while pleading with her to accept his poem ("If I Were King"), he is apprehended by the guards who have been pursuing him— most athletically—since the film's start, for wounding the King's Grand Constable in a tavern scuffle. He is given a temporarily believed alibi by the compassionate Katherine and duly released by his captors.

Having bid her farewell, he returns minutes later to the inside of the church to kneel next to Father Villon, who a moment later emerges from his prayers. He smiles benevolently. "Now, my son, don't you feel better for that?" "Oh, *yes,* Father!" "You see, time in church isn't wasted, my son." "No, it certainly isn't, Father!"

Later he and his companions are caught and sentenced for their parts in the brawl. By King Louis' whim and Villon's own quick wit, his hanging is put off for one week, during which time he is made Grand Constable of France, thus replacing the man he has wounded.

Basil Rathbone hams lightheartedly as the dastardly Louis XI ("We already have one St. Louis; two might cause confusion!"), and a tacit humor seems to run through his scenes with Ronnie. (Rathbone on the set: "I really enjoy this picture. It is the first time in years that I haven't kicked a baby or been killed in reel four!")

Again Colman is giving advice to a king on monarchy: "To abolish despair and substitute hope. To know the people and by knowing the worst in them, bring out the best in them." In fact the prince of beggars is quickly at home in his courtly robes and a great deal more adept at dealing with the problems of the people than the King or his Constable, who created the problems in the first place. Their relationship is that of an old cat and an astute mouse; the King watches Villon's every move with fascination and secret admiration.

Louis: *"You are an amazing fellow. Here in a week, you have made me more popular than I have made myself since my accession. In court, in council, men are pleased to call you paragon."*

Villon: *"I am a man of the people and I know what the people need. A week ago, the good people of Paris were disloyal enough. I repeal the tax on wine and today they clap their hands and cry, 'God save King Louis!' lustily. A week ago your soldiers were mutinous because they were ill-fed, worse clothed, and never paid at all. I feed them full, clothe them warm, pay them well, and today your majesty has an army that would follow me to the devil if I whistle a marching tune."*

Louis: *"But in the meantime, your sands are running out. Is your heart failing? Is your pulse flagging?"*

Villon: *"Not a whit. I have been translated without discredit from the tavern to the palace, and if the worst comes to the worst, I may say with the dying Caesar, 'Applaud me!' You have given me a royal week, and I have made the most of it, lived a thousand lives, eaten my cake to the last sweet crumb, and have known the meaning of kingship. A man might live a thousand years and yet be no more account at the last than as a great eater of dinners. Whereas to suck all the sweet and snuff, all the perfume but of a single hour, to push all its possibilities to the edge of the chessboard, is to live greatly though it be not to live long, and an end is an end if it comes on the winged heels of a week or the dull crutch of a century."*

King Louis had to admire Villon's flair for words as well as his politic dealings with the people!

Heather Thatcher, gravel-voiced and regal as Louis' queen, has my favorite Sturges line in the film. Villon, having opened all the King's warehouses to the starving people of Paris, leaves no food for the castle's occupants in an effort to get them out to fight the enemy. On the following morning the Queen is horrified to see fish upon her breakfast tray instead of the usual eggs. Having sent off her lady-in-waiting to demand eggs from the King himself, she is left staring in undisguised disgust at the bedtray.

"Fish!" she spits. "From the *moat* I suppose."

Villon returns to his rebelling countrymen in an effort to persuade them to help their King fight the enemy, and as the small royal army is on the verge of defeat, Villon marshals the swarms of Parisians to battle and victory, deftly brandishing his sword throughout. (Ronnie had learned his early lesson well, and he moves with all the grace of all the finest derring-doers.) Such stout heart and undaunted humor would warm the iciest of kings, which of course it does in the end: Villon's death sentence is changed by the now wiser Louis to exile from Paris (with the Lady Katherine hurrying in pursuit).

I find myself smiling instinctively back at Villon/Colman, and yet with a lump in the throat, because his is such a wise, tender, lived-in smile, and as he throws back his head, his laugh bursts from the heart. There was much of the poet's soul in Ronnie, as there was poetry in his looks. It was a part of what generated his aura; the idealist in him, mixed with vulnerability and whimsy.

It was the Villon/Colman that later brushed off on me when he read me "Annabel Lee," "The Raven," and Lewis Carroll:

The Shining Thirties

The other night upon the stair
I met a man who wasn't there.
He wasn't there again today;
I do so wish he'd go away.

Benita and Ronnie had known each other for about four and a half years. She was living on a parallel road with her back garden adjoining his, and virtually all their free time was spent together. It was quite obvious to their friends that they were in love, and even Louella Parsons was wondering "when the wedding is going to be" in her newspaper column.

After this length of time Benita had started to judge the situation by her own standards. Whereas to Ronnie, his friends, and even the public, such determined and lengthy an attachment was unique for Colman, his refusal to broach the subject of marriage and the perpetual trips through the back gate must have long since lost their unique flavor to Benita and begun to smart. It had been a mutual understanding early in their relationship that Ronnie did not want to launch into a second marriage; however, such a close involvement over this length of time inevitably led everyone to speculate when he was going to marry the girl. Everyone, including Benita, as she was not cut out to be an unmarried woman, no matter how much she loved a man. If not her pride, her sense of humor would not have permitted the situation to last much longer.

Heather Thatcher was a close chum of hers: "You can't go on after four and a half years! Benita rang me one day and asked me over to lunch. She sounded rather depressed. So I went over and we had lunch on the patio and she said, 'I'm going home. I'm fed up with sticking around after four years of my life. I feel I'm wasting my time and am not doing any films.' So I said, 'You tell him *tonight* that you are going home.' "

Benita told him; with no ill-feeling she started the trip back to London by train to New York. In Albuquerque, New Mexico, there was a telegram at the station from Ronnie saying "Come home and let's get married!" Benita caught the next train returning to Hollywood.

Tim McCoy: "One saw they were in love with each other and took that as an accepted fact, but Ronnie never mentioned marriage, even to me. Then one day he phoned up and invited me around for dinner. 'Old Thatch is coming and there is something I want to talk to you about.'

"So I went over and we all had drinks and dinner. After dinner, we were sitting in the living room, and Benita and Thatch were gabbing and Ronnie stood there and shifted from one foot to the other in an embarrassed sort of way and finally said, 'Tim, there is something I want to tell you . . . Oh Hell! . . . Benita and I have decided to Do That Thing!'

"Thatch let out that raucous laugh of hers, which broke the ice. Then Ronnie said, 'We have to do this very carefully. You know what Hedda Hopper and Louella would do. We are going to fool them. This has got to be very tight and very secret. We have already got the marriage license, and Al Weingand has arranged the judge in Santa Barbara.'

"So he laid it out as though he were Eisenhower planning the invasion. I was supposed to collect Thatch in my car as though I were taking her off on a weekend. ('You mean compromise Thatch,' I said, 'with her monocle!') Then Ronnie was going to call Benita 'as though we were just going to the beach in Malibu, and then we'll keep on going and we'll all meet at San Ysidro. . . .' "

Thatch: "The only people who knew about it were his agent (Bill Hawks) Al, Tim, and I. I was to be matron of honor. Tim would ring me up and because it all had to be top secret, no names were ever mentioned and he would talk in code, saying things like, 'The cases of champagne will be around on Saturday and when they come, give them the empty crates,' which meant, 'Be ready to be picked up at eleven on Saturday!' "

Al: "I had to get the county clerk—a friend of mine—around to the Ranch with the applications for the marriage license, but instead of putting it on the stack of the transactions for the day (the press came in every morning to look them over), he put them under the counter. So he kept it from the press, which is as illegal as hell. But otherwise they would have swooped down and the thing could never have been private.

"Tim and Thatch arrived first, and then Ronnie and Benita, and we all went to Ronnie's house for the ceremony. The municipal judge who married them was so excited that he forgot part of the ceremony."

Tim: "It was all done in a few minutes, and Al had the buckets of champagne there. Afterward, Ronnie told Al to call Hedda Hopper and Louella Parsons and give them both the news at the same time, so everybody would be happy. Al got Hedda first and told her and she said, 'Great, I am just going on the air!' It was late afternoon by this time, and that's when her program came on. Then he told Louella who said, 'Darling, I'm so happy and aren't you kind to let me be the first to know!' Then Al rang Bill Powell (who had not felt well enough to accept Ronnie's casual invitation that morning to 'drive up to the Ranch') and said, 'Bill, Ronnie wants to talk to you.' 'Hell, he hasn't got any news for me, I've just heard it from Hedda over the radio!' Louella's nose was slightly put out of joint about hearing it from Hedda too, but Ronnie placated her later and said, 'Look, we told you both at the same time, but it just happened that Hedda was about to go on the air, and you didn't come out in print until the next morning. We did the best we could do for both of you and showed no partiality.' So they stayed on good terms.

"Thatch and I stayed in cottages at the Ranch that night and then shoved off and left them the next day. That house at the Ranch was rebuilt, but to begin with, it was a two-story house, and the spot they were married in was in the hallway. It was a terrific hallway, and later on we put a bronze star there. We had a thing cast, 'This is where it happened,' and put it right there in the floor. Later on, of course, when it was made into a one-story house, the star had to be removed."

An eternity ring of tiny square diamonds, a bronze star to mark the spot, and two of Hollywood's most eligible finally Did That Thing, a far cry from their previous marriages and hardly one that was entered into without thought.

Benita quipped to playwright Marc Connelly, "Imagine! I not only have that beautiful man, but that voice!" Ronnie chortled and glowed, "About time someone showed me some respect!"

8 ✌

In Perfect Character—and Out:
Lost Horizon,
A Tale of Two Cities,
The Light That Failed

Up until *A Tale of Two Cities* (1935) and *The Light That Failed* (1940), one knew more or less what to expect of Colman and his films. He was always good, sometimes better than the film itself; one was rarely disappointed and as rarely surprised by his performances. However, when he "became" Dickens's Sydney Carton and Kipling's Richard Heldar, the effect was similar to that of looking at cut glass held up against the light rather than admiring it on the mantelpiece. It had always been beautiful on the mantel, varying only with whatever was placed next to it, and offered perfect rather than surprising beauty. Then suddenly came the light, and endless facets, dimensions, colors, depths. . . .

Keeping stars within the framework of their image was, of course, the studio's surefire way of bringing in the money. A star continued to be a star because the public clamored for his/her image, whether that actually had much to do with his real self or not. So films were found and often tailored to fit that image. Though there were many splendid results, there was also much diversity lost in the rut.

With the above-mentioned films as eye-openers, one is saddened by the fact that Ronnie didn't "hold himself up to the light" more often with the wealthy choice of characters from Dickens, Shaw, H. G. Wells, C. S. Lewis, all of whose books he knew well and loved. He was interested in making Lewis's *Perelandra* trilogy into films. Later there were ideas of doing Shaw on radio and film, all of which were thwarted or fell through.

Ronnie's physical appearance hardly lent itself to taking on such classic roles as the Hunchback or Cyrano without hiding behind a makeup transformation. (Ironically, the only time he lent himself to makeup and flamboyancy, playing a schizo Othello in *A Double Life* in 1948, he won an Oscar.) In *A Tale of Two Cities* he did nothing as obvious as that. Without adding a hunch or a false nose, without doing more than shaving his moustache, he transformed himself completely. There were no award nominations for *Two Cities* or *Light;* the performances were hardly flamboyant. However, the subtleties that emerged from each character were as wildly contrasting to Ronnie as they were to each other. The films themselves are fine examples of Hollywood at its literary best. Well-produced, they do credit to what in *Two Cities* is a complex story to transfer to the screen and in *Light* is an intricate portrait of basically unsympathetic main characters.

Lost Horizon, on the other hand, offered a classic example of both perfect and natural casting. It was Ronald Colman stepping into his own image. Not only did Robert Conway fit the public image of Colman, he was also the embodiment of a great deal of Colman's character: his idealism, mystique, intelligence, gentleness, integrity, stubbornness. . . . They had a great deal more in common than the initials of their names. Ronnie effortlessly expanded the role of Conway by opening doors within himself.

This mystical and magical story captured the imagination and framed the ideals of audiences all over the world. The book had already been avidly consumed by readers everywhere, and the film brought yet more attention to

Shangri-La, a hidden valley in the highest reaches of the Himalayas. Many people really believed the place existed. This land of peace, health, and longevity struck a note of longing in the world's heart. It was a tense and uncertain time, with Europe rife with rumors of war, and people desperately needed everything the film represented. (It was hardly surprising that it was not shown in Italy and Germany, lest it corrupt the minds of the Fascists and Nazis with idealism!)

The High Lama of Shangri-La decides that Robert Conway (English author and M.P.) is the man to inherit the spiritual leadership of his valley, having read in one of Conway's books, "There are moments in every man's life when he glimpses the eternal."

It is when Conway is caught up in a revolution in China and helping refugees to escape that destiny takes over. Unnoticed in the chaos of the airfield, one of the planes taking foreigners (and Conway) to safety has a forced change of pilot.

There are four others leaving Baskul that night on the little plane, and it is quickly, quietly apparent that Robert is their natural leader, the one to whom the other three strangers turn, as well as George (John Howard), Robert's younger brother. The cargo of passengers is a symbolic one, suffering from the ailments of the pre-World War II society. A young woman—brassy, despairing, robbed of a future because of TB (Isabel Jewell). A plumber turned businessman; middle-aged, abrupt, defensive, he was bankrupt after a crooked deal and reduced to where he had started as a young man—broke (Thomas Mitchell). A rather older paleontologist, preferring to dig into the past rather than deal with relationships and present day problems (the ever-uncertain Edward Everett Horton). The petulant, materialistic, immature young George, who basks in the reflected glory of his famous brother. And finally Robert, who copes intelligently with his work, endeavors to make life better, searching for truth, for peace, and ever aware of their sadly diminishing quantity in the world.

The plane, having run out of fuel, crash-lands in the Himalayas short of its destination and kills their unknown pilot. Before frostbite and hysteria have time to take over, a rescue team of locals arrives, headed by the distinguished elderly Chang (H. B. Warner). This still, soft-spoken man is surprisingly fluent in English, which adds further mystery to the fact that they were so quickly found in this highest and wildest mountain range.

Through dizzy heights and raging blizzard, the group is led up the rock face until there is no higher peak to climb, and they reach a small arch. The livid sky gives way to a warm, free, cloudless expanse as they pass through to the descent. The scream of the blizzard dies, and the air is filled with the sounds of sheep bells and the tiny whistles on the feet of winging doves. Before them stretches the Valley of the Blue Moon, protected from all elements (including radio) by its surrounding peaks. Animals abound, as do trees and crops in this fertile, plentiful land. Like Chang, the inhabitants speak in soft, lilting voices. The strangers are—understandably—staggered. Robert absorbs it all in silent wonder. One instinctively feels that he has always known in his heart that Shangri-La was waiting for him. It is as if Conway-Colman had come home at last.

The following morning Chang happily shows Robert around the lamasery and its treasures. "Do you fail to recognize one of your own dreams when you see it?" He smiles as his amazed guest tries to grasp the reality of all he sees: the treasures of the lamasery, the happiness and well-being of the people tending their flocks or studying books and music. He is at last summoned by the 200-year-old High Lama, the only man able to answer all his questions, including the reason for their apparent kidnap.

Father Perrault (the High Lama, played by Sam Jaffe) explains the idea behind the valley: to cultivate the inhabitants with the vast, accumulated library of books and music, living by the simple theory of Be Kind. When the world destroys itself, and the remaining people look for a new life, they will be able to turn to Shangri-La, which will then be ready to give of its brotherly love, beauty, and wisdom. Conway at last understands the reason for the "kidnap"; he, Conway, is the Lama's chosen inheritor as the spiritual leader of Shangri-La. He too has glimpsed the eternal. . . .

This place of quiet, peace and comfort, with its wealth of literary, art, and music treasures had been gradually assembled and built by the Lama with both wisdom and love. It was, in fact, a far-reaching equivalent of what Ronnie was already doing at his home, San Ysidro Ranch.

Conway falls in love with Sondra (Jane Wyatt) of open face and warm smile, during sunlit days of swimming in wooded pools, galloping through glades, teaching the children English through songs, and absorbing all he could of the valley's way of life. Sondra, an orphan, was brought up by Father Perrault himself, and what Robert doesn't already know of Shangri-La is explained to him by his companion.

George, meanwhile, has been bewitched by the restless Maria (Margo), who wants only to leave for the outside world. Peace was never meant for her soul. She is the only disquieting note within the valley and echoes George's own sympathies.

Having found his successor, the Lama dies; the valley has spiritually passed into Robert's hands. The same night Maria succeeds in bribing some porters to escort them to the nearest outpost of "civilisation," and with George she tries to convince Robert to accompany them. Desperate to leave with her lover, she cries to Conway that she is very unhappy in this supposedly happy valley, that the Lama was a crazy old man, and that Chang has lied to Robert about her age because he is jealous of anyone who looks at her. Chang had told him that she was in fact an old woman and, like any of the inhabitants, could not leave the valley without physically becoming her true age.

Margo: "It was a hideously difficult little scene when I had to lie and convince them I was terribly young. There was so much to convey in so little time, and I had to be totally honest and at the same time, lie! I was terribly nervous before the scene, and this was the one time Ronnie started teasing me, and of course, what he succeeded in doing was taking my mind off it. He distracted me, and suddenly the scene was on top of me!"

George, who believes Maria's every word and thinks Robert is mad, joins the argument by assuring him that they would not leave him behind in this place, that he would inevitably become unhappy there; Maria, young and radiant, was obviously telling the truth, and Chang and the old man were clearly crazy.

Ronnie, a very private person, had the ability to transmit his thoughts with more subtle coherence than words. Everything he had thought and felt about the valley—the people in it, what it stood for, the Lama's words, Sondra's love, his own concern for his brother, Maria's tears, Chang's warning—everything passes across his face in moments, and the audience is as torn as he.

Several points come into play here—Ronnie's years of experience in silent films, his own maturity as an actor and a man, the depths of his identification with this character, the physical attribute of his large, tremendously expressive eyes—to make these silent moments so filled and true. Finally, faced with the reality of his brother's unhappiness and the realization that this dream does not work for everyone, he puts flesh and blood first and agrees to go.

Unable to entice the other three away from their fulfilling occupations (plumbing and paleontology), Robert, George, and Maria leave with a dubious collection of porters while the torches of the Lama's funeral procession light the valley.

They pass through the distant gate, and after days of trekking, their porters are killed by an avalanche. The beautiful Maria, now well away from Shangri-La, shrivels up into an old woman, as Chang had forewarned, and dies. An unforgettable, horrific moment of truth. George, upon seeing her withered face, runs screaming into the blizzard and tumbles down a ravine to his death. Robert falls blindly on, finally collapsing at the bottom of the mountain, where he is found by some local tribesmen. Stricken with amnesia, he only remembers Shangri-La after he has been taken on board ship by his British colleagues in Singapore. He finally manages to escape them and make the long journey home to the Valley of the Blue Moon. Happily, the dream is not lost to Conway; he had that rare chance to return to it and to all his finest aspirations.

In London Lord Gainsford tells their fellow Members of Parliament of Conway's fantastic determination to return. When they ask if he himself believes such a place exists, he speaks for everyone in the theater audiences when he says, "I believe it because I *want* to believe it," and makes a toast, "Here's my hope that Conway finds his Shangri-La. Here's my hope that we all find our Shangri-La!"

Ronnie himself, having searched—perhaps unconsciously—through his mature post-Thelma years, had found his Shangri-La, far from the Himalayas and yet very familiar: the joy of Benita, the warmth of his friendships, the expansive peace of San Ysidro, the refined intelligence with which he tackled his work, the search for beauty in his photography, painting, books, and houses, the art of living behind each day that made his life an art in itself. He fulfilled his life by giving to it as much as he gave to himself of what was important and dear to him. He found Shangri-La, not only because he wanted to find it, but because he created it, from the inside out.

In its present state *Lost Horizon* suffers from being cut a great deal since its early screenings. The present television print runs about one hundred minutes, winding up abruptly after Robert, George, and Maria's disastrous trip down the mountain. We are simply told of Robert's subsequent amnesia, his recovery, and repeated efforts to escape from his colleagues and return to Shangri-La. This was all originally on film. In not seeing it, one is left with a frustrating sense of missing the end of a shared adventure and of being obliged to enjoy it vicariously through Gainsford's description.

Even so, the magic remains; it is a heart-lifting, ageless story, and cast, script, production, and direction do Hilton's novel proud. There is a sense of atmosphere and pace throughout. The story will always strike the eternal chord of mystery in everyone's mind; like Lord Gainsford, audiences will believe it because they *want* and need to believe it.

More than a year of study went into the making of the film, with director Frank Capra and Robert Riskin (*Mr. Deeds Goes to Town, It Happened One Night*) working together on the script. The American explorer Harrison Forman was technical director in charge of research work and made an extensive trip to Tibet, taking photos of life and lamaseries, writing notebooks of details, gathering trunks full of material. This bewildering assortment must have been delicious to unpack, ranging from ceremonial costumes of Tibetan peasants, farming implements, native bracelets, and necklaces to wigs with 108 braids of long hair. The costumes were faithfully reproduced in the film by Dan Grossbeck.

Although the director had trouble casting all the extras

(not a single Tibetan had ever been known to take out a passport for America), there were never any doubts about his star:

Frank Capra: "My great respect for Ronald Colman began when I saw him in *The White Sister.* With his performance in *A Tale of Two Cities,* my respect matured into a love affair for a fine actor. There was a man who could convey his innermost feelings just with silent reactions.

"Came the matter of casting *Lost Horizon,* I could see only one person in the role of Conway and that was Colman. Ronald was English, a perfect gentleman and above all, he was an idealist with a tough mind—the perfect combination that would justify the High Lama's kidnapping him from the world and bringing him to Shangri-La as his successor. Colman would understand Shangri-La, and *why* he was kidnapped. There might have been Leslie Howard, Bill Powell, not Cooper because he didn't have the intellectual capacity for this part. He would agree with Shangri-La, but to lead it was far beyond his intellectual attainments. Warner Baxter was another, but none of them added up to Ronald Colman.

"He wanted to play the part from the very first time the idea was broached, but he was worried about Columbia. It was Poverty Row. And it was Harry Cohn—an executive known for his crude, bullying tactics. Under my insistent urging, Ronald agreed to play the star part in *Lost Horizon,* but only after demanding—and getting—many small protective clauses in his contract to make certain he wouldn't be abused or taken advantage of. It was his way of defending himself not only against Columbia, but against me. I had a reputation of doing everything myself, of changing scripts and scenes on the set, and of asking actors to ad lib scenes without rehearsals. One of the contract items he must have, he said, was to be furnished with script changes at least a week before the scenes were to be shot.

"But all this self-defense business was quickly forgotten once we started to work. He quickly found out that I had an enormous respect and love for his work, and right away there was something symbiotic between us. We got along famously. We became very fast friends.

"When viewing our rushes, Colman was always there. And to my delight, he took a very active interest in his part, and in the parts others were playing. He was not the kind to come right out and say, 'I think this,' but he would make suggestions—always sensible ones when we'd go over his part alone. We didn't discuss things in front of people.

"I did a great deal of discussing with individual actors in dressing rooms; questioning the parts, making certain the actors *knew* who they were, what they were after, and what the coming scene was all about. I wouldn't tell them how to play the scene; we probed only the *what* and the *why*. The *how* would then come out of them naturally—and no two actors would do it the same. He knew where his character was at any one time. (With a little more brass, he would have made a fine director, because he had knowledge, understanding, and appreciation of scripts—how a character grows in virtues or faults. And when Ronnie made a suggestion, wise directors listened.)

"He was much more compelling on the screen than he was in person. He would do a bit of acting that didn't look much on the set, but it would leap out at you on the screen. You could see Ronnie's brain working on the screen. He held you, compelled you to watch him.

"Although he didn't mix much, he was not aloof. Far from it. For instance, the way he helped Jane Wyatt. Jane was frightened; it was her first big film role. She was twenty at the time, and for a young girl to play opposite Ronald Colman was an extraordinary experience. But Colman helped her; he helped her loosen her nerves, to understand her part. Helped her most by being just kind, for he was probably the kindest, gentlest man I ever knew.

"When we had finished the shooting, I knew in my bones that we had made an important film. And Ronnie thought so too. I think he felt he was revealing himself on the screen in *Lost Horizon* more than he ever had done—or would do again. He shared Conway's dreams. He always talked about the Conway part later on. I'd say he was quite sure he had played himself in it.

"We never worked together again, principally because I couldn't forget him as Conway. I couldn't see him playing any other character—unless we made a sequel to *Lost Horizon*. Ronnie was very keen to make a sequel, wanted to keep on with this guy that was really Ronald Colman. He had many great ideas about a sequel: a modern thing where those in Shangri-La thought it time to go out into the world with their message of peace and beauty, only to be defeated and come back again and say, 'Let's wait another thousand years!' But the author of *Lost Horizon*, James Hilton, died soon after, and so did our sequel idea.

"If I were to film it again today, I would still go about it in the same way, in terms of the sets, etc. I think you need that kind of mood expression—in the free air, the pigeons with tiny bamboo flutes on their legs (this was Ronnie's idea —something he remembered from Bali), that exterior quality of natural beauty and peace with old wisteria and ivy and large libraries, spaciousness and an endurance of something that had been there and would be there, not subject to the frailties and winds of storm. There is no doubt that you could play Shangri-La as an idea, you could play it in a whorehouse. It is a place to go where you can get away from things, a place in your mind as well as in actuality. However, I never have been tempted to do a remake in wide screen and color and everything. Frankly, I felt we had done it. Besides, where could one find another Ronald Colman?"

Conway certainly magnified the mystique of Colman, or perhaps it was the other way around. . . .

Sydney Carton was one character Ronnie had wanted to play since becoming an actor, and Dickens's books lined a shelf in his library not far from Kipling's. He knew them all and perhaps identified more with the characters of Carton and Richard Heldar, not only because they are exceptional, but because each of them was, like Ronnie, very much a man's man.

Watching *A Tale of Two Cities* today, over thirty-five years since it was made and over one hundred since the story was written, I can't help but feel that Dickens would have approved of it as much as present-day audiences. His main story has been kept intact, and the characters are true to their Dickensian selves, with never a face, accent, or performance out of place.

MGM had had an enormous success the previous year with *David Copperfield* (1934) and were quick to follow in its wake with another Dickens spectacular, including some of the same cast (Elizabeth Allan, Basil Rathbone, Edna May Oliver). Both films were produced by the same man:

David Selznick: "In adapting *Copperfield,* the problem was principally one of eliminating a sufficient number of characters and story tangents to bring this work within the limits of a single photoplay, and still give an impression of preserving the original intact. In adapting *A Tale of Two Cities,* there was no such problem, because the story itself was not too long for picturization. Different problems, however, confronted us. For instance, there are long stretches in the book in which the character does not appear. As we worked on the script, it became obvious that, granting an interesting portrayal, the audience would become intrigued by the character of Carton and would expect to follow him, the more so because of casting Colman in the role. The cure for this lay in a rearrangement of the sequences.

"Intensifying the romantic interest between Carton and Lucie, played by Elizabeth Allan, was another major problem. Dickens left this attachment almost entirely to the imagination of his readers. On the screen, it is given more stress. Transferring the vivid scenes, working in the important characters—the De Farges, La Vengeance, the Woodcutter, Gaspard—without lessening the focal interest in the major characters, was still another problem of no small consequence.

"Dickens stresses a strong resemblance between Carton and Darnay—in fact, he makes them facial doubles. In a picture, the only way this effect could be obtained would be to have both roles played by the same man.

"This matter was discussed at length . . . and we finally decided there was nothing inherent to the basic story elements that made it necessary for Carton and Darnay to look exactly alike. We also decided that an audience would be conscious always of the camera trick of double exposure with the subsequent loss of realism, and that it would be very difficult to get an audience excited about Ronald Colman going to the guillotine to save Ronald Colman playing Charles Darnay.

"Following this decision, we found that our problem was not so great. There are only two places in the picture in which the resemblance really matters; one in the Old Bailey trial, the other in the substitution at the prison in the final sequence. . . . We feel somewhat sustained in this decision by the history of *Two Cities* in the 'legitimate' theater; without exception, Carton and Darnay have been played on the stage by two different actors." *

Ronnie knew Dickens's novel virtually by heart and had longed to play the role of Carton for many years. Seven years before he was finally cast for the film, in an interview with a magazine writer, he said: "In Sidney Carton, he [Dickens] conceived a character that only a genius would know; a whimsical, sardonic, bitterly disillusioned fellow who successfully—or almost so—masks his emotions beneath an unmoved exterior. Dickens wrote of this man with a glorious power. He has lived for me since the first instant I discovered him in the pages of the novel. . . . It has a charm that is greater than magnificence, the charm of intimacy in the midst of spectacle."

He considered Carton to be literature's prime example of the man who truly believes in Be Yourself. "He was never anything else than entirely natural. It was impossible for Carton to make compromises with others, with himself or with the problems of life. He was the most unheroic of heroes, but he had the fundamental fortitude to walk to the guillotine with a grin on his face, because he was strong enough to be himself. He lacked utterly any desire to court popularity although he was a man of brilliant talents. Indeed, he lived his life without a thought for the impression he was making on those around him. And it was this trait of character that, in my opinion, has made him live vividly for almost a century." *

At the end of each day's filming Ronnie took home his script and compared passages with the book, often making alterations to the former.

He became so interested in the filming that he broke one of his professional habits—that of never visiting the set unless he was actually working. During *Two Cities* he was

* *Picturegoers Weekly Supplement.*

there virtually the entire time. Liz Allan remembers him as always having a very serious attitude on the set. "We might have been playing tennis together the day before, but it was almost like a Jekyll and Hyde. He was very unjokey on the set, and we never had lunch together to go over the lines or anything."

Carton/Colman first appears after the film has been running for almost half an hour, and is on the screen for relatively little of the film's two hours. However, one might only realize this in retrospect. During the film one is totally involved with this powerful character, who quietly, steadily dominates every scene he is in. One's thoughts are with him during most of the story, whether he is on camera or not. It is a subtle and complete character portrayal: pensive, drunk, sardonic, morose, finally happy, ever shrewd. The actor gives a rare insight into this unusual hero with triumphant strength of character.

His moustache was shaved for the second time in his film career for *Two Cities,* and this Colman/Carton face, with bemused eyes and tousled hair, seems more broad, open, and interesting as a result. Rather more lean-looking than in *Clive of India,* three years earlier.

Charles Darnay (Donald Woods) has always reminded me rather of a grown-up Oliver Twist. Both are good, true-hearted Dickensians, each surrounded by a shining wealth of interesting characters. They are not the doers; rather, things happen to them. They are the passive people of the plot and have little incentive and interest themselves. In fact, examined on their own, they are quite boring.

Lucie Manette is equally good and true but has more character—her quick interest and affection for Carton and their subsequent close friendship are enough to prove that. Liz Allan has exquisite hats, hair, and costumes; she is photographed with the most delicate, perfect lighting and looks altogether like an English dream. When it comes to the romantic scenes, however, the difficulty of the part becomes apparent:

Liz Allan: "I had to keep looking aside during those speeches. The words were not supposed to be making any impression on me. From my point of view, the difficulty was that I found it hard to imagine that any girl could possibly fail to be attracted to Ronald Colman's charms. His position was even more difficult because he had the task of making the speeches romantic without being too impassioned.

"I was greatly impressed when watching him acting to see how tremendously seriously he took his work. I had been inclined to imagine that he'd slip into his part easily and without worrying. I soon discovered that he regarded the studio much as a businessman regards his office . . . It seemed to me that he could do more with an expression or a gesture than any other actor that I have ever met. . . . He'd act in pantomime a scene for which most talkie actors would require at least a line or two of dialogue." *

Isabel Jewell won the small but difficult role of the seamstress who recognizes "Darnay" as Carton in the dungeon and who dies just before him on the guillotine.

Isabel Jewell: "I had played rip-roaring comedy stuff before then, and Jack Conway (director of *Two Cities*) would say to me, 'You're a marvelous little comedienne, but you can't play the part of the seamstress.' He refused to give me an audition, but I knew this was my part! So finally I went over his head to Selznick, who knew my work. He couldn't understand why I hadn't been auditioned and he arranged one for me. Conway refused to direct it. I did the dungeon scene with one of the assistants directing, and the crew were crying at the end of it. Conway had a great deal to say about the

* *Film Weekly*, April 18, 1936.

casting on the film, but Selznick always had the final say—
thank God! It was *Two Cities* that finally broke through my
comedienne image.

"The day after I had tested, Ronnie came to my dressing
room and said, 'Isabel, I asked Mr. Selznick if I could come
and tell you we have just seen your test of the seamstress and
I am so happy that you are going to do the part.' And I just
stood there with my mouth open!

"Ronnie wanted our scene together—the dungeon, then
the tumbril and guillotine—to be shot in continuity. They
were difficult scenes, and I felt singularly fortunate that we
did them in sequence. I said to him when we were working,
'You know, I have to be very careful when working with
you, because I get so spellbound watching you think!'

"The night *Two Cities* was previewed, he wrote me a
letter which was one of the most lovely things that have
happened to me in my life. Only he knew how I had suffered on that picture with Jack Conway. It said, 'I feel that
your performance as the little seamstress is the epitome of
all the innocents that have gone down in world holocausts.
What you did for the film can be recognized by humanity and
what you did for all of us in the picture will always be one
of the things I shall cherish.'

"I've worked with most of the great artists, but Ronnie
was my idol, and the two pictures (Gloria in *Lost Horizon*)
I made with him were the two most important of my life and
my most cherished experiences."

A Tale of Two Cities took five months to film. Luckily
for MGM, Dickens was prone to detailed description, which
was invaluable to the producers. The styles of furniture,
tableware, clothing were carefully examined in the pages by
various departments. This, plus all the information gathered
by cameramen dispatched to France and England to photo-

graph everything from 200-year-old buildings to wallpaper, was entered in lengthy reports that resulted in the sets and costumes.

The film was a critical success and up for the 1936 Oscar for Best Picture of the Year (*The Great Ziegfeld* won it). Elinor Hughes, critic for the Boston *Herald* had this to say:

"Looking back over the years he has spent in the service of the cinema, both silent and talking, we cannot help but be impressed by this reticence which Mr. Colman has been able to sustain from the first, regardless of the goldfish bowl publicity forced upon most of the prominent players in Hollywood. To be sure he hasn't become a legend like Garbo, nor does he flee the press with quite the perseverance she has displayed, but he has kept himself to himself and caused no offense in doing so. The man must be a miracle of tact.

"No one can maintain the position that he has without starting some sort of dispute concerning his ability. We had engaged in them upon occasions, feeling more than once that Mr. Colman was getting away with polite murder and walking through his roles with an agreeable smile and a display of personal charm that was not precisely a substitute for acting. British reticence, we could not help but feel, was being carried too far. With the release of *Two Cities,* the actor in Mr. Colman got the better of his policy of understatement and he offered the best screen portrayal we have ever seen him do. Sydney Carton is a character rich in opportunities for the display of feeling vivid humor and sympathy, and it is to Mr. Colman's credit that he took full advantage of them without becoming awkward or embarrassed." *

The filming of *A Tale of Two Cities* was well timed. Ronnie was not only the perfect age for it, he had sufficient experience (both in life and in films) to bring the wise, "lived-in" quality to Dickens's character that gives him a rare rich-

* The Boston *Herald,* January, 1936.

ness. He is a golden character yet very human, and Ronnie fills him with balanced amounts of wonder and knowledge of himself.

Carton's cynical laughter, which is contradicted by his smile, the sadness behind his eyes, his joy at being restored to the best in himself by Lucie, and so to the "far far better thing I do than I have ever done" all stay in the mind long after the film has ended. The gesture of his hand, note of his voice, tilt of his head. . . .

Unlike the character of Robert Conway, none of Sydney Carton is identifiable with Ronnie himself, who was never cynical and rarely sad (during the second half of his life, that is). But he lives and breathes and obviously loves Carton, and this shows in every frame of the film.

It is watching *Two Cities* that I find myself consciously missing him. I remember him organizing a screening of it for me (aged about twelve at the time) at the studio and he, Benita, and I went to see this role of which he was so proud, only to have the projector break down after the first reel— in which he does not appear. There was no hope of it being mended that day and the opportunity simply did not arise for arranging another showing. We drove back up to San Ysidro with me pumping them with questions about the plot. I saw Ronnie as Sydney Carton over twelve years later and was amazed and very moved by his performance. Twelve years too late for him, though the Hollywood screening would probably have been almost that much too early for me. This praise comes belatedly, but his performance has been a joyous discovery to me, and has greatly increased my respect for him as an actor.

Around the time *A Tale of Two Cities* was first being discussed, Ronnie was approached about filming *Anna Karenina* with Garbo. It was inevitably a role that was second to Garbo's—a leading man always played "in support" of her, and MGM was already puzzling how they would bill these two equally major stars. It must have crossed Ronnie's mind as well. He said he would do it for twice his normal fee (then about $150,000) plus a percentage. Though the opportunity of making a film with her was thrilling, playing any kind of second fiddle wasn't, plus the fact both male parts were quite unsympathetic characters (the husband, Karenin, and the lover, Vronsky, who take turns in deserting Anna). It was rather a difficult situation to resolve, and the studio finally decided that the roles didn't balance sufficiently to warrant such a major star as Colman (and at his asking price) playing opposite the title role.

Three years after *A Tale of Two Cities,* Colman joined with Paramount to make their second film together (the first was *If I Were King*): Rudyard Kipling's *The Light That Failed.*

Kipling was twenty-six years old when he wrote *Light,* and was already known as a master of the short story. He ran into disagreement with his editor over the tragic ending of this early novel. For years the public was agitated as to whether it was better for the hero, Richard Heldar, to die a blind and broken man in the battle-swept Sudan (Kipling's preference) or to regain happiness in the arms of his cold, ambitious childhood sweetheart, Maisie (the version preferred by his editor, but totally inconsistent with Maisie's own ideas throughout the story).

Kipling lived to see his original unhappy ending favored by the reading public, but in the first two film versions (1916 and 1923) the other prevailed. In 1939, three years after his death, Paramount converted his book into a film that is faithful in every detail, relentlessly somber to the inevitable ending that the Empire-proud Englishman first conceived.

Kipling the fatalist, the man fascinated by the desert and with the strong bonds between men, more than between men and women, is reminiscent of the mystical Lawrence, strikingly so in *Light.* Throughout, the hero's closest relationship is with his kind and compassionate fellow-soldier, Torpenhow, played in the film by Walter Huston, and his soul remains in the desert long after he's been invalided back to England. It is to the desert and Torpenhow that Heldar returns, when blindness has finished his career as a painter and fate has relieved him of hope. He chooses to end his life in the heat of a wild Sudan battle, where "his luck held to the last, even to the crowning mercy of a kindly bullet through his head."

The film studiously avoids any of the common Hollywood traps; the hero is not transformed into an all-round charmer, nor is his sweetheart all love and devotion. The desert battle scenes don't overwhelm the story with undue length, size, or gore. The characters are indubitably those created by Kipling, not the producers, and a great deal of the dialogue has been neatly transferred from the novel to the screenplay by Robert Carson. It is a "thinking" film that moves at a pace concurrent to the development of its characters and their relationships, never rushing yet never lagging.

It seems inevitable that William Wellman should be involved with this picture. With his war background of the Foreign Legion, a daredevil pilot shot down and then stitched together in a French hospital, he "fought" rather than "grew" up, and resembles a fiery character from the film itself. A contemporary of Ronnie's, he still fills a room with his electric energy, and his moustached good looks, though more lean and angular, are very reminiscent of Colman:

Wellman: "I was a kind of a wild guy. I'm housetrained now and have been for some years; however, the time during which I directed *Light* was my wildest time of all. A lot of people didn't want to work for me, nor did I want to work with them.

"Now we come to Mr. Colman. He and I didn't like each other from the very start. When they called me in and said they wanted to do this film with him, I said I loved the idea of doing *Light* but I thought Wellman and Colman wasn't such a good idea. It was a most unusual combination! I was a crazy guy, and he was very much the gentleman.

"He had the most gorgeous voice I have ever heard in my life. I appreciate a good voice. I have been to the Boston Conservatory of Music and I had a lovely voice. Voice to me is always wonderful. I remember once, early in the picture, he had a very important scene, and when it was all over and I yelled 'Cut!' he said, 'What did you think of it?' and I said, 'So help me God, I don't know. Your voice is so wonderful to me that I close my eyes and just listen to it! I remember it sounded great!' And he just looked at me strangely. . . .

"He was a funny guy, to me he proved very hard to know. Now, Frank Capra and he were great friends, but Frank was such a nice guy and I wasn't. He was accustomed to someone that took great pains; I took great pains too, but I probably printed more first takes than anyone in the business. I know the business of being a director, and sometimes when I thought I had a 'sleepy' man, I might not let him know it. Let him do a little thinking for himself; it would show. I often found that you could get a certain inspiration from a first take that you could never get again, and this way everything didn't become parrotlike.

"Ronnie liked to know everything and I said, 'I just want you to know enough so that you help me.' He said, 'Well, I'll help you more if I know more.' I said, 'No you won't. You know what you are up against.' He had Dudley Digges, Huston, and Lupino. I said, 'You're going to be on your toes. I'm not protecting you. You're the star, and I'm certainly not going to let anything happen that won't be good for the picture, because the picture to me is of great deal more value than you or Huston or anything else. You took this job with me, and you knew what you were up against. You made your decision and have to stick by it. I can't change; if I had to rehearse over and over I'd say, 'Oh, to hell with it!' and go out and get drunk or something.

"I know that I had the weakness of impatience, a desire to get that one wonderful scene that you can sometimes get if you work them all up and then if there's a mistake, you can cover it in another odd angle or a close shot. I knew how to cut a picture. I had worked as a cutter, and I knew exactly what I wanted and how I did not have to use it if I didn't want it. Well, it was awfully hard to explain this to him. I said, 'The hell with it. You're just up against it, that's all. You've got to take it easy and relax yourself.' Well, he wasn't a fighter, you know. I don't think I ever saw him really mad. If he was he did it beautifully, and I didn't. Everybody would know within blocks of the place with me! So it was rather an odd combination.

"We had one argument that went to the studio, it was so bad. He wanted me to use Vivien Leigh for the role of the waif. Just before Jimmy Townsend had brought her up to my office, Ida Lupino had burst in. She went by my secretary and everyone and said to me, 'You're doing Kipling's *Light That Failed,* and this is my part. You have *got* to give me a chance. I know it right now. I know the whole script, because I stole it!'

"Then she played one of the greatest scenes (where Heldar breaks her down completely to bring out what he needs in the portrait he is painting of her). I played a very very bad Colman with her, and I have never seen anything so terrific in my life. I said, 'You've got the part.' And I went to tell Schulberg and said, 'This is my girl.' Then Ronnie wanted Vivien Leigh and said to me, 'I think you've made a big mistake.' I said, 'Well that's one of my faults. I make mistakes, but occasionally it sticks its head out of the ground and amounts to something.' He hadn't seen Lupino do her stuff; he'd just heard me talk about her. So, he then went to Schulberg and complained about it and said, 'If I can't get

Vivien Leigh, I want another director.' Schulberg said, 'Well, I cannot do that. Wellman has made some great pictures, and he is very capable and this is his type of picture. I have a hunch he will make a great picture out of this, and I'm running this studio. I'll call in Wellman and see if I can't talk him out of it.' So then I said, 'No, get yourself another director. The hell with Colman. If he is going to cast the picture for me, then you don't need a director, you need a messenger boy. How am I going to direct a guy like that? If you want to do it, I'll go home and you get me somebody else.' He looked at me and said, 'No, you've got Lupino.'

"So that's the way it was; we started out on the wrong foot. I'm completely in accord with the way Ronnie felt about me. If I had been Colman, and Colman had been Wellman, I would have felt the same way.

"Ronnie was a male Stanwyck; he never blew his lines. Stanwyck knows the script from beginning to end; he was the same way. You never had any trouble with him forgetting lines. Come Lupino's big scene, where she has to work herself up into a state of hysteria while he is painting her portrait, he forgot his lines right in the middle of it, right in the middle of her hysteria. So I said, 'Cut!' and I thought that maybe he had been as affected by her performance as I. So we rested for a few minutes and I started again and he forgot again. Then I got mad. I cut and went up to him and said, 'Let's you and I take a little walk together.' So we got away from the others. 'Look, Mr. Colman, I know there is a reason behind this. I don't give a goddam what the reason is. My reason for anything good or bad is to try and make a good picture. Nothing else means anything to me, but I've got to tell you this, if you do it once more, I'm going to make a character man out of you. I'm not kidding, that lovely face of yours is not going to look the way it does right now!' And I walked away. Now he is not that kind of a screwball; we did the scene again and it was done beautifully.

"From then on, we spoke to each other as Mr. Colman and Mr. Wellman.

"Now, I don't know about this, but it tickles my sense of humor, so if he did it for any other reason, he didn't get to first base, but in *The Halls of Ivy* the heavy's name in the script was Wellman. [This was chance, not design.]

"After the film was over, we didn't see each other for a long time. Frank Capra and his wife are very dear friends of ours, and we went to dinner there one night (we used to go about every week) and there was Ronnie. Well, my wife and Ronnie had a great singles ping-pong match. They played as if they were playing for their lives. He got beaten and she got beaten and they were both damn good players. When we had a doubles match, he went up to her and said, 'Would you mind playing with me?' and she said, 'I think that would be a great idea.' They beat everybody, and you know why? She is very polite, and of course he was very polite, and they were so polite to one another that they always got out of each other's way. It was just fantastic.

"Later on we had several dinners and we got to know each other and became friends, so it ended beautifully. I don't think he would have wanted to do another film with me though. I had the same kind of trouble with Gregory Peck. We had very little to do with each other, yet that picture was also very successful!"

Though Ronnie enjoyed filming *Light* less than his other pictures because of the friction with his director, it is without doubt one of his most interesting roles, and one to which he does great credit. In fact, of all his films it is my personal favorite. Kipling's unusual story, the faithful screenplay, Wellman's shrewd direction, and the subtle, excellent performances given by Colman, Huston, Dudley Digges, and Lupino combine to make an unforgettable motion picture.

Perhaps it is coincidence that the first film character

Ronnie portrayed after his marriage is not only my favorite of his roles, but one of the finest performances of his career. However, I like to think that the depths to which he was able to reach for the character of Heldar were more developed—and perhaps more accessible—now that his relationship with Benita was secured. She had certainly sparked him into a finer awareness of himself, and it would follow that this would eventually encompass others. Ronnie plays Richard Heldar from the inside out. Watching the film, one knows Heldar rather than the man playing him. Ronnie was equally knowledgeable of both.

The following rather uncertain review from the Richmond *News* always amuses me, and probably encompasses the opinion of those not quite on the same wavelength as the film, even up to confusing an English star with an "English picture."

"This picture drags in spots and is dotted with intervals with suspended action in which the spectators are given an opportunity to reflect or conjecture (imaginatively if possible) upon the problems presented. That's because it is an English picture, and English pictures have acquired the annoying habit of puzzling American audiences." *

The New York Times critic was more precise: "Mr. Colman has rarely handled a role with greater authority or charm, manfully underplaying even the sure-fire melodramatics of the sequence in which he goes blind—a heaven-sent infirmity for 99 out of 100 hard-pressed actors!" †

Around the same time as *Light* was being filmed, Thelma opened a novelty shop in Laguna Beach (outside Los Angeles), having been for some time the recipient of a highly sufficient alimony. She had not mellowed with time, however. Her first name for the shop was "The Original Mrs. Ronald Colman," but she was dissuaded from using this by her friends. Then,

* Richmond (Virginia) *News*, March 2, 1940.
† December 25, 1939.

with her inventive sense of indiscretion, she threatened to publish her memoirs, entitled, of course, *My Life as Mrs. Ronald Colman the First*. Considering the amount of time she had played the role, this could hardly have been more than a short story.

Though she preoccupied herself in Laguna Beach for some time, the book idea was squelched. Ronnie had long since dealt with her only through lawyers and felt a great deal less vulnerable since his marriage to Benita. Also, he had lived in Hollywood long enough to have firmly established his reputation. He was liked, admired, respected by friends and public alike, and no gossip Thelma had to offer would have been appreciated by anyone. Thelma was fighting a lonely, vindictive battle, never in sight of her opponent and with no one to agree with her.

9 ✑
The Forties

A Californian colonial for over ten years, Ronnie was feeling unquestionably at home. He flourished in the warm climate and in the way of life that his adopted country had made possible. Surrounded by good work and friends both English and American, he had every intention of continuing to make this his home, and quietly applied for an American citizenship. Shortly before the final stage of his Americanization, England declared war on Germany. Ronnie instantly canceled the proceedings, instinctively not wishing to "desert" his native country at such a crucial time. Throughout the war years he helped with his money and his time, and although he never moved from California, he maintained his British citizenship for the rest of his life, as did Benita.

His friends had noticed a welcome change in him during the time he had known Benita. He became far less restrained and moody, more open, more widely social, and clearly more relaxed. Now that the marriage step had been braved, he awoke to the fact that he was thoroughly enjoying it. At a New Year's Eve party, sitting out a dance with Fay Wray, who at that time was on the verge of marrying Robert (*Lost Horizon*) Riskin, Ronnie recommended marriage highly: "It's really marvelous at breakfast . . . *and* in bed!"

194 ·

As far as raising a family was concerned, he approached the idea as warily as he had marriage; certainly neither he nor Benita had ever thought along the lines of a large family. Having one's first child when approaching middle age is a major unrehearsed step for any man. Someone growing up alongside someone growing old provides a lively, changing situation in which to be involved, and one that Ronnie did not find easy several years later. At present, however, he found his life sufficiently full and fulfilled with his wife, as well as an increasing amount of radio, bond drives in the States and Canada, supervising the San Ysidro house plans, and forming a company with Bill Hawks for which he made two films.

The war inevitably brought an economic crisis to Hollywood, and by the end of the thirties, stars' salaries were being slashed. The solution lay in contracts for smaller fees plus a percentage of the profits, or the stars' agents forming production companies consisting of the star, director, and writer of the film(s), who then worked on a profit-sharing basis. Ronnie and Bill chose the latter solution.

Lucky Partners and *My Life with Caroline* were both directed by Lewis Milestone, a friend and neighbor of the Summit Drive area. A man of tremendous humor, which is belied by the films for which he is most famous (*All Quiet on the Western Front, The Front Page, Of Mice and Men*), he was not praised by the critics for these two.

Lewis Milestone: "The critics always expected something weighty from me, so whenever I did a comedy—like these two—they'd usually say, 'Milestone takes a holiday!' These two films had to be made to keep Ronnie's production company active. It was just Go, and we had to find stories at pretty short notice.

"The screenplay of *Lucky Partners* was written by John van Druten and Allan Scott, based on a play by Sacha Guitry.

We had Ginger Rogers playing opposite Ronnie, and I brought Jack Carson into it. I remember having a little squabble with Ginger because she didn't want him. 'He was an extra man in one of my pictures!' she said. 'I can bring up pictures where you were an extra girl! Everyone starts where he can.' 'What does Ronnie say about it?' 'Ronnie says what he always says: 'You're the doctor.'

"So I put him in. For the first few days I had a terrible problem getting Jack to assert himself. He was so in awe of these two stars. Finally I got through to him. He gained confidence in himself, and soon both Ginger and Ronnie went crazy about him. And Jack took full advantage of it.

"One morning, we were rehearsing a scene with Ronnie and the judge. The judge was being played by Harry Davenport, then about seventy-five years old, a member of the Barrymore and Drew clan. A wonderful old man. Ronnie kept blowing his lines. Davenport became very indignant. 'Mr. Colman, I know that you have a valet around. The least you could do is to make him run the lines with you. I don't expect a world-shattering performance from you; just remember the jokes!' Then he took off his robes and marched off the set, leaving the very reticent and always correct Ronnie completely embarrassed.

"I rushed off the stage to halt the old man's flight. 'Mr. Davenport!' The old man stopped: 'I don't want to discuss it! Everything I had to say, I've said to Mr. Colman. I don't want to be in his picture; I'm through.' I tried to calm him down, but he raved on. 'There is nothing you can say that will change my mind.' But I had a sudden inspiration, so I went on: 'I won't even try. I just want to tell you a little story which I think will amuse you.' He relaxed. 'Okay—but no tricks!'

"The story dealt with a friend of mine, Octavio, a man of the world, a great gourmet and expert on wines. While he was visiting Beverly Hills, I invited him out to dinner at a gambling club on Sunset Strip where they served very good food. Octavio addressed our waiter in French, but the waiter didn't speak one word of French, so when Octavio had gotten through his order, he said, 'I'm terribly sorry, but I don't speak French, so you'd better tell it to me in English.' Octavio wanted a paillard of veal, with a purée of carrots. The waiter took down the order, but when the dinner arrived, the paillard turned out to be a veal cutlet with spaghetti on the side. Octavio practically passed out at the sight of the dish. Just then the maître d'hotel stopped by the table and in perfect French asked if everything was satisfactory. Octavio complained, 'This place lays claim to fame about cuisine, and look what he brought me!' The maître d' listened sympathetically and finally said, 'May I ask you, sir, how long have you been in this restaurant?' Octavio looked at his watch and said, 'About an hour.' The maître d' shrugged. 'So you have been here one hour and you are complaining. I have been here for five years; you should feel sorry for me!'

"So Davenport roared with laughter and said, 'I can see the similarity. Okay, I'll go back.' On the set, he put his robes back on, apologized to Ronnie for blowing his top, and told him my story. We finished the picture with no further trouble.

"I liked Ronnie's qualities. If you took the trouble to wait until you got through that first layer of defense, he was warm and friendly. A couple of times he invited me and a few other people to have a drink with him after the shooting. He had a wonderful sense of humor which he would project on the screen.

"I think he and Ginger were only professional friends. Running rushes with her was an experience! She insisted on coming to see them, then the minute the lights went out and a scene of hers came on the screen, you could hear her start groaning. And she kept groaning, sliding down further in her seat until just the top of her head was visible. She always found something wrong with the way she looked."

My Life with Caroline (van Druten's adaptation of the French comedy by Louis Verneuil) was started directly afterward, each film taking around six to eight weeks. The picture begins with Ronnie confiding to the camera in a brief monologue about coping with marriage to Caroline. The idea blends with the French farce rhythm of the film, and of course has been used many times since, most memorably perhaps in *Tom Jones*.

The young English actress Anna Lee, in her first Hollywood film, played the rather childish, flirtatious Caroline. She made a hit with the company, if not with the public.

Milestone: "The poor girl, if there was nothing in her way, she would nevertheless find something to stumble over. You couldn't help but be amused by her; she was an original. Ronnie never expressed an opinion of her for fear that it would come across as criticizing a fellow actor.

"I enjoyed making both films with Ronnie. There was never any tension between us. If I wanted to talk to him, I always could. He wasn't a recluse who hopped into his dressing room and locked the door, but like all actors, when he had a difficult scene, he liked to be alone beforehand. Whatever the scene, he would throw himself into it wholeheartedly and do it as well as he could.

"He hated gossip, especially if it involved him. If anyone said anything about him that wasn't true, he would find it very difficult, if not impossible, to forgive him.

"I used to live behind Ronnie's house at Summit Drive. Across the street was one of Marion Davies' houses which was rented by Horowitz, the celebrated pianist. My cousin is a famous violinist, and he shared the house with him. He would practice upstairs and Horowitz would be downstairs playing the piano. When I came to visit, he showed me his workroom and there I saw two concert pianos. 'Why two pianos?' 'Rachmaninoff plays this one.'

"It was that kind of a household. They promised to have a musical evening with Rachmaninoff, Horowitz, Milstein, and Barbirolli, the famous conductor who had just arrived from abroad (this was during the war). So I told Ronnie about this, and he said, 'Can you get us invited? I would love to be there!'

"So Ronnie and Benita were invited. What nobody reckoned on was that Charlie Chaplin would also be there. When Charlie came in, all those great musicians sat at his feet, and he spent the whole evening telling them anecdotes. Mostly about his own life. They were so fascinated there was not one note of music played!"

Ronnie was not particularly happy with either film, especially the second. The critics agreed. Playing opposite a starlet twenty-five years his junior was not his style. It was certainly contradictory to his character as well as to his image to be enamored of a flirtatious young girl, and the result on screen was as uncomfortable to the public as it was to him. He looked older under such sharp contrast, and a touch silly.

Dissatisfied with his efforts as a producer, he decided not to continue with his company and to put his time into radio and his other ventures rather than force out another film. There was certainly much to do until a good script appeared, at which point he could take a percentage, if salaries were still being cut.

At the same time as the new plans were being drawn up for rebuilding the San Ysidro house to one level, Ronnie and Al were considering the idea of opening a restaurant in town. The Ranch, run on the American plan, offered only a dining room, and they were thinking along the lines of something rather more elegant in Santa Barbara (which at that time offered nothing in that category): a restaurant that would be a good property investment as well as an attractive alternative for the Ranch guests.

They chose a defunct yacht club on the Santa Barbara wharf, a location overlooking the harbor, the Pacific, and the palm-lined oceanfront. The Harbor Restaurant is now quite well known in California, although all its originators have long since pulled out. Ronnie bought it with a New Yorker who had already financed a couple of restaurants, and again Al was on hand as supervisor. Benita, not having the time herself, suggested that Jessica (Mrs. Richard) Barthelmess do the interior decor, as she had a flair for design, and the results were downright deluxe!

Al: "I ran it myself for a while; then on December seventh, a few months later, Pearl Harbor happened, and the Army put up a barrier at the entrance to the wharf. The only people allowed out there were those with identification. So business, after a very good start, went to nothing, and fifteen days later we had to close the restaurant. I went into the Navy, and Ronnie, not being able to get into uniform, did war bond sales. Later on we sublet and ultimately sold the lease and furnishings. We just broke even on that venture."

It was the only one of his real estate ventures that did not yield either money or pleasure; there was time for neither. Other investments in properties at Big Sur, Hidden Valley (near Los Angeles), Bel-Air, and Palm Springs all paid well in their time, but Ronnie was never destined to be a restaurant-backer.

Al: "He traveled all over America and Canada on those bond drives for Britain and the Allies, and this was very valuable. He had that deep-rooted love for Britain that all expatriates have, but I don't think he ever regretted not living there. He liked the tropics and warm places, and at that time California was a smog-free area! It had become so much his home and he knew it all. My wife and I would go traveling with them a lot to Palm Springs, Lake Arrowhead, Death Valley, San Francisco. Once we went to the Grand Canyon. We rode mules down to the bottom of the canyon, then spent the night there at the Paradise Lodge on the Colorado River and came up on the mules the next day. He was a fine rider.

"He used to talk about when and if he got married he would leave Beverly Hills. He had bought Summit because it was a good investment, though he realized at the time it was too big for one person. He always had in mind San Ysidro as the place he wanted to live. That's why he kept developing the house. Benita developed a love for San Ysidro but never the intensity that he had."

San Ysidro was something deep-rooted to Ronnie. It was a natural extension of his own backyard, to which their friends gravitated on weekends. It was his ideal base from which he would go "out" to work, drive one hundred miles down to Hollywood when he needed, yet keep his own life quite clear of it. The Ranch was the sanctuary where dark glasses were used just for the sun; where he had his beloved privacy and yet was close enough to Hollywood to appreciate from precisely what he was being private.

Benita recognized his need eventually to make the move to San Ysidro; his whole life pattern pointed toward it. She was also aware of his desire for her to share his love for the Ranch, if not the need. Had she been a less social and gregarious person and as independent as Ronnie, no doubt they would have moved to San Ysidro a good ten years sooner than they did. However, Ronnie also appreciated her desire to live in what had become her second home within reach of most of her friends. So they continued to use the Ranch for weekends and spare time, while maintaining Summit Drive as home base.

The tennis group was now disbanded because most of the members had joined the forces and many others had left town—Dick Barthelmess and David Niven had joined the U.S. and English forces, respectively; Clive Brook had returned to London, as had Percy Marmont. Bill Powell had remarried and was living in the desert in Palm Springs. Although there was the occasional match, Ronnie was now putting Beverly Hills spare time into photography and painting in his Summit studio. Meanwhile Verbois (the San Ysidro house) was being rebuilt, and time was passing busily. With travel and radio encompassing more and more days, the *Dragoon* was sitting sadly in the harbor unused for longer periods and no longer worth the expense of her upkeep. Ronnie sold her with a fond farewell.

Though the film scripts continued to pile up on his desk, those that interested him were fewer and further between. War stories were popular, but he felt he was doing better work for the cause outside of films rather than accepting roles with which he wasn't entirely satisfied or in which he felt miscast. Though he did not look his age, he did not want to repeat his last mistake, and made certain his next choice suited both his age group and character.

At the beginning of the forties a script arrived that had passed through the hands and typewriters of various writers from Irwin Shaw to Sidney Buchman. Finally George Stevens, already an established and distinguished director (*Alice Adams, Quality Street, Penny Serenade*), decided with Sidney Buchman to put some final work into the script and film it under the title *The Talk of the Town*.

The story's main interest lay in the interplay among three principal characters; two men and a woman, each as different and dogmatic as the others, yet hardly the typical "eternal triangle." The elder is a legal whiz, a more intellectual than practical professor (and ultimately a Supreme Court justice); the younger is an escaped convict, a ne'er-do-well wrongly accused of arson and murder, whose theories on criminals and justice are in wild contrast to those of the professor. Lastly, there is the local schoolteacher, who finds herself sandwiched between these two opposites, equally attracted to both. They are all brought together when she rents her house to the professor for the summer. He is in need of seclusion to finish his thesis on criminals and crime; unknowingly, the convict has chosen to hide in the same house. The schoolteacher, who believes in his innocence, protectively recommends him the role of the gardener, while she stays on in the house doing the professor's cooking. His guise is inevitably realized by the professor:

> She: *"How are the zinnias doing?"*
> Gardener: *"Dying!"*

However, all ends well in the lives of both justice and convict, and the audience remains uncertain until literally the last frame as to which man's affection will prevail over the schoolteacher's indecision.

Major stars Jean Arthur and Cary Grant accepted the roles of the schoolteacher and convict, and Colman stepped in as the professor in *Talk of the Town,* his second film for Columbia.

Director George Stevens had an arrangement with Columbia whereby he worked for them on the condition that he did not have to talk to Harry Cohn, which made great sense to Ronnie.

Stevens: "I think what made the picture something other than the design indicated was Colman coming into it. Cary and I had discovered each other before this, and of course Jean and I had worked together, but I had never worked with Ronnie. We had considerable conversations as to the screenplay being less than complete, and he wasn't sure at first that he should engage in a situation with these people being starred. (The actual billing wasn't very important; I mean, three people like Jean Arthur, Cary Grant, and Ronald Colman, however they are put, distinguish one another in association). Opportunities were everywhere for all three of them, and they would really choose their pictures on the basis not only of the character being right for them, but that the experience would be a pleasant one.

"Although the picture was perhaps a little too light for him, he didn't alter it; he intended to treat it lightly without being comic, for the way it was written, one could read it as such. Being rather a sparse film, there was not an awful lot of rehearsing; just the understanding of what was going to happen was important. It wasn't a picture that has that wonderful element of doubt, where everything is disproving it and then, all of a sudden, it comes off. In the back of my mind, I knew it was going to come off all along. It didn't have that hazard in it; it was more of an understood flight with a take-off time and an arrival time and not too much headwind.

"The only time I saw any sensitivity between the three of them about who was doing what was at the very end. Cary became very uneasy about walking down that long Supreme Court corridor with Jean following him. I don't know whatever got into his head, but he figured that she was upstaging him, doing all kinds of witty things that must be fantastically interesting, because people were laughing around the set. They were amused because it was a very funny scene! Dilg is walking away, being very noble, but he can't shake the girl off; his magnetism is taking her along and is quite disturbing to him. There was never a moment that Cary worked with Ronnie when that happened, worrying about which man was doing what."

The Talk of the Town still works today, even if it is perhaps a trifle melodramatic in those scenes surrounding

Dilg's escape and, later, the tracking down of the guilty man. However, the essence and interest of the film lies in the three characters, their contrasting beliefs and personalities, and their effect upon each other. With the amount of ideas thrown around the house on law, love, and life, some are bound to take root, and each character benefits from knowing the others. The justice ends up far more a part of this world, tackling his new job in the Supreme Court with more realism and happiness than he previously possessed; the radical Dilg gains a tempered respect for both the justice and for what he stands; and the schoolteacher, largely responsible for helping remove the justice's nose from his law books, ends up with the reformed Dilg.

The justice was Colman's first mature (rather than romantic) role and as he had passed from silent films to talkies, so he continued on to this next stage of his career with both style and grace. In the stuffy but likable role of the professor who has the courage not only to admit his faults but to do something about them, the Colman mystique, now enhanced with dignity, is still in evidence.

Jean Arthur has a similar indefinable charisma about her, and their mutual attraction in the film is as understandable as it is apparent. As much is said in their silences together as in their conversations, and they blend so naturally that it strikes a wrong note when she ends up with the very definitive character of Grant/Dilg, even though he is nearer her age. In this new, mature role Ronnie's attraction to women was (both on screen and off) very much in evidence.

The Talk of the Town was one of the most popular films that summer. Ronnie was pleased with it and returned to more radio and war work. Being fifty years old and an expatriate, he felt strongly about not being able to join the armed forces. He was riveted to the papers and radio for the latest developments of the war, and directed all his energies to the cause in his own way. He had sent a wire to the Secretary of the Treasury, volunteering his services to the Government in any capacity. The reply had been that the Government valued the offer and felt he could best serve by lending his voice to their broadcasts. His voice was in fact only a part of what he offered: he became a member of the Hollywood Victory Committee, president of British War Relief in Los Angeles, a worker for the American Red Cross and the bond drives. Personal appearances were a major phobia of his, and these tours consisted of hardly anything else. Thousands of miles by train across the States and Canada, waiting in countless stations, little sleep, endless lunch and dinner banquets, exhaustive handshakes, autographs, and general chat.

Though he had no immediate family in London (his brother and sisters were in Australia), he felt a deep-rooted concern for his country's involvement, along with his old familiarity with the horror of war. With personal appearances as well as radio, with about a third of his own income, with bundles and packages of food and clothing, and with continual correspondence, Ronnie and Benita did all in their power to help support those involved—servicemen, friends, and relatives alike—throughout the war years. In fact he broke down from sheer nervous exhaustion and strain after his last bond drive, at which point his doctor ordered him to rest.

Ronald Colman was one of the first major film names to be connected with radio. His voice as well as his stature made him a natural choice as far as the networks were concerned, and he himself appreciated and enjoyed the wide range of plays, books, and other works that this medium laid open with such relative ease. His voice covered a great range of characters both young and old. He appeared in the Screen Guild Theater and the Lux Radio Theater, but he was most occupied with programs for the war effort: the shows for the troops such as *Yarns for Yanks* (this was a fifteen-minute late-night series that consisted of stories read by such familiar names as Laughton, Marshall, Tracy, Cagney), the English-American Amity programs, a U.N. commemorative program, and *Everything for the Boys,* in which Ronnie starred.

Written and directed by Arch Oboler, this was the most expensive show on the air; it had a thirty-five-piece orchestra, a twenty-minute dramatization with Ronnie and the week's guest (such equally big names as Bergman, Colbert), and ended with a telephone conversation with overseas GIs. Though an enormous success with both the servicemen and the public, it was not an enjoyable experience for Ronnie. Milton Merlin (later to write much of the Colmans' *Halls of Ivy* series with his wife Barbara) first met Ronnie on this show:

Merlin: "I was called in on *Everything for the Boys* because they were having trouble with what they called Colman's 'champagne and caviar.' So I came on and wrote a lot of special material, and got to know Ronnie through that. Oboler was really a character. Rated as one of the top radio writers and producers of the period, a reputation he had earned by prolific and inventive talent, he had also created an image which was fashionable at that time—the role of the eccentric. He'd dress in dirty dungarees, no socks, thong sandals with his big hairy toes sticking out, a fishnet T-shirt, and a hat with a grease-stained band. When Barbara and I went to dinner at his house, he'd be wearing a suit, so this was all an act. And you can imagine Ronnie's reaction! Ronnie the immaculate, on a big posh show, with a director who would appear in bare feet and dirty sweatshirts! It got down to nasty clashes, like one day when they weren't speaking, Oboler said to his assistant director: 'I wish you'd tell Mr. Colman that is not the way to read a line.' Ronnie turned to Tommy Turner and said, 'I wish you'd tell Mr. Oboler to get his pants pressed!' "

Established playwriting partners (Jerome) Lawrence and (Robert) Lee first met Ronnie on the Screen Guild Theater and through their respective agent-friend, Nat Wolf. (Lawrence also knew him from working on *Everything for the Boys,* for which he also wrote some material.) They sold Ronnie on the idea of acting as host as well as main interpreter on a weekly classical series. *Favorite Story* was a half-hour program, and the stories (adapted and directed by Lawrence and Lee) were either favorite plays or novels chosen by a different well-known person each week: Einstein, Mrs. Roosevelt, Sinclair Lewis, H. L. Mencken. (In one of them Benita played Elizabeth to Edna Best's Mary Queen of Scots.) Adaptations were made using a great deal of narration, accented with music and sound effects. There were new roles for Ronnie, including Phineas Fogg in *Around the World in Eighty Days,* the man who married Anatole France's *Dumb Wife,* Deburau in *Gift of Laughter,* and *Cyrano.* Later there were adaptations of *A Tale of Two Cities* and *The Light That Failed.* He tried to get clearance for some Shaw that he particularly wanted to do; however, it proved too difficult and expensive to manage.

A tale that he dined out on for some time was Lawrence approached by an English writer in London:

"Mr. Lawrence, you are an American radio producer-writer-director—can you sell our adaptation of *A Tale of Two Cities* over there? It's 148 two-hour episodes."

Lawrence: "I hate to tell you, but we have already done both a Decca album and a radio show with Ronald Colman, and each version is half an hour long!"

"Oh, you Americans!" replied the Englishman disdainfully.

Lawrence: "We often had conferences ahead of time about specifically what we were going to do on the stories. When we were doing a show in which he starred, we'd go up to the

Summit house and read it out loud first. He'd say, 'Yes' or 'This is a little awkward here.' He was good to work with, creative and never temperamental. He did a job and had a conscientious feeling about his work. He wanted to be artistic as well as be able to reach people. He always was a tremendously creative actor. A member of the team, he never pulled the star bit, except to say, 'I don't think that's for me.' Ronnie knew better than anybody else what he could do and what he could not do. He'd say, 'No, this part is not Colman.' That voice was a Stradivarius—you didn't play Yankee Doodle on it!

"One of us would pick him up and drive him to the studio and he had a mania about punctuality. We had to be exactly on time. He used to say, 'Punctuality is the courtesy of royalty!' We'd rehearse four or five hours, then time it, then do a 'dress rehearsal' where we usually had to tighten things up, work with the musicians, work with the sound effects. We didn't have tape in those days. If something went wrong, it was very difficult to dub, unlike now. As with *Lux* and later *The Halls of Ivy,* we played *Favorite Story* straight through. That series was distributed all over the English-speaking world and was immensely popular.

"Ronnie had a far better sense of humor than most people gave him credit for, and I think he was a far better actor. The variety of things he used to do on radio helped prove it. But a lot of people thought it was just that voice and those looks. It was always an adventure doing a program with him, and it always brought the other actors up to a kind of height of professionalism. Of all the film people, he was the most in demand on the radio. Even when he was at his height of film fame, he was still a top radio choice; he didn't do it because times were slow in film, he had them running almost simultaneously.

"Later on, when Bob and I were just out of the service, we had a New Year's Eve party and invited Ronnie and

Benita and Edna Best and her husband, Nat Wolf, and a bunch of other friends and we played charades. We gave Ronnie, who was on the other team, *Ronald Colman* to dramatize, to see what he would do and how he'd do it. He drew a bottle and nobody could get it. He wouldn't point to himself or anything. The bottle was Colman's mustard! Nobody got any of his clues and he was furious. Then he drew a plate with a circle at the edge. Edna was furious with him, she kept saying, 'What are you doing, what *is* that, Aunt Jemima's pancakes?' At the end he said, 'How was I going to portray *Ronald Colman* except by doing Colman's mustard?' He didn't really like the game. . . ."

After his two poor films at the beginning of the forties, Ronnie's position was well redeemed by *Talk of the Town* and he was back on his enduring pinnacle with its successor, another James (*Lost Horizon*) Hilton novel that had recently been published and quickly bought by MGM. *Random Harvest* (the title is a quote from an official German report: "According to a British Official Report, bombs fell at Random") is a guaranteed tear-jerker set in England after World War I, about an Englishman who, stricken with amnesia for over twenty years, marries the same woman twice. The much married wife was played by English actress Greer Garson, who had made her U.S. debut three years before in another Hilton adaptation, *Goodbye, Mr. Chips*. Well cast in *Harvest*, she managed convincingly to carry off the progression from music hall dancer-singer (where we see her doing an unlikely knees-up in mini-kilt) to secretary and wife of an M.P.

An amnesiac soldier (Colman) escapes from his asylum-hospital and is taken in and cared for by a compassionate actress (Garson). They fall in love, eventually marry, and move to a cottage in the country, all without his knowing who he is or where he belonged before the war. Shortly after the birth of their child, he is knocked out in a car accident, and when he regains consciousness, his past comes back, but his present is lost. He returns to his parents' home and a promising political career, haunted by but unable to trace his actions of his lost years.

Meanwhile, Garson, their child having died, has tracked him down, realized the situation, and become his secretary. She patiently hopes that one day he will remember what the strange key is on his chain, where those lost years went, and who has been typing his letters! His career prospers and he becomes an M.P., proposes to his most indispensable and lovely secretary, who has wisely—under the circumstances—annulled their marriage. She accepts him. Years elapse with no break in his memory. His frustration slowly turns to sadness, despite their subdued but happy marriage, as instinct tells him he has left someone behind. Then, his business takes him to the town in which they first met on Armistice Day twenty years previously.

In a similar rowdy atmosphere, this time with striking workers filling the streets, pieces fall back into his mind: the crowds, the noise, the tobacconist, the dance hall, the asylum, and at last their now empty cottage in the country. The gate that creaks, the bough that needs trimming, his key fits the lock, and her name bursts from him. Greer is not far behind, and having sat through the entire film longing for her to *tell him,* one's throat becomes decidedly lumpy as he "sees" her for the first time in twenty years.

Mervyn LeRoy (who had made the sensitive *Waterloo Bridge* the preceding year) directed, and thanks to him, what could easily have become an overindulgent, sentimental story was handled with subtlety and tenderness throughout its two hours. The director was already a friend of Ronnie's:

LeRoy: "When *Random Harvest* came along, Ronnie and Greer were the first choice for the roles; it could have been written for them. (The film still holds the record for the longest run at the Radio City Music Hall in New York.)

"There was nothing of the ham in him. He'd always

make a lot of suggestions about script and dialogue, always good ideas. He'd never be definite about it though; he didn't want to hurt you, and you didn't want to hurt him, so we would walk around the set and talk things over. I always had about two weeks of rehearsals before we started, just reading out loud, and then you get a lot of ideas. He was very businesslike on the set, a real pro. He didn't talk too much.

"He wasn't a man that you kidded. You'd tell him jokes, but he was serious about his business. An exciting guy even though he was quiet; he had a real bounce and sparkle to him, and great expression and power in his face. He was always very calm and knew what he was doing.

"*Random Harvest,* which was all shot at MGM, cost around two million. (Today it would cost over five.) Sidney Franklin (the producer) and I worked so well together, and we all got on so well, it was a wonderful picture to make. When we did the last scene at the cottage gate, which was also the last scene we filmed, Ronnie said to me, 'This is one picture I hate to finish!' "

Besides being a delight for them all to make, the film was a smash. The Academy nominated it as one of the Best Pictures of 1942 (as well as *The Talk of the Town*); Colman (for the third time) received a nomination for Best Actor; Susan Peters (his niece in the story) for the Best Supporting Actress; and Greer actually won Best Actress that year—for *Mrs. Miniver.*

About ten years after *Random Harvest* was made, Ronnie ran it at Summit Drive, chiefly for my benefit, as I had only seen *Prisoner of Zenda.* Much to his disgust, I missed the story line completely, being far too fascinated at the time by how red Miss Garson's hair was (she had also been invited to see the film) and whispering incessantly throughout to my neighbor. It was not until years later that it occurred to me how much it would have pleased Ronnie to have his only child appreciate him "in his business," as it were, but it had not happened. I often feel that the lumps that have been choked back the many times I have since seen the film will never make up for that evening, lost in whispered giggles.

Verbois was now completely rebuilt onto one level, and in celebration of their virtually new house and of the major source of money that paid for it, Ronnie rechristened it Random House. Benita, having already redecorated Summit, now launched into the wood-beamed, fireplaced rooms of Random and replanted the garden. This descended in tiers, and now began to flourish with multicolored flowers, bushes, and trees, the only continuous hazard being the deer that persisted in their haute cuisine invasions for rose petals. Trumpet vines and honeysuckle started their trellised climb around the patios. A croquet lawn sprang up on the first level, and a large flagstoned wisteria arbor on the bottom one. At the far end of the house, before the olive trees took over, a goldfish pool was dug with a center fountain, the paths leading to it thickly bordered by calla lilies and oak trees. Farther down another pond took form and was fenced in for the fat and noisy ducks. The chickens, headed by a rooster called Bucket, crowned the hill next to Ronnie's studio, and the fan-tailed pigeons nested in the barn loft, gossiping while he painted next door. Woodpeckers sent their Morse code from pine to pine. All the right scents and sounds kept the air full. Harry M., who had been Ronnie's driver for many years, had now become Random House cook as well; he would ring the ship's bell outside the kitchen door when lunch was ready, bringing Ronnie down from the studio and Benita up from the garden. It was altogether a very civilized way of life—if only on weekends!

The war years were drawing to a close. Benita was thirty-nine and Ronnie fifty-three when they decided it would not do to wait any longer for a child. Random House was ready and so were they. It was around the time that Ronnie signed to do *Kismet* that she became pregnant. "What will Hollywood say?" reflected Ronnie, dazed at the actual prospect of fatherhood. Benita took to knitting (for the only time in her life) and arranging the nursery rooms at Summit. They pondered on the names Timothy, Melinda, and Juliet.

Ronnie started filming as Hafiz the beggar king in this Arabian Nights fantasy, swathed in turban, robes, moustache, and beard. In a famous play by Edward Knoblock, the role had up until now been solely identified with its original interpreter Otis Skinner, who had played it on stage as well as in a silent and a talkie film version. This third version was a lavish MGM film, Ronnie's first in color.

Co-star Marlene Dietrich arrived in a flurry of red carpet.

"Do you have a side of your face?"

"How do you mean?"

"A left side or a right side that's better on camera?"

"Well . . . yes."

"Darling, you are so lucky. I have none! I have to face the camera."

"And you know," related Ronnie, "it was perfectly true, she played every single scene looking straight ahead!"

Dietrich, playing the dancing princess in the ivory tower, seems to have little to do with the film, except lend her hair to the unbounded imagination of the hairdresser, her body to the wardrobe department, and her name to the billing. Between the tight intricacies of her looped and braided locks and the gilded, wired, bejeweled clothes, she is about as seductive as a rosebush. Her wild dance of the veils in the court of the grand vizier with legs sprayed in gold paint is amusing but does little to change the impression.

Ronnie seems to enjoy himself throughout in the role of the rhyme-spouting beggar king who foils a plot against the Caliph's (James Craig) life and wins the hand of the dancing girl (Dietrich). This general enjoyment must have been partly due to the number of magic tricks the part called for him to do. He never looked back after *Kismet,* and always had a new trick up his sleeve with which to surprise friends (when pressed, of course!). Watching scarves, jewels, doves, etc., appear and dis- in happy random from his hands during the film, one can't fail to notice both his dexterity and glee.

It was a mid-summer evening in 1944 when Benita was whipped off to the Cedars of Lebanon Hospital, and while Ronnie paced the corridor until well after midnight, I finally arrived. He had hoped for a daughter and was overjoyed, giving the proud Mum a square blue-white diamond to mark the occasion. A christening ensued a few weeks later at the church in Beverly Hills with godfathers Tim McCoy and Warner Baxter. Benita chose her good friend Sylvia Ashley Fairbanks and her own sister as godmothers.

Feeling perhaps more indulgent than usual, Ronnie gave a rare interview to the drama editor of the Los Angeles *Times* on the present state of his career:

"It's twenty-two years since I made *The White Sister,* and that's a long time. I'm not ambitious to make too many pictures today, but I have never put any actual restriction on the number. I am guided entirely by the character of the stories which come to me from the studio. Of necessity, one thinks in terms of a picture a year, or at the most three pictures every two years under those circumstances, but as far as I am concerned I would have no antipathy toward more if the subject were obtainable. A director might be something to consider for the future, but I am quite satisfied to remain the actor as long as there seem to be assignments at fairly regular intervals." *

(Unmentioned was the fact that films involving water-soaking sequences, knife-throwers, and camels stood little chance.)

* Los Angeles *Times,* September 17, 1944, interview with Edwin Shallert.

For the two years following my birth Ronnie made no films, working on radio and, in his spare time, on his painting. He also took full advantage of the new, most challenging subject for his camera. Benita, having married the confirmed bachelor with his own house and his own servants, felt at last truly established in their home. Bringing her child into Summit, she felt instinctively that the house had become hers too.

She was constantly delighted watching father and daughter. Any inhibitions or shyness were dissolved in dealing with his child. He became an expert on nursery games and noises, and it was difficult to say who was more intrigued with whom. Only Benita was aware of feminine guile already at work.

Tennis started up again at Summit, though never quite as assiduously as before the war. Croquet and golf took place at the Ranch, where the family now drove more often with the Nannie and Harry M. in tow. Entertaining continued in Beverly Hills with dinner parties of old friends and new, all of whom would be tiptoed proudly upstairs to the nursery upon the slightest inquiry.

Their chum David Niven returned from Europe and the war with a beautiful wife and two small children (Primula, David, and Jaimie) to a warm Summit Drive welcome . . . and tragedy:

Niven: "Within six weeks, Primmie was killed in an accident. We had rented a house very near, and when I came back at 2 A.M. from the hospital, having been told she had died, I wandered round the streets completely dazed until Bob Coote came and found me and took me to Ronnie and Benita's house. They were marvelous. They took me in and looked after me, continuing to do so all through the ghastly funeral time, and indeed, till I'd pulled myself together and went back to start picking up the pieces of my life. I can never forget what they did for me.

"He was a wonderful friend; steady, true, full of wisdom

and humor. I don't ever remember seeing him angry, though he held very definite and often unyielding views. He was generous and completely unbitchy unlike so many actors. A great actor, the master of the understated playing, and one many people (including me) tried hard to copy. A glorious speaking voice, dirty great brown 'fan' eyes, a smile that lit up the whole of Beverly Hills, and a man who could give a lame dog or a struggling actor a lift with never a thought of self-congratulation."

It was 20th Century-Fox's production of *The Late George Apley* that brought Colman back to the screen. This Pulitzer Prize-winning book by J. P. Marquand was already a hit Broadway play, and the main character matched Ronnie's years. ("I've averaged one picture a year for the past six years and that suits me. If I don't get a set-up I feel sure of—producer, writer, director—I don't want to make the picture.")

Set in Boston during the early 1900s, the story revolves around the Apley family, headed by a stuffy patriarch ("Boston's not just a city, it's a state of mind!") in whose life everything and everybody has a place—established and unvarying. It is a subtle satire on Boston in which no attempt is made to appease the Bostonians, who no doubt enjoyed this humorous poke as much as everybody else.

The film opens with preparations for Thanksgiving dinner and the annual family gathering. Mrs. Apley (played with tender acceptance by Edna Best), in a moment of festive madness, arranges different table decorations for the first time in twenty years, at which her husband gasps: "Snapdragons and pumpkins?" And she wavers: "It just came over me, George!"

In his leisure time George Apley is a bird watcher, president of the local bird watchers society, in fact, and is given to quoting Emerson at every available opportunity. He accepts no other college than Harvard and no other eligible match for his children than native Bostonians with similar views to his own. Examining an envelope addressed to his son from his girlfriend, "It's postmarked Worcester; the girl's a foreigner!"

As the story progresses, however, one realizes that under that stuffed shirt there is a more human husband and father trying to get out. His mind is blown by the outside influences of both his daughter's boyfriend and the father of his son's girlfriend. The love for his children eventually overcomes his stifling prejudices; he lends himself to new ideas and mellows considerably, later admitting to his wife, "I've been thinking . . . Worcester isn't Boston, but it *is* in Massachusetts!" The end of the film sees him arranging the elopement of his determined daughter (Peggy Cummins) to the man she loves, neither a native of Boston nor an admirer of Emerson. One assumes that the following year, snapdragons and pumpkins would be accepted as part of the Thanksgiving table.

There was never any doubt that Colman was wanted as first choice for George Apley; the only doubt was whether or not Joseph Mankiewicz was going to be the director. They knew each other socially and had a mutual dear friend in Edna Best, but Mankiewicz became fraught with tension when Ronnie asked to see *Dragonwyck* before giving his approval. (This was JM's first and only film, as at this time he was best known as a producer and screenwriter.) All went well; having seen it, Ronnie said "Fine, let's do Apley!" marking the only time in his career that Mankiewicz was approved by his cast.

Ronnie made a few alterations to the script, but by and large it was a George S. Kaufman adaptation of the Marquand novel. Marquand came on the set during the filming and approved greatly of Mr. and Mrs. Apley. During the many rehearsals the principals felt that some of the cast could have been better, that they could have been stronger. It was a little bit difficult for Peggy Cummins (who had originally been brought to Hollywood to star in *Forever Amber*) to play a Boston girl, a little bit difficult for her not to be a star. Also Richard Ney (then married to Greer Garson) was a very successful stock actor but not about to set the screen on fire.

They managed to have a ball, nonetheless. During the filming *Time* magazine wrote something about Mankiewicz, referring to him as a "Hollywood old-timer," which Ronnie thought was very off indeed. (By 1946 JM had been there for some time, having started very young as a writer.) So he and the rest of the cast wrote a letter to *Time* objecting to their calling him that, and enclosed a picture of them all around a director's chair, which they'd had made with "Old-Timer" painted on it.

Mankiewicz soon recognized Ronnie's obsession about a certain side of his face which one came to expect in stars. Rex Harrison has it, and nobody has ever seen Claudette Colbert come on screen from left to right. If Ronnie's right side were on camera too often, he'd just pout a little bit, but that was about all. However, the continual efforts to get the left side in led to inevitable teasing. In the scene in which one of the young Apleys gets married, Mr. Apley escorts his wife down the aisle, and a plot was laid by Edna and Mankiewicz, with the other members of the cast clued in. Edna picked a fight with Ronnie after they'd rehearsed the scene:

"Goddammit, Ronnie, I'm just not going to have any more of it, that's all!"

"Any more of what, my dear Edna?"

"You are not *look*ing at me when we play the scene. You are looking away from me—never once do I see your eyes while we are walking down the aisle talking."

"Well, my dear Edna, of course I do, I look at you!"

"You're a damn liar, you don't!"

Finally, Mankiewicz called to shoot one, and Edna went off to the makeup women, leaving Ronnie going over his lines to himself, pouting slightly. She returned seconds before Mankiewicz said "Roll it," and walked directly into the scene, where she stood next to Ronnie wearing a full black beard. The wedding started and Ronnie played the whole scene, walking down the aisle and talking to Edna wearing the beard, without ever noticing. Edna never stopped telling that story. It was about the middle of the filming and by then they were all having a marvelous time!

Of course, Ronnie didn't pay any more attention to looking at her after the beard experience; as far as the audience was concerned, he *was* looking at her, the actors being the only ones who notice. Having grown up in the jungle of Hollywood, where you fought for that camera and you weren't sure the director was going to protect you, it had become instinct. As Rex Harrison used to say, "If you can't see the lens, the lens can't see you." Ronnie had made *not* looking at the actor a part of his technique, but it was no longer a conscious part, so that he was able to walk fully twenty feet alongside Edna, talking to her without noticing that she was wearing a fat black beard.

Outside of the British studios at Shepperton and Pinewood, there has never been more to-do about teatime than on *Apley*. Ronnie had to have his afternoon tea, as did his English leading lady. Edna knew where to buy some scones, and suddenly Mildred Natwick turned up with some homemade cookies. This developed into a competition for the most elaborate contribution. Peggy Cummins arrived with a chocolate cake, and soon after the grips and electricians were invited, so ham sandwiches had to be provided and pretty soon someone brought in a liverwurst on rye. A fullfledged buffet had taken over every afternoon—provided and consumed by the entire cast and crew, all of which started with Ronnie's cup of tea.

He retained an eye for the ladies—not too seriously, he simply wanted them to know he was enchanted by them.

When Peggy Cummins first entered into the filming, she was feeling rather insecure and thought that it would help if she could get all the men on the set winging. She was being extra sweet to everyone. Ronnie was telling Mankiewicz and Percy Waram about making *The White Sister* in Italy, when Peggy came over.

"Oh, I remember *The White Sister!*"

"You couldn't, my dear, that was in 1924."

"Oh my God, that was long before I was *born!*"

It took Ronnie several teas and scones to come out of the depression.

His reviews for *Apley* were excellent. When a stuffy actor plays an Apley-stuffy part, the result should have been very stuffy. *Apley* would never have succeeded if its star hadn't been an actor who wasn't basically humorous and witty. On one level you had to know exactly what you were doing to make it work.

Mankiewicz believed Colman would have made a wonderful producer but not a good director, because a director must quickly evoke the equipment of an actor, must wind up with an assessment of what his equipment is, and then has to help him attain the director's ultimate objective with that equipment. He found Ronnie had a special attitude toward things and wasn't prepared to try them two or three different ways. But as an excellent judge of scenes and scripts, able to appraise material, he possessed all the qualities necessary in a producer. They remained friends after *Apley* was completed. Mankiewicz paid frequent visits to San Ysidro Ranch; in fact it was there that he wrote *All About Eve* and *A Letter to Three Wives*.

A couple of weeks after he finished *Apley* Ronnie had his first serious fight with pneumonia. He was susceptible to any infection of his lungs and throat, from colds and laryngitis on; respiratory problems were to trouble him throughout his life and were ultimately responsible for his death.

After two weeks in St. John's Hospital with Benita in an adjoining room, he returned to the warm sun and blue air of San Ysidro. Later, completely recovered, he was seen off on the train to New York by his family to revive the George Arliss role in *The Green Goddess* (in which over twenty years before he had played a temple priest) and the Colin Clive role in *Libel,* both for the Theatre Guild on the Air. Daily telephone calls from east to west usually included a brief chat with me, the highlight of which was a rousing chorus of "My Darling Clementine," with a lot of wrong notes coming from California. Benita, who could never bear talking long distance for long, would be laughing in despair, "The cost of this call—don't you dare go into the fourth verse!" He returned some ten days later to welcoming hugs at the Los Angeles train station and more broadcasts for Lux Radio Theater, including *Prisoner of Zenda* and *Rebecca* (with Ida Lupino), and guesting (with Benita) on Jack Benny's weekly show for NBC.

Christmas came with a flurry of green and red and silver, towering trees, and presents to everybody from everybody, including the dachshund Hansie, the Persian cat Pinkle Purr, and the two nameless tortoises that roamed the Summit gardens, defying age. Good friends and their children abounded, and there were parties whether Christmas, birthdays, or Halloween. Ronnie's enthusiasm for games had long since been doubled by Benita and inherited by their offspring.

Square dancing became a rage in Beverly Hills, with everyone dressing the part—checked cotton shirts, bandannas around the neck, and jeans. Ronnie and Benita, Edna Best and Nat Wolf, led by the rotund and beaming Andy Devine do-si-doed their way around many a room and patio, with a fiddler holding forth and a caller clapping out his words. Had an outsider seen Ronnie at any one of these gatherings, he would certainly have done a double take!

Ronnie and Benita were briefly reunited with the Mc-

Coys on the occasion of Ronnie becoming godfather to their first child. Tim and he saw relatively little of each other during their respective second marriages. Although later Tim had a successful children's television show in Hollywood for a while, he was usually traveling around the States, and for holidays he disappeared to the ranch in Wyoming.

Despite their rare times together, a strong bond remained, and Tim's first son was christened Ronald (as I might have been Timothy!). I talked to my godfather (who was exactly as I remembered him from almost fifteen years earlier) in the hacienda he has built near the Mexican border in Arizona. He still lives in his much-loved West and continues —though in his early eighties—to tour the country indefatigably with his Wild West shows. Only recently has he done without a horse. His precision with gun, rope, and knife remains excellent, and he has a wealth of fascinating tales of the people he has known, both Indians and white men!

After many hours of talk in front of the Thanksgiving fire in his library, I asked how he would sum up his memories of Ronnie, whom he had known over a period of thirty years, for someone who had never met him.

Tim: "When people ask me what he was really like, I say, 'You've seen him on the screen, that's exactly what he was like off the screen.' He was the same gentleman; a man of fine character, great integrity, and principles he never compromised. If he were ever worried or depressed, he never allowed anyone to know it. He was quite self-sufficient. He built a little wall around himself, and those of us that were his good friends could share his best moments. He didn't wear his emotions on his coatsleeve at all.

"I don't think he had any failings. . . . We speak of failings and we say, 'Sure, John Barrymore was a great actor, but he used to get plastered all the time when there was no reason for it.' Well, Ronnie never did that. He never did anything to excess. I think if there were anything that could have changed him or anything that could have made life better for him, it would have been that he should not have taken life as seriously as he did. But that was the way he was, and how are you going to change a man?"

Over a year after *Apley* was released, an exciting original screenplay was handed him by Garson Kanin and his wife, Ruth Gordon. It was going to be a "family" film, with Michael Kanin producing and their friend George Cukor directing. The story revolves around a famous theater actor who begins to live the roles he plays. He takes on Othello and in a moment of madness strangles an innocent girl, then later —on stage—nearly kills Desdemona, who is played by his wife whom he wrongly believes to be unfaithful. Finally he stabs himself and dies.

Ronnie was thrilled with the script but not with the idea of playing Shakespeare, whom he had never felt either the desire or ability to tackle. Here was the crunch—a challenging, different, interesting role with excerpts from Othello essential—integral—to the story.

He wrestled and meditated and ruminated, until one weekend at the Ranch, Bunny and Willie Bruce were prodding him for information and the subject came to a head. It was the Shakespeare that scared him. Amid their and Benita's combined encouragements of "You can do it!" "You should do it!" "You will be throwing away a marvelous opportunity if you *don't* do it!" he finally agreed to accept it. His mind was still not completely at rest; as far as Othello was concerned, however, he was sufficiently cheered to take on the challenge.

Though basically a rational, intelligent man, Ronnie was ever prone to the root-shaking uncertainties of his profession. The first day of filming, he set out for the studio most successfully camouflaged in hat, dark glasses, and coat collar pulled high, only to be refused entrance by a new gateman. Without a word he turned his car around and drove directly home. The studio telephoned in a panic, thinking their star either ill or in an accident, and instead discovered him in great need of being reassured that he *was* wanted back at the studio. After a hearty coaxing he returned.

Swedish actress Signe Hasso had been signed to play his wife/Desdemona, and auditions were still going on for the role of the young waitress he strangles in the story. Their friend Lilli Palmer had recommended a coach for the Othello sequences, a German lady who was supposed to be an expert on Shakespeare. She arrived on the set, and a look of terror came over Ronnie's face. The idea didn't go down at all well, and she was politely excused. Walter Hampden came from New York instead, and coached him line for line during ten days. The Othello scenes, rehearsed very carefully, were shot in continuity, separately from the rest of the film.

George Cukor: "He played Othello the way he saw it, within his vision, his strengths and his limitations. In *A Double Life* he wasn't playing Othello for the camera, he was performing as though he were doing it in the theater. He wore stage makeup as opposed to screen makeup; Signe Hasso did so as well. The contrast was deliberate. He would have played Othello quite differently had he acted it for the screen. He also indicated that the line between the reality of life and the reality of the theater was blurred.

"At the time of *Double Life,* Ronnie was still a tremendous star. He was respected by the profession and retained his importance at the box office. He selected what he wanted to do very carefully. He had not only an eye for what he hoped was going to be popular, but what was suitable for him.

"He was born for motion pictures. He was that unique animal that had a face that was photogenically perfect; his eyes, the way the light entered them, the bones and the skin.

He was a wonderful instrument. I think all great movie stars are creatures of the screen; when they come on the screen, there is a sort of excitement.

"He had learned the technique of acting *for* and not *to* the camera with enormous discretion and taste. He once showed me how Fairbanks Sr. would make a certain exit—with grace just right for the camera. He had enormous economy in his acting. Once a young actor made a rather busy exit, and Ronnie said, 'May I show you?' Then he stood on a dime and gave the impression of movement, whereas the actual movement would not have achieved that. One didn't know whether he had covered a great deal of territory. In fact, he hadn't. He moved wonderfully, and that was all out of knowledge; it was self-taught. To think of this man's intelligence and taste and hard work that had turned him into a very distinguished actor.

"I would love him to have given courses in acting for the camera, because he knew all about it. He simplified everything. It was spontaneous and fresh, but disciplined and never mechanical. He knew it would cause an effect. At the end of the film, in the death scene, I suggested that just before the man dies, there would be a surge of strength and vitality in his eyes. The camera was standing right over him, and to my eye, it didn't happen, but the next day in rushes, it jumped at you from the screen. He knew that every thought of his would register.

"He had the technique of an artist—not the tricky stuff, but knowledgeable. He would never do a scene in which he didn't believe, which he thought was not right for him. There was a scene in *A Double Life* where he was supposed to be in pajamas, and he said, 'I can't do that, it looks messy.' It wasn't vanity, there was no vanity at all; he just knew that everybody looks like hell in pajamas, especially men!"

During the making of the film Ronnie was in every day's shooting schedule with the exception of two and a half days:

"I was absorbed by it. During the week, I came home, saw Benita and Juliet, had a couple of drinks and dinner, then there was work to be done for the next day's shooting, and early to bed in order to be at the studio by eight A.M. No social life except for Saturday nights with a few close friends.

"The lunch break at the studio is bad for me. It's very hard to get into concentration again. I'd sooner go right through but that can't be done because of the union. I like to get to work early and prefer a late lunch because it shortens the afternoon. In England they have Saturdays off and at seven P.M. on Friday, they have to find their way off the set in the dark—they have thirty seconds to get off!

"My manager, Nat Wolf, helped keep the set clear at Universal—of press, people, visitors. You get into an interesting conversation and twenty minutes later you have to get into concentration again. I can sense it when someone is out there. Between a camera change or move-up for twenty minutes, I don't go outside the lights and join another world. I stick right on the set in order not to lose the mood or anything.

"Having done so many pictures, it becomes monotonous unless I can find something inspired like this, that I can get my teeth into. This was almost too much for me, but the hard work itself made the whole thing worthwhile. Everything stems from the material. Every character is someone you are interested in. All the people in the picture had something to give—no outside influence came into it." *

A young stage actress from New York auditioned for the role of the waitress. Thinking they were bound to test hundreds of girls and end up "giving the part to somebody who looked like Lana Turner," she had convinced herself she would never get it.

Shelley Winters: "I had called up Garson Kanin in California

* RC interview with Ruth Waterbury, early 1948.

to ask about understudying Judy Holliday in *Born Yesterday:*

"Hello, Garson Kanin, this is Shelley Winters in New York. . . . How's the weather there?'

" 'Fine. How is it there?'

" 'Fine!' and I hung up. I was too scared to ask him about the part. Finally, I called back, and he said something like, 'Oh, it's the weather girl again.' He told me that Jan Sterling was already understudying Judy Holliday, but that he and his wife had written a screenplay, *Double Life,* and suggested I come out to audition for the waitress. So I went to Hollywood and met Michael and Garson Kanin and George Cukor.

"Adolf Zimmerman was directing the tests. Cukor had rehearsed them, but he had already started shooting. They had tested six or eight stage actresses by the time I auditioned, and I was amazed when they called me later on to say I'd gotten the part.

"The first day on the set, Ronnie introduced himself, and we started to rehearse. I was so terrified; suddenly acting with Ronald Colman in the flesh. I had a Brooklyn accent; I was the kid from Brooklyn who had finally gotten a big Hollywood part and was absolutely dumbfounded. It was the scene in the restaurant and he said something like, 'How's the chicken cacciatore?' and I said, 'It's *your* stomach!' and then poured him a cup of tea or something, and I couldn't do it, the things were rattling so much. I did ninety-two takes.

"So Ronnie took me to lunch while I think the casting department was looking for another girl. By the time we got back after lunch, I was completely relaxed, and I was fine in the scene.

"We had these scenes in bed later on, and he was always so proper about the whole thing—it was so sweet. In the scene where he is strangling me, they wanted the implication of sex, but it was only legally possible if he did it with one foot on the floor—that you could see—and one on the bed. He thought that was pretty ridiculous and so did everybody else!

228 ·

"He had a gentle way of teasing me. He was patient and kind. I was rather scared of George (Cukor), who would get impatient with me. He would never let me wear false eyelashes, and I used to go in the corner and cry because I wanted to look glamorous. He wouldn't even let me curl my own eyelashes; here I was finally in a Hollywood movie, and I looked awful!

"I remember Ronnie taught me how to hit marks. You do it technically with your feet and then you feel it, when the light is the hottest, then you are in the right place. You develop a kind of seventh sense. If you see a shadow on someone else's face, you know you're not on your mark. They never teach you that when you're a starlet in school, and that's exactly what they should teach you.

"The story of *Double Life,* about an actor not being able to separate his roles from real life, is true about a certain kind of actor. It's very true about method actors. I was married to Tony Franciosa, and in *Hatful of Rain* there is a scene where his father wants to fight with him because he's given money to his brother. His father says, 'Come on, I want to fight,' and in the scene he says, 'Ah, come on, Pa, cut it out!' One night he just said, 'OK, come on, let's fight!' right there on the stage—Frank Silvera could have killed him!! In that play I was madly in love with Tony. I married him after the play was over.

"Actors so often fall in love with each other, so often marry each other, but more in plays where they see each other every single night for a year or so. You create the reality from the work, you create the offstage reality, and that was what *Double Life* was about.

"I'm rather disappointed with something in my own career, that I didn't develop a style. It's a different thing from just being a character. It has to do with discipline and glamour. Ronnie came onto the set with his carnation. Actors early in the morning usually come in and go to get dressed in their dressing rooms, but he always looked like he was going to a party. Later on I approached acting as though it were a terrible experience that you put yourself through, but he always made it seem as though it were a joy. Each new day was approached as though we were going to have the most beautiful experience. He used to say to me, 'They pay us for this; if they only knew!' "

The theater used in the film was none other than the Empire in New York. Between shooting in the lobby and the main entrance, Ronnie sat inside in the stalls, remembering *La Tendresse.* He climbed onto the stage, then drifted into his old dressing room and to the office where he had asked Henry Miller to release him so he could sail for Italy to make *The White Sister,* twenty-three years earlier. It was a lifetime away from Cukor, the Kanins, and the Hollywood pros who were setting up the next scene outside. Almost too distant and foreign for nostalgia. . . .

Cukor: "Ronnie had a mind of his own, he had that English stubbornness. He was realistic and sharp, discreet, scrupulous, very careful about committing himself. He never did anything for money and yet he made plenty of money. His career was a masterpiece of discipline and management. That's why it lasted so long. He made a success of everything—of his career and of his personal life. A lot of actors are talented, but very few are artists."

Shelley Winters left for New York to take over Annie in *Oklahoma!* on Broadway, having seen the rough cut of *A Double Life* and hating the way she looked, despite Louella Parsons's promises of a starry future. Ronnie was happy to have done it, but as happy as Benita to have finished with it. He had been hell to live with during its making! Universal rubbed their hands together—they had a hit performance on their hands.

Ruth Waterbury was at that time doing the movie reviews for Los Angeles' leading newspaper, the *Examiner*. As Universal believed they had a potential Academy Award winner on their hands, they decided to release the film in Los Angeles in time to qualify it for the voting (whereas the rest of the country would have to wait until the time of the actual awards to see it), and asked her to see a private preview of it one night.

"It was just before Christmas, a cold night, and I wasn't relishing sitting in a projection room all by myself, but I did and was completely bowled over by his performance, and said so with much elaboration in the paper the next morning. Later that afternoon, a tremendous basket of pink tulips arrived at my house with a card from him saying, 'Thank you for my wonderful Christmas present!'

"I wrote a thank you note and said that tulips were my favorite flower. So the next day he rang and said, 'Are pink tulips really your favorite flower?' I said, laughing, 'Really yellow ones are, but I love all tulips!' And it seemed to me not more than ten minutes later, another tremendous basket arrived—of yellow tulips."

Ruth went up to the Colman house shortly thereafter and Ronnie talked, among other things, about his daughter:

"Juliet is nearly four—not at her best, but not at her worst! We'll wait until she's sixteen and we'll see what she wants to do. She has a sense of humor and goes along with a gag, and it's remarkable, I give her a deadpan gag and she looks at me as if to say, 'You're not fooling me!'

"She hasn't seen me in any movies except for the home movies we make in the garden. After the color films they have at some children's parties, she comes home and can't sleep, they're so frightening. We get tired of running the same pictures of the baby in the garden, though, so I went into a camera shop the other day and thought I would get a Mickey

Mouse. I told the man I didn't want one that would frighten the children, and he said, 'They *are* pretty awful, but maybe you'll like this one,' but it was awful too. . . . Another cartoon we watched I thought was bad for children because it was sadistic with them banging each other over the head. Juliet wanted it run again, but I told her that the machine had broken down."

Three months later the Annual Golden Globe Award dinner was given by the Hollywood Foreign Correspondents Association at the Hollywood Roosevelt Hotel. Ronnie won for Best Actor *(A Double Life)*, Roz Russell for Best Actress *(Mourning Becomes Electra)*, and Zanuck for Best Film *(Gentleman's Agreement)*.

March twentieth brought the twentieth annual Oscar night to Hollywood, and all six thousand seats of the Shrine Auditorium were filled. The building and its surroundings were fraught with stars, press, dazzle, and tension. All the reviews for *A Double Life* had not only raved about Colman in such an unusual part, but cited him as a natural winner. This was his fourth nomination, however, and he had heard these words before. He was in stiff competition with not only his friend Bill Powell *(Life with Father)* but with 20th Century-Fox's *Gentleman's Agreement,* which had gained nominations for Best Film, Best Actor (Gregory Peck), Best Actress (Dorothy McGuire), and Best Supporting Actress (Celeste Holm). It actually won Best Film and Best Supporting Actress, losing to Loretta Young in *The Farmer's Daughter.* When Olivia de Havilland read out Ronald Colman as winner, he stood up to an ovation. It was a moment he had long hoped for and cherished.

In the backstage hustle around the winners Ruth Waterbury was newsgathering amid the throng of cameras and poised pencils. "I ran straight into him. He was holding his

Oscar. He almost gasped, 'Oh Ruth!' and then he began to cry. That dignified, handsome man."

After all the tension and emotion of the night itself came the flood of letters and telegrams, from as near and dear as the Nivens ("A million congratulations and a big wet kiss, incidentally it's about time too") and the Kanins ("Congratulations and thanks now we must plan to start from the beginning and do it all again for in addition to that statue you have won our hearts") to the Mayor of Topeka, Kansas, and Jack Warner ("I rarely write fan letters . . .") and Sam Goldwyn ("An award well deserved for an unusually fine performance. I'm particularly pleased for nostalgic reasons. You are getting better all the time").

The Oscar itself went onto his mantelpiece at home. As Ronnie said to Cukor, "I hope you've noticed how inconspicuously I've placed it!" With such a crowning success amid his colleagues and in his profession, he must have felt that his past career had been confirmed. He carefully answered the stacks of mail, enclosing photographs when specially requested. Hollywood's Masquers Club set a precedent by holding their first dinner for the winner of the year's Academy Award. Jack Benny emceed this stag dinner with an eminent collection of British and American film people around the table, all of whom were either chums of Ronnie's or colleagues with whom he had worked.

A week later Ronnie and Benita left for New York to sail on the *Queen Elizabeth* for the London and Brussels openings of *A Double Life,* accompanied by their close friends Edna Best and Nat Wolf (Edna's husband, and Ronnie's agent).

It was his first trip to England in over ten years, a nostalgic visit, both proud and happy. Crowds queued alongside derelict bomb sites for four hours to see him arrive at the Leicester Square Theatre (with Benita, Edna, and Nat) for the black-tie premiere. He took the time to visit his one surviving sister, then living in the country, and soon afterward left Benita to visit her parents while he took the boat-train with Edna and Nat to conquer the next capital, Brussels. More crowds, the premiere, interviews with the press, guest-of-honor dinner, speeches, and off to rejoin Benita the next day in Paris before sailing home.

The Cadillac drive to the Los Angeles train station with the nannie and Harry M. Waving down the platform to meet the two figures waving up. Mink and tweeds hugs, and explosion of local news such as Pinkle Purr's new litter. Tales of distant boats and trains. Later the surprises secreted in the depths of the large trunks, and deafening new verses of "Clementine."

Ronnie and Benita's guest appearances on the Jack Benny radio show expanded along with their success with radio audiences. They were doing their third season. The programs were pleasant for all concerned; Benny was flattered, Benita positively glowed at working again, and Ronnie just enjoyed the lighthearted comedy. The Colmans were written into the script as Benny's neighbors, and were often referred to on the days they did not actually appear. This started the popular misconception that spread even to friends invited chez Colman for the first time—that they actually did live next door. In fact we lived several blocks away, and Benny's neighbors in Beverly Hills must have often rued the day the idea had ever been conceived.

Benny: "The reason we wanted them as next-door neighbors in the show was because they made such a beautiful contrast to me—with Ronnie's lovely speaking voice and Benita's lovely humor. They were so English and so aloof, so far above me that they could dislike me all the time and never understand my meanness. They were the right team, the contrast needed, that the gags just followed. For instance, if I visited them, they'd be too nice to tell me to get out. They'd suffer me very politely and nicely, but anything to do with me and my household next door, they really didn't want to know about! One big laugh we had was once when we were having dinner and for some reason Ronnie mentioned Phil Harris (my band leader on the show) and Benita said, 'Oh, please, Ronnie, not while I'm eating!' Any mention of me or anything to do with me, they could *just* tolerate. Like when Ronnie would complain about my stinginess, Benita would say, 'He tries to be nice, but he just doesn't know how. . . .' I'd always be going next door for sugar and things. One day I went over with my tin cup, humming a little tune, and suddenly you could hear footsteps coming along and a coin dropped, and I'd just say, 'Thank you.' That broke up the audience.

"I had a butler in the show, Rochester, and Benita could never get his name straight, and she'd be saying 'Manchester' and 'Dorchester.' On one show I had asked them over to dinner and they were too nice to refuse, and when I answered the door, Benita said, 'Where's Manchester?' and I didn't know what she was talking about and told her, 'It's two blocks down and then you turn left at Pico.'

"I wanted Ronnie on the show because he was nice, he had a beautiful voice, and we all knew he was a great actor. I was very proud of myself that he liked working with me. We must have done twenty shows together. He was not a fiery personality, whereas Benita was all over the place, the life of the party. If I had a dirty joke to tell, I couldn't have told Ronnie. He'd have said, 'Oh, yes—funny!' I would rush to tell Benita because I knew she'd just roar with laughter and she could tell it to him!

"Jimmy Stewart and his wife took over the Colman gag as my neighbors years later on television. When people ask me which were my funniest shows that I enjoyed most, I still say the ones we did together with the Colmans on radio. . . ."

Both Ronnie and Benita were interested to see how listening to the shows would affect me, as it was the first time I'd heard them in their own element (still having seen none of Ronnie's films). When Ruth Waterbury asked him about this, he confessed:

"Juliet doesn't pay much attention to us on the radio. She listens to the Jack Benny Show at home and is very puzzled by it. We leave the house and then we come out of the box in her room and she has to be told that it's Mummy and Daddy, but she wants to know about Mr. Benny. When we come back an hour or so later, she asks us what Mr. Benny is like. Benita took her for a walk the other day past his house and said, 'That's where Mr. Benny lives!' and Juliet said she had to go in to see him, but he wasn't there. Benita thought that maybe Mary would be in, but there was no one and Juliet was very disappointed . . . and continued to be puzzled." *

As far as I was concerned, Jack Benny was the star of the show and the only person who interested me!

A Double Life really was the climax of Ronnie's career; in fact the films that followed could almost be considered postscripts. Few good films were around in 1949–50. It was neither a vintage time for Hollywood pictures nor good from the box-office viewpoint. The industry lulled for nearly three years in the television doldrums. Quiz shows were the rage, and that was the basis of the comedy screenplay, *Champagne for Caesar*.

An unemployed Ph.D., refused a job by a soap company, sets out to bankrupt them by winning a fortune on the soap-sponsored radio quiz show. It was a well-timed film and a moral one in the fact that it showed up the business side

* RC interview with Ruth Waterbury, early 1948.

as not caring the slightest about anything (or one) other than selling their soap. Offered the role of the brilliant Ph.D., Ronnie was intrigued especially after the many inappropriate, indifferent, or just plain bad scripts he had been offered over the preceding two years. This was lighthearted and looked as though it could be good. The film was backed by Harry Popkin, an independent producer for United Artists, and ex-actor Richard Whorf (*Till the Clouds Roll By*) was to direct this ill-fated piece.

A fine stage actor who had turned to films played the villain of the story, and began his friendship with Ronnie and Benita during the filming:

Vincent Price: "I don't think I had ever missed one of his movies starting with *Beau Geste,* and when I first became a part of his profession, I was sent to a drama coach to study his and Charles Boyer's technique, for according to her, they were able to convey everything with the greatest economy and to resolve most of the problem of motion picture acting in the eyes. Their example was especially beneficial to me, as I had a bad habit of overacting with my mouth which was very distracting to the eye of the beholder. So Ronnie became not just an actor for me, but a way of life.

"My first day on *Caesar* was one of abject misery. I was co-star to Ronald Colman, and the thought was not as ego-building as it should have been, but rather I was overcome with a kind of humility, which I have long since been able to camouflage. Dick Whorf recognized my dilemma and did a very sweet thing: he rearranged the schedule so that I didn't have to do a big scene with Ronnie on the first day. One day 'in the presence' and I was all right, for he had the confident actor's ability of putting everybody at ease. During the filming, we all became great friends—Ronnie, Benita, my wife, and I. I suppose I never met two people who seemed to so complement each other as Ronnie and

Benita. She sparkled all around his steady gleam, and one left them feeling happier and with a sense of great rightness."

The lady of the plot also began the film in slight awe and ended in a "family" friendship:

Celeste Holm: "I think Ronnie took *Caesar* for the same reason I took it. I had been offered five pictures in a row (this was the year when it was better to be an Alp than an actress); producers were looking for a gimmick, instead of recognizing that it was basic values that audiences respond to. But not knowing what the basic values were, how could they find a script? So they started making crazy films, crazy comedies. Actually this one *was* a funny picture, and perfectly timed with all those quiz shows on the air then. Richard Whorf was a fine actor and a good painter, but as a film director he was just all right. If you have a brilliant director who is so inventive that he sparks you, you take what he gives you and you go on from there. That can be the most exciting thing in the world. You can hardly wait to get to rehearsals in the morning. But if you have just a good journeyman director and you realize that he is not going to give you all the lovely little goodies that you would like, then another kind of stimulus takes over. You know you're going to have to deliver, and you know that you're going to have to find a way to do it. Neither Ronnie nor I ever discussed this with each other, but we understood it completely.

"If we didn't quite like what the director said, we would always suggest an alternative. We didn't make any suggestions as to how to play our scenes, we just did them, and Dick would say, 'That's it!' We would run through the lines several times before the take, and occasionally we would have Dick in the room with us, and he'd make suggestions on how he thought things should be and we would agree or not, depending.

"Ronnie was the truest actor. There wasn't a word he said that you didn't believe. He made his role an extension of himself, as all good actors always have done. There is far too much talking about acting nowadays. I don't care what brings an actor's imagination to the surface, just so it happens. I frankly consider that all homework and not to be discussed. Suddenly, something has happened, psychiatry might have been the springboard for it, where every piece of dreary information that you can dredge up out of your psyche, you present to the psychiatrist like a dead mouse and say, 'Look what I found, isn't it marvelous!' because you are so rewarded for this sad kind of confession. It seems to me that this has begun to be a social—almost an exhibitionist—thing in people. As a result of that, you will find people telling about things which, when I first started in the theater, they wouldn't dream of discussing. We all used the same things to springboard emotion, but we didn't talk about it, and so it was with Ronnie.

"In between takes we would go over scenes together, but I was always the one who asked to do it. We had lots of peripheral discussion. You're sitting around waiting for the lights to get fired and start talking lightly about things, but you try not to get deeply involved, because it's kind of like a cocktail party, somebody's going to interrupt you and say, 'All right, let's go now!' Some actors read a lot in between, though I didn't notice Ronnie reading during this film. I can't read a serious book if I'm doing comedy—it gets in the way.

"I remember during one of the first days of the shooting, as his portable dressing room was next to mine, I could hear much of what was said in his; the door was open and he was being interviewed by an earnest and rather awed young lady. She asked him what he thought was the most important thing for an actor to retain, and he said after only a moment's pause, 'His amateur's enthusiasm.'

RONALD COLMAN

"I don't remember the exact occasion when he confessed that his greatest fear was at the end of each engagement when he would close his makeup kit (or whatever) and would wonder whether he would ever be asked to open it again. This I found terribly identifiable to any actor. Any actor who is worth his salt has felt this way. Ronnie wasn't a selfish man, which is why he was such a good actor. I have a very definite theory that an actor or actress can only be good when he is so sure of himself that he is no longer competitive: he has developed a trust and is free to give the ball to someone else without worrying how it is going to land.

"Someone visited the set once, someone not of enormous imagination, and I said to Ronnie that it is difficult to communicate to someone the importance or rather the basic principles of what you are doing when those standards are not apparent to that person. And Ronnie said, 'Yes, and it gets harder and harder.' I really felt that I understood him. Some women don't have men friends, but I have always had them, because I know what a man friend is. It's someone to whom you could be tremendously attracted, but wouldn't consider pursuing that attraction because it would be inappropriate. In other words, with our situation in life, I would never in the world have ever given it any conscious thought. I admired him, and I had a tremendous closeness in feeling to him; his sensitivities and sensibilities were familiar to me.

"Most films are shot out of sequence, so we were surprised to find that our last scene, which was in the car, was the last scene on the last day of shooting. Ronnie said, 'That's a take!' and I said, 'Let's drive away and never go back!' and we both laughed and Ronnie kept on driving several blocks more than we had to. I had admired him so much before finally working with him in *Caesar* that I was still a little in awe of him. I don't think he knew that, and I certainly didn't like to make him uncomfortable, but I did admire him that much.

"There was no party at the end of the picture, no limp sandwiches or champagne out of paper cups or any of that. It was all over; we kissed each other good-bye, and that was that. It seems to me that before the picture could have been dry or out or anything, Harry Popkin sold the entire thing to television and disappeared.

"I was paid a flat fee at the beginning and was supposed to get another fee after it had made its first—what—run or after it had been paid for, and the same applied to Ronnie. Neither of us got our second fee, and Ronnie got lawyers and talked to MCA, who said there was nothing they could do. It was suddenly in the public domain; a little picture that everybody could show—and everybody did!"

So *Champagne for Caesar,* which might well have been the comedy hit it first promised, had only a brief screen airing before disappearing into television. Neither Popkin nor the other half of their money was ever tracked down. Whenever we drove past his house in Beverly Hills, Ronnie and Benita would shake their fists and we'd all join in with, "That's where that son of a bitch Harry Popkin-with-all-my-money used to live!"

That summer was our first family holiday. Benita and Ronnie had already gone to the East Coast on a spring visit of business and pleasure; the business in Chicago and the pleasure in visiting Dick and Jessica Barthelmess, as well as a quick trip to see Washington for the first time, in its smother of cherry blossoms. With a nannie to govern the ungovernable, we all met in New York and sailed on the *Independence* for Naples, with a great deal of Colman ping-pong and shuffleboard in between.

After Vesuvius and Pompeii, Ronnie behind his dark glasses, cap, and camera, shunning the paparazzi, we continued up the coast to Genoa. By car to Portofino, then uncrowded and unspoiled, where Rex Harrison, his wife Lilli

Palmer, and their son lived in a cliff-hanging house, and Alexander Korda (a director with whom Benita had worked years before, and a friend of them both) had his yacht in the harbor. Breakfast on sunny balconies, Ronnie's occasional but voluptuous outbursts of Italian; *pedalos,* swims, octopus, fishing, wooded picnics with a donkey laden with baskets of food, Ronnie avoiding interviews and relaxing with friends, Frascati, and spaghetti.

The Colmans and Harrisons went on together to Venice, and we met up in the south of France with Benita's sister. Taking in the local sights as well as friends, sun, and sea, Ronnie planned to rent a villa on the next occasion, rather than staying in a hotel. Still avoiding planes, we returned the same way we had come—surface, with a ping and a shuffle. Another night at the Plaza Hotel in New York, and then to Chicago and the Super Chief once again, for three days east to west. Harry M. and the Cadillac were waiting at the Los Angeles station with news of Pinkle Purr's new litter of Persians.

It was during this trip that his old friend and contemporary, Warner Baxter, died in Beverly Hills. An American actor with the same dark, moustached good looks as Ronnie, he is perhaps best remembered as *The Cisco Kid,* whom he played with wide sombrero and upturned moustache in three films. A dear friend—and godfather—he was much missed.

Around the same time as *Champagne for Caesar* was born, a far more important idea sprung to life in the bar of Hollywood's famous Brown Derby restaurant. Nat Wolf and Don Quinn (creator-writer of the established radio series, *Fibber McGee and Molly*) evolved an idea for a series based on a college professor. Quinn, essentially a joke writer, was a great lover of words. Prodded by Nat, he elaborated, bringing into outline the professor and his surroundings. It sounded like an excellent basis for sophisticated comedy and intelligent talk. Not long afterward, their idea took on the solid form of an audition with Edna Best and Gale Gordon as the college professor and his wife. The networks, however, did not go for it. Then Nat approached Ronnie and Benita, who did go for it, and with the Colmans involved, the networks were very quickly sold on the idea.

Dr. William Todhunter ("Toddy") and Mrs. Hall of Ivy College were born. Hall was just as much a projection of Ronnie as "Vicky" was of Benita. He was an astute, intelligent, well-read professor and college president for whom Ronnie had the highest regard and with whom he took great care. Mrs. Hall, a live-minded, equally well-read and witty woman, was quickly snapped to life by Benita, thrilled with working once again. As the couple were themselves so interesting, not to mention the college and home characters around them, a very simple situation was all that was required to make each half-hour program work.

Most of the early *Halls of Ivy* scripts were written by Jerry Lawrence and Robert Lee with continuous ideas, jokes, etc., streaming in from Don, Nat, Ronnie, and Benita. Ronnie had total control over material and casting throughout the series—something that rarely, if ever, occurs today. If he wasn't actually in on the preparation, every new idea was put to him before it was developed. Thus, with supervisory authority on the scripts, he was satisfied before anything was actually recorded.

The first reaction from the critics was "lovely, but should be put on Sundays for institutional advertising." To the critics' surprise, however, the public appreciated and enjoyed *Ivy* from the start. They enjoyed the comedy and appreciated the intelligence of the material, which never patronized or talked down to them. In fact, the show was an excellent example for disproving the ever-popular theory, in any medium, that the level of intelligence should be brought down to meet that of the general public's in order to sell. Letters from *Ivy* listeners from coast to coast and from the Middle West contradicted just that. This weekly show ended up with a big fat rating in the top ten, finishing only with the "death" of radio, toward which time it was the only show that gave television any competition at all in New York, continuing until the spring of 1952.

Always played to live audiences, every show was a special occasion for the Colmans and as close to theater as either ever were again. Flowers were in abundance everywhere in the studio, and everyone followed their example of "dressing up," including the audiences.

Barbara and Milton Merlin joined as writers after *Ivy* had already been running ten weeks:

Milton: "The thing that struck us about it was that it was a complete departure from anything that had been done before. There would be eight or ten minutes of repartee, conversation bouncing back and forth between the two of them. This threw everybody at first, but it became the hallmark of the show. Every show was a Broadway first night! You've never seen such a response. They played to the audience, and they loved it. From the first reading in rehearsal, everyone gave a performance, or Ronnie didn't approve. He always looked completely composed and was totally aware of all his cues. His cadence and accent were so contagious that other actors would start picking him up and say, 'I'm picking him up—I can't rehearse in the same room!'

"Sometimes he'd come in in the morning uncomfortable about the script and say something like, 'Seems dry. . . .' He would never say it arbitrarily. So we would sit down and finally find together what was wrong. He was unusually objective and critical about material, which I've found with only two or three people in all the years I've been in the business. An almost impeccable instinct, and that critical two-headedness which you rarely find in actors.

"Quite often he would come down and say, 'Good morning!' in a very dry manner, and Benita would say, 'He didn't like his breakfast this morning,' and give me a nudge. So we'd start rehearsing and finally he would say something to Benita or something to me and then everything was fine and it was a joy. But I always warned new actors before they came on the stage to have their coat buttoned and their mouth buttoned and to wait for Mr. Colman and they would find their cue. 'Don't come up and slap him on the back and call him Ronnie!'

"During rehearsals, new words and lines would come out. Benita would have some wonderful lines, and then Ronnie would have to top them and we'd put those in. We got to the point where we would write it so that he would have the last line, because if we wrote it so that Benita had the last one, he'd say, 'That's much too big for you, Ducks, I'll take it.' And she would say, 'You're leaving me with nothing but "buts" and "wells"!' But they were publicly very good-natured about it.

"Nat Wolf was Ronnie's agent and friend and closest confidant in professional terms. When he left the show to return to New York, I assumed a position of a kind of body-guard in terms of material, because everybody in town had an idea for Colman. Sometimes a story line came from out-side. Once a professor in Pennsylvania sent a script instead of a fan letter!

"I directed the shows after Nat left and was completely in charge. I was expansive and I fell in love with Benita, so I made a fuss over her. That was great, but after about three or four weeks, she came over to me and said, 'Milton, for heaven's sake, will you do this on one side? I go home and Ronnie won't talk to me! I love praise but take me to one side and tell me!' It's divine, because it's so human. That's why you loved the man. He was devoted, he helped, but it was still his show, and you had to be careful!

"Don Quinn was a terrific joke writer, but he couldn't

have handled a plot or an overall design. He was happy and cheerful and a real joy to have around. He established a climate. When he came on the set, you could hear the ripples of laughter; he always had a joke for everybody, saving the best one for Ronnie at the end of the line.

"Ronnie wrote three scripts for the radio. I'd come into my office in the morning and find the most beautifully typed and arranged script that I'd ever seen on my desk, without a name. I'd read it, and it would be very good and require no changes. Ronnie wouldn't tell us that he'd written it; it was just left there and I would read it and could tell from the language that it was his. Then I'd call him up and say, 'You know, I found this anonymous script on my desk today.' 'Oh, really?' 'Yes, it's about so and so, do you like the idea?' 'Sounds good, let's discuss it.'

"Barbara and I created a marvelous character on the radio show—the maid, played by Elizabeth Patterson. She thought in shorthand; for instance, she would come into a room saying, 'They're brown on one side,' and then leave. So Ronnie and Benita would be left trying to figure out what she was referring to. She'd have two lines and there would be an ovation. She left the show before we went into TV, because Ronnie was saying that she was 'too old to stand the pace!' whereupon she took an enormous part in a Broadway play which had a huge success and even went on tour!"

Halls of Ivy fans were as widespread as they were varied. Governor Adlai Stevenson, in his first presidential campaign, was criticized for speaking a witty language over the heads of his audiences. When taken up on this after a speech at the University of Wisconsin, he said, "You may be right; but you see, my favorite radio show is *Halls of Ivy,* and I was speaking to that public!" Fredric March, doing a Broadway show during the series, would tune in every night while he was making up, and knew every single story by heart, virtually line for line. Not long after the season ended, the Merlins were rescued by a feisty young garage mechanic when their car broke down on the San Diego Freeway. When he discovered they wrote *Ivy,* he threw down his wrench and started swearing: "Where do you write to, who do you talk to? That's the only show my wife and I ever listen to and they took it away from us!" When they asked him what he liked about the shows, he said, "They spoke the English language. They assumed we were intelligent. You know, we're not idiots!" Which was the conviction shared by the Colmans, Merlins, Nat Wolf, and Don Quinn—that everybody out there understood as much or more than they did. It was on that basis that the show had its wide appeal.

Milton Merlin: "It had a profound influence on the universities, and sometimes not to the good, because a lot of university professors would try to be witty and fell on their face! The professors and all the educators liked it, but to my mind the most rewarding thing was just the people in the Middle West, Northwest, etc., who all wrote in to say they liked the language and the fact that we assumed they were intelligent people. It had a kind of reverse snob appeal on the people who might not have understood all of it. They liked it, and maybe it taught them something. They weren't about to admit that they might not have understood all of it, that they might have to go and look something up."

By the end of the series, *The Halls of Ivy* had won the most distinguished of radio awards—the Peabody, as well as a Citation of Merit from the Chamber of Commerce, and Benita won a green-enameled and gold ivy leaf brooch with a diamond dewdrop from Ronnie. Having contributed enormously to the *Ivy* scripts, Benita's writing talent was well in tune by this time. With Ronnie doing his "desk" business in the mornings and me at school, she and Barbara Merlin settled down to two or three mornings a week at Summit, turning some of Benita's ideas into TV scripts.

Barbara: "She had a fantastic writing talent, a wonderful sense of fun and imagery. Ronnie emerged from his study around noon; he'd come downstairs and sail through the 'Chinese Room,' where we worked, feeling very jaunty: 'Good morning, ladies, and how is the little writing going?' Then if it were nice, we would all have lunch outside in the patio. One day when he said, 'Come on, lunch is waiting!' Benita said, 'Just a minute, Ducks, I want to get this in,' and I was scribbling away like mad in my shorthand. Ronnie sat down next to me and said, 'I do shorthand.' 'You *do??*' 'Yes, what system is that?' I said it was nothing he'd ever heard of since it was only taught at one semester in my old business school and then dropped. 'Well,' he said, 'I do Gregg.' Whereupon he took my notebook and did the most impeccable Gregg shorthand. He had never forgotten this shorthand that he had learned when he was a clerk in England, and he was so pleased to show me!"

Benita and Barbara wrote three scripts (which with their wealth of ideas could have developed into a delightful series) based upon the things that happened to Ronnie when he was "let out alone." Benita called the first one *The Unlikely Customer,* which sums up these fatal sprees.

Buying Christmas presents for the crew of *Ivy,* for instance: It was Tommy Turner's day off, and Ronnie had dropped the two girls off at Saks in his car, saying, "Take a cab back to the house."

"Why don't you come back and pick us up?" said Benita. "Very simple—we'll be inside the entrance at the handbag counter at five-thirty."

Ronnie was a bit early and they were a bit late. Standing at the handbag counter with his hat pulled way down in his perpetual effort to look like part of the crowd, he self-consciously picked up a handbag. It turned out to be the handbag belonging to the lady standing next to him—a large, loud lady who at that very moment turned around and screamed at the top of her lungs, "HE'S STEALING MY HANDBAG!" It was dropped like a hot brick as Ronnie's wild-eyed glance caught the back of a familiarly minked lady at the entrance. He rushed hysterically forward, leaving a small crowd behind him, and swept her toward the car, saying, "Darling, where *have* you been?" only to realize as she was ensconcing herself in the front seat, that this mink had a totally unfamiliar face. It was a speechless, overwhelmed stranger, who had little intention of budging, as being swept off her feet by Ronald Colman had clearly figured in her dreams for some time.

On another occasion he set off to Beverly Hills to do some shopping, cautioned as usual by Benita.

"Please don't."

"It's perfectly all right, I am just going to buy a pair of black laceup shoes."

So she let him go. He arrived at the shoe store inconspicuously, yet instantly produced a window crowd. "I'd like a pair of black laceup shoes," he said to the salesman. They produced Italian suede moccasins, alligator loafers, everything expensive they could lay hands on.

"No, just plain black laceup shoes, please."

At this point the salesman took off one of Ronnie's shoes to see whether he was getting the size right, and disappeared with it. So Ronnie was left in the shop with one shoe off and one on, trying his best to look invisible, desperately conscious of customers and passersby staring and smiling at him. Not knowing what to do about his shoeless foot, he tucked it under him. That didn't work, so he crossed his legs and noticed a little bit of gray fluff at the end of his sock. He picked at it fidgetingly and, without noticing, managed to unravel the entire bottom half of his sock, at which point the salesman returned to gasp, "Oh, Mr. Colman, you have a *hole* in your sock!!' Needless to say, he never did come home with his plain black laceup shoes.

These Keatonesque happenings caught up with Benita and Barbara even as they were writing them down. One morning, Ronnie passed through to say good-bye on his way to play golf with David Niven. David had promised to honk when he arrived at the bottom of the driveway, and Ronnie, having heard a honk, was on his way. He strode briskly down, covered as usual with dark glasses and low-brimmed hat. At the bottom of the driveway he blindly opened the car door and sat right in the lap of a lady from Iowa. It was one of Hollywood's tours of the star's homes.

Why these *Unlikely Customer* scripts were never actually produced still remains rather a mystery to me, though I suspect that Benita was satisfied with having had a thoroughly enjoyable time writing them and didn't really go into selling them with much effort. She and Ronnie moved to Santa Barbara shortly afterward, and the Merlins became involved with something else in Hollywood. According to Barbara the network people that did read them thought they were "hysterically funny but too good," which seem rather cynical words for such early television days.

One of the Benita-Barbara scripts was in fact filmed with Merle Oberon on *Four Star Theater,* an early television series set up by Dick Powell, Charles Boyer, and Joel McCrea, who had realized they would rather switch than fight. Ronnie was to be the fourth star, but he was wary of signing up for an entire TV series. David Niven joined as the Fourth Star.

Summit days were drawing to a close, but the memories remain: a first shining blue bicycle from Ronnie with a bow on it; the presents we could tell he wrapped because his bows always turned out flat; discovering Santa Claus *was* Daddy. The cause of this was Benita's Pekinese, who strongly disapproved of everyone but her mistress (she was known to keep dinner guests out of the downstairs ladies room until they screamed for help). Milk and cookies were left outside the nursery door each Christmas Eve for Santa's benefit and were in fact consumed by Suki. This Christmas of disillusionment, Ronnie had filled the stocking and picked up the tray without noticing that Suki had not finished her repast. The result was a noisy attack on his hand (she was never very clear about which side her bread was buttered on). Ronnie dropped the tray with a shout of disbelief and Suki set to furious barking, which brought Benita out of her room and threw her into a fit of giggles, at which point I awoke, catching them all in the act.

Endless series of illustrated notes with more drawings than words were relayed from Ronnie's room to mine when either of us was bedridden for any reason. There were ball games on the lawn and in the pool, hide-and-seek all over the house, and as many piggyback rides and bedtime stories as could be wheedled. My first encounter with poetry was my father reading me Poe's "Annabel Lee"; I believe it was what started me dreaming. We never stopped singing the favorite duets-trios for many years—"Clementine," "Be Kind to Your Web-Footed Friend" (for a duck may be somebody's mother, etc.), and "You've Got a Hole in Your Head," which could be sung to various tunes. Ronnie's most successful stocking present ever was a royally sequined cork with embossed card, "For the Hole in Your Head"; I treasured this marvelous find for years!

I remember the first day of school and quickly picking up a hardcore California accent, to his disbelief and horror. Ice skating, ballet and tap lessons, of which he was always keen to see results; "Now do it *prop*erly . . ." Seeing *The Prisoner of Zenda* at Summit, loving the sword fights and action, missing the plot and not associating any of it with Daddy. Spectacular birthday parties on the patio and lawns with herds of children, nannies, and some of the parents, which must rather have resembled a Broadway opening with the Boyers, the Chaplins, Farrows, Rubinsteins, etc. On one occasion a dog trainer was mustered up for entertainment with his troupe of incredible Hollywood poodles, each of which was far more sophisticated than any younger members of the audience! Another year either Ronnie or Benita discovered the most sensational seal that could do anything (and did) in the swimming pool, being rewarded by its trainer with small fish. This tireless beast had never had a more enthusiastic audience. However, after an afternoon of tricks, the swimming pool smelled so pungent that Ronnie was obliged to have it drained. And later my swimming teacher—indeed, the swimming teacher of virtually every child in Hollywood —Mrs. Finney, who sat on the edge of the pool swathed à la Isadora Duncan in hats, veils, and dark glasses, offering directions and encouragements from a deck chair. On no occasion do I remember her in the water, yet we were all crawling, doing the breast-stroke, and diving from the age of five, so she must have been doing something right!

The expense of running Summit—the house, property, and staff—was becoming prohibitive for someone whose first love was elsewhere. Ronnie's promised direction was now a timely one. Benita agreed. San Ysidro was especially ideal for a child, and there was a fine local grade school. Summit was smoothly sold, and the minimum of staff and animals made the move to the Ranch in the summer of 1953: the two Harrys came (one the rosy-plump English gardener with his even plumper brown poodle, one the chauffeur-now-cook-as-well) and the nannie. The Summit cook, maids, and Tommy Turner were bid farewell.

Pinkle Purr came with one of her long-haired Persian sons, along with Suki, the perennially disgruntled Peke. The rabbits at Summit were given away, and the tortoises could not—as usual—be found. A new duck, which had been temporarily installed with the rabbits, came to join the rest at the Random House pond. Some of the furniture came, and all of Ronnie's accumulated paintings and magnificent collection of books, their large record collections, and Benita's Bluthner piano.

We all drove away from Summit Drive and pointed our noses to the fresh sea air, to chosen friends and new.

10 ❧
Home

When the Summit duck that had been living with the rabbits was released amid its fellows at the Random House pond, it was baffled, indignant, and quite determined to stay away from the water as well as its companions. After a week of this self-imposed exile, it was firmly thrown into the pond by Harry W. There were deafening squawks and splashes indicating near drowning, until it suddenly realized that it could float and was not, after all, a rabbit.

The rest of the Summit company certainly took to water without hesitation. Pinkle Purr instantly had another litter of kittens in the barn. Suki chased the chickens whenever possible, and settled possessively into the main bedroom. The many and varied books nestled into one end of the living room, around the piano, and into every wall of Ronnie's study. The Constable and the Zoffany portrait of George Colman now greeted guests in the entrance hall; the Munnings coach horses looked quite at home against the wood paneling of the dining corner. Benita's flowers, tended scrupulously by Harry W., appeared in ubiquitous bowls. Harry M. enlarged upon his cooking capabilities, coached by Mrs. C., and on his day off Ronnie donned his chef's hat and apron and knocked up one hell of a spaghetti.

Their now nine-year-old daughter disappeared to the Ranch stables to become, almost completely, a horse. (Ronnie bought me one of my own the following year so that I could differentiate.) He invested in a second car, a two-seater Jaguar, in which he could nip about locally and to the golf course, a sport that Benita had also taken up. Having over the previous years petit-pointed an original assortment of cushion covers and rugs, she had started delving into sculpture at one corner of Ronnie's painting studio.

Now that the house was being lived in year-round, further improvements were made. A summery living-dining room grew around the old veranda, overlooking the garden and distant Pacific. Plans for a swimming pool took shape, one that would not disrupt the contours of the lawn. The pool was shaped rather like a fat comma with a diving rock (instead of a board) at the fattest end and a flat stone bridge at the other, separating a round lily pond from the pool itself. What appeared to be floating flat stones crossed the shallow end. These stepping-stones were in fact supported by round, stumpy pillars, ideal for sitting, legs in water, or for underwater slaloms. The whole effect melded in with the garden, which swept up to a flowered wall around the deep end and to the close-cropped croquet grass around the shallow end. Beyond the croquet, under an ancient Spanish oak, a ping-pong table was planted, and the family took up playing with a vengeance for the championship of Upper Montecito. Ronnie, a fine player who had once patiently shown me how to hold the paddle, now found himself losing to exhausting competition. It was many months before he left the defending to Benita and returned to the calmer climes of the croquet course.

Our free time together moved from ping-pong table to study. Besides my strong affinity for horses, I became addicted at a relatively incoherent age to writing poetry and short stories (illustrated at that) and found a reliable colleague in my father. We would sit for hours in his study, me dictating from my "notes" and he seriously, meticulously typing, suggesting the correct word, inserting appropriate spelling and punctuation. Our longest epic, meriting a binder all its own, was *"The Adventures of Bill and Carrotina* by JBC with a little help from her father." Hardly the most generous acknowledgment, but those hours of considerate advice, help, and love have endured.

On clear summer nights when Ronnie was in the mood, we would all stretch out on the patio chairs and stargaze, armed with his powerful German binoculars and his astronomy book. This was an enduring pastime, as he was an expert at explaining how to spot the constellations while Benita could relate the myths leading to their names, and I was generally wild about the whole idea. It was usually the mosquitos rather than the hour that drove us inside.

He became enamored of king-size jigsaw puzzles with minute pieces. These were spread over a special card table in the living room, and here he hovered for a few minutes around drink time—Scotch in hand. Once, a new governess, in ignorance and zeal, stayed up all night completing the current puzzle, proudly showing him the results of her labor the next morning. He nearly fired her on the spot.

Puzzling, writing, golf, croquet, ping-pong, and painting took up many pleasant hours, but they were never accompanied by "retirement." It would hardly have been typical had Ronnie remained uninvolved with television for long. The medium had too firmly established itself as something with which radio and film (and their actors) had seriously to reckon. His first introduction was a local one: four Santa Barbarans got together with Ronnie and Al Weingand to put up the money for a station. KEYT, the only station in this booming community (and still very much in existence), was started in 1953 with Ronnie as one of the directors as well as a shareholder. Legally one has to be a U.S.

citizen in order to be a director of a television station, but everybody had a voice in the directors' meetings, including Ronnie. When a vote was taken, he'd vote right along even though, being an alien, he had no power whatsoever. Nobody ever convinced him that he was completely powerless. Not that they tried. When he and Al sold out in 1956, for every $1,000 they had put in, they received $4,000 in return.

The next step inevitably led to the other side of the cameras, through *Four Star*.

Milton Merlin: "One night I called him to talk about an idea. It was TV and he was very cautious about actually doing TV. But he couldn't help get inside this story because it was an entire half-hour of just one man, a dramatic tour de force. It was called *The Man Who Walked out on Himself*. His role was a wealthy man (amiably released by his enlightened wife of many years to marry a younger woman) who was spending the last few days before the wedding at the club. All of this was revealed through one-way telephone conversations (Colman's) and his soliloquies. Having satisfied himself that all details have been reasonably and pleasantly worked out, he decides to take a walk outside. He puts on his hat, looks into the full-length mirror to adjust it to its favorite jaunty angle, and his image turns and walks out of the shot in disgust. In a panic he tries a hand mirror, sees no image, then checks his wallet to assure himself of his identity. Finally, after another conversation with his ex-wife, in which she casually mentions that she thought that she had seen him crossing the garden earlier, he comes to a decision—to declare a change of heart. He then prepares to go out, adjusts his clothes, and stands again before the mirror. His image, lost for a moment in abstracted approval, barely makes it back in time to match the motion of Colman putting his hat on at that jaunty angle.

"Ronnie loved the story, but as it was quite a thing to take on, he wanted to do something else first—sort of a TV testing ground. I had a favorite story of Lord Dunsany, called *The Lost Silk Hat,* which I adapted. It was only about nine pages, a one-acter. *Four Star* did it, and that was the very first thing he did for television.

"The first day he came on the set, he lost his voice completely. It was psychosomatic. Fortunately, the producer just paid everybody and said, 'Come back tomorrow.' We went up to the house and still no voice. Then after a couple of drinks, it came back. He laughed about it afterward, and everything was fine the next day. It had been purely nerves about doing his first TV. He enjoyed doing *Silk Hat,* and when we subsequently did *The Man Who Walked out on Himself,* he gave a great performance, rated high by the critics and by the audiences. I think it went through some fifteen or more reruns, a record for that early period."

There followed—also for *Four Star*—a third Merlin script, *Ladies on My Couch,* in which he played a psychiatrist sorting out the problems of three women patients, played by Patricia Morison, Elizabeth Fraser, and Hillary Brooke. Benita made *her* television debut playing his wife.

Merlins: "In the story he explained very carefully to his wife, before going to the office, that he never became involved with his patients. In each case, as the patient lay on the couch talking to him, his involvement was choreographed, quite an innovation for the time.

"The first woman was frigid, and as she told him her problems, we locked camera and went at half-speed and Ronnie did a dance—waltzing around with her doing much the big love scene. The next woman complained that her husband didn't understand her and was jealous of everyone that walked into their house. She ended up chasing him from one end of the stage to the other. What was such fun about this was that Ronnie devised the choreography—all the movements! The third woman was poisoned by him in his fantasy. He brought out a bottle and poured some into a pot of lilies and the lilies died; he did it all with Chaplinesque touches and a great glee.

"It was still early days in television, and all three of these shows were very unlike what Ronnie usually did. Of course he was in seventh heaven working with those three lovely girls for *Ladies*.

"Benita was miserable about doing this show, and very nervous. She had not yet lost the weight that she eventually lost for *Ivy* TV, and she still had the brown hair that she thought would photograph terribly. She hated her dress and couldn't find anything she did like in the shops and hated Milton avidly because he was the one who had talked her into it. Ronnie was unhappy about it too, because he really would have preferred doing it on his own.

"We had about a five-day shooting schedule because of all the special effects, so they scheduled Benita's two little scenes on the afternoon of the fifth day. By then Ronnie had been cavorting around the set having swooping love scenes with the girls. They didn't get around to Benita until 3:30, by which time she was desperately nervous, and Ronnie had developed a migraine. They started rehearsing and he hadn't learned his lines! She was ready to brain him. He was being absolutely no help and they had to do take after take with him feeling so sick he didn't know whether he was going to be able to make it, and meanwhile Benita was just dying. Everybody was rushing out getting him aspirin and he was being terribly selfish about it all. That night we finished shooting and they had invited us and Pat Morison and a few other people from the show back to dinner. We got there early and Barbara went up to Benita's room; she was charging up and down the bedroom with nothing on but a pair of pink satin mules saying, 'That dirty rotten son of a bitch of a Colbox' (Colbox was one of their nicknames). She was furious, but she got it all out of

· 259

her system. Then she got dressed and went downstairs and she was perfectly charming. 'Poor Colbox, how is your headache?' "

When *The Halls of Ivy* finished on radio, Ronnie had assumed that that was the end of it. Don Quinn soon developed other ideas—he wanted to sell the series to television. When it was first offered to Ronnie, he turned it down, thinking TV would be too much of a hassle and the pace would be too much. At the same time it is unlikely that he thought they would accept this No at face value. He needed to be coaxed a lot, whereas they only coaxed him to a certain point and then dropped it. He certainly did not think they would offer it elsewhere.

It was at this point that he became interested in adapting Somerset Maugham's stories and obtained the rights to *String of Beads*. The Merlins again did the script and Angela Lansbury co-starred. The show proved to be another success, and he enjoyed the role of host who could also become a protagonist. The old idea of a rep theater had resurfaced with television as the medium, and using the finest actors and material available. (This, in fact, had been the original idea for *Four Star*.) "Only the best!" he enthused to the Merlins. "I know how I could get Garbo, and Olivier of course would do it. But I must play Socrates!" They all discussed the idea over a period of a couple of months at which point they became involved once again with *The Halls of Ivy*.

During this period *Ivy* had been offered elsewhere; first to Rex Harrison and Lilli Palmer, then to Dick Powell, all of whom were close chums of the Colmans and rang up Ronnie in astonishment: "Aren't *you* doing *Ivy?* They've just offered it to us!" Ronnie was furious. It was as though one of his cherished possessions had been grabbed to be sold. He snatched it right back.

Don Sharpe and Don Quinn were clearly anxious to effect a sale to television, though Quinn had at first priced it completely off the market by asking one million dollars, excluding his own participation in the property itself. That sort of money did not exist in television then, and finally the rights were sold for $430,000 to a producer with more money than taste.

It was, indeed, much to everyone's surprise that Eddie Small bought *Ivy*. Previously involved with shows of the *My Life with a Chain Gang* ilk (and more recently with a Christine Jorgensen film for United Artists) he knew neither what he was buying nor the nature of the show. He only knew that Colman was a big name that spelled money. Needless to say, there was little hope of communication between Colman and Small. After the initial conferences they spoke only through intermediaries.

It would probably have worked out far better for Ronnie had he pursued the idea of the Maugham series and the television rep rather than entering into television *Ivy*, which had an uncomfortable feeling about it from the start. There was a tension throughout that had never existed during the radio series, and the schedule meant a great deal of time away from the Ranch—in a Hollywood flat Ronnie rented in order to cope with commuting to the studio.

During the preliminary conferences, there was talk of having someone else play the role of Mrs. Hall. When Benita was ultimately decided upon, Ronnie insisted she use her maiden name rather than Mrs. Ronald Colman, which she had used on radio. It developed that one of his reasons for this was in case she didn't work out on television. Benita, in on the meeting, stood up with a "Well, you son of a bitch!" and left the room. (Later he was very happy with her playing the part, though rather taken aback and jealous if she got too many laughs.)

Her dark hair photographed badly, and it was decided she should "go blonde," which took endless hours at different hairdressers before she was happy with the color. Then the big diet started; twenty-eight pounds came off, and she was hungry throughout the entire series.

It was a killing schedule: two shows were filmed back to back with one day in between. Each show took three and a half days, then they had three days off. Ronnie was now in his early sixties, though still looking a good ten years younger, and his health faltered under this strain, more and more plagued by his respiratory troubles.

They began with arguments with their sponsors, International Harvester and National Biscuit Company, about canned laughter. One sponsor agreed to do without it, whereas the other demanded it. Colmans, Merlins, et al were strongly against the idea, being entirely out of character with the show and never used on the radio series, where the live audience did all the work. The result was that one week it sounded as though they had a vast and noisy audience, and the next week—with the other sponsor—as though the house were empty.

One of their directors, the brilliant William Cameron Menzies, was making his launch from films to television. He was an inarticulate man who drew out all the camera situations, hardly ever speaking, which made almost everyone impatient. Nobody realized he was already ill with cancer, and in fact died shortly after the series ended.

Small complained constantly about the scripts—"They are all words, what are all these words? We want action!"— and was always on the verge of firing both the director and writer.

Milton Merlin: "He called me in—about ready to fire me— and then discovered that I had been an assistant to Harry Rapf (an MGM producer) for years, and this changed his entire opinion of me: 'Well . . . then you must know the motion picture business!'

"He was on his way back to New York that particular day, and he practically had his arms around me all the way to the airport. Shortly afterward, in the middle of a scene, an assistant on the set yelled, 'Is Milton Merlin there? Mr. Small wants to talk to you from New York.' I just happened to catch Ronnie's face and he was livid, thinking I had gone over to the enemy camp! He didn't talk to me for about a week and I had to explain that I was on Ronnie's side and we just had to cope with this man and that I would keep them away from each other. Small did not come down to the set, but his executive producer would be around saying, 'Words, words, what are all these words?' Our line was, 'Well, when you find another way of communicating . . .' This was the climate in which the show operated."

Benita with her blonde hair, and in a new wardrobe, starving, and wearing the recently invented "lifts" that smoothed any hint of lines in the face, could have been in her thirties. People were constantly rushing up to her on the set saying, "Oh my God, darling, you look so wonderful!" and passing Ronnie right by. He took this very remiss and seemed not to notice how she looked at all. Edna Best, who usually made a point of just wearing an old coat, came on the set one day not having seen Benita since the transformation. When they saw each other, Edna burst into tears hugging her.

Merlins: "Benita's lifts or 'nylon fishhooks,' which Ann Sothern's hairdresser had devised, were the cause of more ruined shots! They were stuck on the hairline, then tied behind in the hair and were camouflaged. She'd get all gussied up with these things so that the chin was pulled up. But the lights in those days were very hot and if there were a long take, one of them would come flying off; the chin would go and we'd have to start again.

"All rushes were the same; Benita would be saying 'Double chin shows, double chin!' and Ronnie would be saying, 'Wrong side!' (of his face). Milton is a devout coward and used to sneak into rushes late to sit in the back; I'd get there earlier to sit in between the two of them. One day, there was a perfectly gorgeous close-up of Ronnie right at the end of the rushes, and when the lights went up, I said, 'Oh, Ronnie, that was the most beautiful close-up; you didn't look a day over thirty-nine!' 'I should hope not, my dear girl!' he said and then walked out in high dudgeon. Then I'd say to Benita, 'How did you like the way that scene played?' and she'd say, 'What scene, what play? All I ever see is my chin!'

"For twenty weeks we couldn't get a reverse angle because Ronnie would not allow it. We couldn't get an angle of her over his shoulder. On his 'bad' side, he had three wrinkles on his neck which bothered him and then he had more crow's feet on one side than he did on the other and he didn't think he looked as good on that side. Benita's double chin showed more from one side also. I remember seeing him in a bathing suit at the Ranch when we went swimming, and he had the body of a young man of about thirty! I've never seen anybody as young—his eyes, that walk!

"He resisted vehemently anything which required any physical activity in the show. It was a major problem to get him to make adjustments, to make changes. He'd take the radio script which he knew. I'd say, 'We have to make an adjustment here. We have to get movement.' Now if somebody else were playing the scene, he'd get behind the camera and move them all over the place, but the minute it was him again, he'd sit in that sofa or chair and Benita would move around. It took me twenty-five weeks to get a crab dolly to move around. As a result, those early shows are very static when you see them now. It was nobody's fault, just the circumstances of the time. Neither of the directors knew anything about television, and there Ronnie entered into his realm. He would get behind the camera and often knew more about it than they did, though he would never question or challenge a director in a field in which the director was familiar. It was also a time when the crew and cameramen were not adjusted to this pace. They were mostly from motion pictures and everybody was confused; the techniques of the time were so primitive.

"It was difficult to have confidence in the crew or the equipment or the directors at that time. To get him to throw away a line was also a problem. He wanted to make sure he was in camera, and I think if it had been a movie, he wouldn't even have thought about it.

"He insisted upon the Teleprompter naturally, because there was such a lot to learn in such a short time. Invariably, when he wasn't looking at the Teleprompter, it looked as though he were reading the lines; he got to be so adept at that damn thing! Now they have become routine, everybody uses them. But he was the first big star to make the adjustment to television and it was difficult to adjust himself to its small intimacies and requirements. Radio was no problem, he was quick in thinking but not quick in action. Nothing was impulsive; everything was calculated, every move was calculated, and there was not time for that in television. I think this pressure closed him in more.

"Neither Benita nor Ronnie ever read anything but their lines in the scripts. Once Barbara came up with an idea for an opening which was all visual; there wasn't a line for three or four pages, but it was a funny, visual joke. Ronnie rang up in a rage, 'I'm not in this opening at all; it's bad enough you giving Benita all the funny lines, but now I'm not in here at all!' 'Ronnie, it's all about you, it's a sight gag!' Practically every week one of them would say, 'I don't understand this,' as they read their line over the telephone. 'Did you read the qualification, the description?' Never, just the dialogue!

"I [Milton] have worked with many stars, but I've never known anybody who was as interested, as earnest and as concerned about what he was doing. In the first script we did, for instance, he had to recite a verse of John Donne, and we spent two days discussing this. He had to know the meaning of a word that is now archaic. He had to know why the author used a semicolon instead of a comma. This was a sheer delight to us.

"He'd call up from the Ranch, when they had the scripts (Barbara did the final copying of them), and say, 'Now, Barbara, on page twelve you have a semicolon after this . . .' This was extremely important to him in its context."

Once Milton identified a Shakespeare quotation as "Scene One, Act Two." Ronnie telephoned him as soon as he'd read his script: "I think you have made a little mistake about the scene number." (The public would never know the difference, but *he* had to know). "What edition of Shakespeare are you looking at?" The arrangements of the scenes are fairly arbitrary, and they had been referring to different editions. When a letter from a viewer queried the pronunciation of a word, Ronnie himself would check, and if someone challenged him on it, he would write him a personal letter. This meticulous approach to his material remained natural to him.

For the lunch break a small group of them congregated at their corner table in the nearby Brown Derby restaurant. At one such lunch Ronnie took Milton to one side to tell him that the Oxford Debating Team was coming to Los Angeles to debate with the University of Southern California and had asked him to be moderator. "That's wonderful!" enthused Milton.

"But, old boy, I'm not qualified!"

"What do you mean, you represent the college professor to them!"

In fact, nobody on *Ivy* had been to college. Ronnie refused the invitation, feeling that he would be acting under false pretenses; Dr. Hall was a fictional character and Ronnie was not a college graduate.

Television audiences liked *Ivy* for sentimental reasons, because they liked the Colmans, they liked the subject matter, they liked the words. When the vice president in charge of advertising—and responsible for buying the show for International Harvester—came to Hollywood, they asked him why he had chosen the show. The company had made a survey of their largest body of clients, and it turned out to be the farmers who buy one tractor rather than the big complexes. So a survey was made of all those farmers in the Middle West, as to which television show they preferred, and *they* chose *Ivy*. After the triumphant radio series, however, television *Ivy* was poor. It did not succeed as well as it might have under more favorable circumstances.

Ronnie was not the same during the last half of the series, which ended because of his exhaustion more than anything else. His longer silences and his close-ups at the end of the day showed how very tired he was. After completing the last show, he put his arm around Milton's shoulders: "Well, we've made it!" He had completed the challenge, and his relief was obvious.

Milton: "Benita handled him flawlessly. This was the greatest performance. She was there. She was lovely. She was a great hostess, always bright and entertaining and never tired, but never in the forefront when Ronnie was around. Sometimes he would be sitting looking at a picture or something, and Benita would turn and say, 'Isn't he the goddamnedest most wonderful looking man you've ever met!' I have never known a relationship like it. How much he was aware of it, I don't know, of how she played this role. He must have chosen it as a man should and thought, 'This is the role I want!' "

In March, 1955, Ronnie wrote to Al in Hawaii, belatedly congratulating him upon his second marriage:

"I heard of the event after it happened, hence no roses!—and

the incessant work on *Ivy* gave me no time or thought for anything else. My belated and most sincere good wishes for your
permanent happiness, to you both. The TV series finished at
last two or three weeks ago and I am still recovering. You
will notice some improvements in our house here when you
next visit, and they are now busy re-landscaping and repairing
our entrance. The Eucalyptus outside the front door has been
taken out. After four days of demolition we had a good rain,
hardly needed, so work was held up and at the moment our
entrance looks like a battlefield. The rest of the place is perfectly lovely, of course, and the gardens are blooming.

"We are planning a few months in England and the
Continent during the summer, and believe it or not the old
man has been offered a fat juicy film to be made in Berlin
in the Fall. This surely must be my celluloid swan song!"

The trip to Europe came about three months later, to
London this time, to see old friends and family. Benita often
missed living in England. It held for her a more recent, solid
nostalgia, whereas to Ronnie it gave the vague, unsettled feeling of returning to an old home now renovated by new ten-
ants. He had English roots, but they were from a completely
alien past, compared to Benita's more recent ties and emotions. She never became a Californian at heart as Ronnie had.
Indeed, he would very likely not have returned on these visits
had he not been married to Benita, whose love for England
was as unspoken and complete as his for San Ysidro.

What the Berlin film was, I am not certain, though it is
possible that it was Shaw's *Back to Methuselah* of which there
had been talk. In any case the film did not happen, and though
he was still to make a couple of appearances on the screen as
well as television (Jack Benny shows), Ronnie's health and
vitality never bounced back after finishing *Ivy*. It had been
a tough haul and it showed; he did not feel well and was
inclined toward being crotchety and moody with his family.

Old enough to dine with them, I was often chastised at length for not having appropriate dress or hair for the table, as was Benita for putting back the weight she had lost for *Ivy TV*. Never shouts or arguments, there were just ill-tempered, sometimes unkind remarks that managed to throw a pall over the rest of the evening. Unfamiliar with ill-temper, I turned instinctively toward my mother.

His wildly un-English daughter had become estranged with her horses, tennis, and schoolfriends; he could not manage to catch up with her. Benita's natural vitality and ease had never permitted any distance, while Ronnie, shy and rather jealous at feeling left out, realized he needed to make an effort, but in which direction puzzled him.

It was a joy and relief when he was his familiar self. He and Benita would both come in to say good night, and he would sometimes stretch out on the bed, pretending to be asleep before I emerged with brushed teeth. Patching up and puzzling, "Let's talk about things daddies and their little girls talk about." *(In spring when woods are getting green, I'll try and tell you what I mean . . .)* Ronnie was shy and unfamiliar with the new life, centered around school events and horsey young tennis friends, in which he played no part *(. . . in summer when the days are long, perhaps you'll understand the song . . .)* At ten, wary of his moods and ignorant of illness, I was suddenly rather in awe of this often stern gentleman, and unable to think of something that might interest him to share. *(. . . for this must ever be a secret kept from all the rest between yourself and me . . .)*

A slight uneasiness developed at not being able to find this secret, and I became more conscious and cautious of his moods. Upon return from school I would usually find him in his study, patio, or studio, and if he were ominously quiet or morose, I'd go and find Benita—most often in the garden—to share the latest news and giggles. If, on the other hand, he were lighthearted, we might go off for a drive in his Jag with the top down, into the evening hills. There were domino and Scrabble games (he and Benita were expert players), not to mention endless problems that required solving in arithmetic homework, something I had a lamentable habit of failing without his help. Or we might walk up the steep hill to his studio to have a look at his latest paintings, he pausing often to catch his breath, me leaning teasingly against his back, pushing him up; "Ooo yes, that's lovely!" Leaving him there with his brushes, canvases, and delicious faint odor of turpentine, I would dash off to the stables. . . .

The Hollywood apartment proved convenient for Ronnie's perpetually unretired state, as both he and Benita had cause to spend occasional nights there during the week. They continued to make "neighbor" appearances on the popular Jack Benny Show, now transferred to television, and when Mike Todd started putting together his *Around the World in Eighty Days,* Ronnie was invited (as well as thirty-odd other stars) to do a cameo performance for either a Cadillac or a token check. He accepted the role of the official of the great Indian Peninsular Railway in immaculate white uniform and safari hat, and a new yellow Cadillac joined the family.

At a Beverly Hills party shortly afterward, a woman quizzed him about it: "Is it true you got a Cadillac for just half a day's filming?!" Cocking an eyebrow, he answered, "Not at all, madam, for the work of a lifetime!"

When producer-director Irwin Allen offered the role of the Spirit of Man in a film of Van Loon's *Story of Mankind,* Ronnie was captivated. He already knew Allen's Oscar-winning film *The Sea Around Us* and had been impressed with it. He was also familiar with Van Loon's book and fascinated by the idea of presenting man on trial in a heavenly tribunal. Only a few weeks' work were involved, virtually all his scenes with his friends Vincent Price and Cedric Hardwicke (as the devil and judge, respectively), so the atmosphere was bound to be a nice one. The script (Irwin Allen and Charles Bennett) of the tribunal sequences was intelligent. Ronnie accepted the offer optimistically and drove down to the apartment soon afterward to commence filming at Warner Studios.

The sole inconvenience that developed during the shooting was the eternal clouds that were required in Warners' "heaven." Although these knee-deep, wafting billows had been passed by the Board of Health and the insurance men, they were still aggravating to both Ronnie and Cedric, each of whom had weak lungs. Every moment off camera was spent inside Ronnie's air-conditioned dressing room, where he held small open house. The otherwise pleasant weeks of filming gave no reason to suspect the extraordinary finished product.

As the Spirit of Man—wise, compassionate, honorable— Ronnie presents a case in defense of mankind, putting examples to the judge and tribunal of its inherent goodness, and valid reasons for prolonging its existence, which is in serious question. As the detractor, Price shows up the world's wickedness and intolerance, maintaining it should be destroyed. Cedric Hardwicke presides over the tribunal with tolerance and objectivity.

Irwin Allen: "We wouldn't have made the film without Ronnie, because he was so truly the spirit of man. He had lived a full, varied, and interesting life. He was the ideal person to fight for the proper judgment of man.

"He never seemed to tire and was always aware and concerned. He had a way of making suggestions on scenes very quietly. They were usually subtle changes about staging or a word in the script. He was the most fussless man I have ever worked with; the total pro, he knew every line of script the day we started and was very responsive to the finished result.

"If I had a chance of refilming it, I would have made the picture tighter, made the pace better and recast a few people, but not Ronnie, Cedric, or Vincent Price."

During the course of the filming Ronnie talked to Allen about acquiring the rights to *Man and Superman,* which he was keen to film. Allen investigated, but due to the eternal complications with Shaw's estate, the property was simply not available. Ronnie must have thought this just as well when he saw the completed *Story of Mankind.*

Man's and the devil's "pieces of evidence," filmed quite separately, were wildly incongruous when sandwiched between the intelligent deliberations of the tribunal. They ranged from Hedy Lamarr as Joan of Arc to Groucho Marx buying Manhattan from the Indians ("How?" the chief greets him. "Three minutes and leave 'em in the shell!" Groucho flashes back). The end result, showing a wild indecision as to whether the film should be treated as drama, comedy, or farce, came as a surprise to everybody, the public included. Ronnie summed it up when asked by a reporter where the story came from: "From the jacket of the book by the same name by Hendrik van Loon."

There continued to be Ranch weekends of friends, mingled with croquet, piano, swimming, etc. Benita was actively involved in redecorating many of the Ranch's guest cottages, and Ronnie's idea of turning a storeroom under the Ranch dining room into a pub-ish bar was being most successfully realized.

The weekenders included chums from radio and television as well as business associates, family, and film friends: the Carl Esmonds, the Brian Ahernes, Joseph Cottens, Boyers, Patricia Medina, George Sanders, the Ronald Reagans,

Sylvia Fairbanks, Bunny Bruce (whose dear Willie had recently died). Nat Wolf always came on his trips west (he and Edna now lived in New York). The flow was strong and steady.

Ronnie became interested in real estate around Palm Springs and rented a house in the desert the following Easter vacation. We all drove down, with Harry M. and dogs in tow, finding familiar faces on and off the golf course. He "cased the joint" and bought some property for investment purposes.

On the next trip to Europe he was not as eager as Benita to stay in a London hotel, so this time they rented a house in the country within an hour and a half of town. It was protected by gardens and fields (even a croquet lawn) and well equipped with staff and general comfort. However, with the exception of a few lovely picnic days and boating-on-the-Thames afternoons, the English summer was wet and windy. He became uncomfortable and grumpy and suffered from recurring coughs and colds. It was difficult for Benita to entice him to go out to the theater or to London; most socializing was done by their chums visiting them in Berkshire. At the end of this trip they flew rather than sailed home, planning the following summer to rent a villa in the warmer south of France, which would coincide with establishing me in my first year of boarding school in Switzerland.

Ronnie did some pleasant work at home, recording all of Shakespeare's sonnets for an album of records and intermittently considering the idea of writing his autobiography. His career had covered many eras, and he had been involved with each: theater and silent films in England and America, talkies, radio, television, two World Wars, a wide scope of people, travels. But a book is inclined to be a long and painstaking task, and he didn't really feel well enough to take up the work.

His own thoughts on actors and their profession had

been noted and shared by Al, who although he had never had any direct interest in the business himself, had shared many of Ronnie's friends over the years:

"Actors should be expected to interpret life, but cannot observe objectively when everybody's eyes are on them. Their every move is noticed, reported, and blared through the world, yet everyone demands better acting, giving the actor no opportunity to really study things objectively. It's particularly tough on the young people in the business who succeed to early fame, thus having no chance of study, concentration, and observation, so essential to the improvement of the art."

He thoroughly disagreed with the idea that he, or any star, owed something to his audience, that they "made" him: "Audiences attend pictures solely for their amusement, not to make the stars famous. They go because he entertains them. Consequently, instead of the star owing the audience gratitude, they should be grateful to the star for their debt, should respect his sincere and reasonable desire for privacy."

Occasionally Ronnie was accused of avoiding publicity for the sake of getting some, but this was never the case. He ironically considered himself the least likely man to have gone into his profession, as the one thing he did not like to be was an exhibitionist. "But I have to; it's my trade!"

He had often been intrigued with the idea of returning to the stage or starting a repertory company, but at the same time he was fearful it might not come off. With his tremendous reputation as a film actor, he was reluctant to take the risk. Not that he ever had much time to dwell on the subject, being continually interrupted by either film, radio, or television.

Several years earlier Ronnie had been voted America's handsomest man by a periodical. Hedda Hopper picked him up on the honor in a brief interview:

"I have absolutely nothing to say on the matter."

"Oh, yes, he did!" cut in Benita. "Mr. Colman pointed out the matter to his wife and said, 'Now perhaps you'll show me some respect!' "

This was an ever-recurring family joke. When either of us would tease him about something, he'd join in with a despairing, "No respect! no respec' for your Dad!" Though it was a family joke, it was one with roots. The respect of friends, colleagues, and indeed everyone is something hard won and retained in any career, and certainly in his profession. Ronnie had achieved it. He was a self-made man in a complete meaning of the words. At this late stage the idea of losing any part of that respect (especially that of the people closest to him) would have made a mockery of his beliefs and achievements, though this instinctive reaction was to his own imagination rather than to any actual threats. Thelma's demasculinizing manner had left a lifelong imprint.

He needed teasing and the right reasons to be able to laugh at himself, which only the people dearest to one can offer without offense. To know Ronnie on any level was to respect the man, and it was something that was preserved by everyone who knew him.

His favorite way of teasing his family was a casual reference to intentions to shaving his moustache, at which we would explode with threats of immediate divorce. It was usually an exit line, and he would leave the room chortling wickedly. He never shaved it, though. . . .

Benita, a woman of many talents and roles (actress, pianist, writer, wit, artist, sculptress), had one that outshone all others, and that was as Ronnie's wife. She never co-starred, but hers was in no way a secondary role. She had not pursued her career because Ronnie, *his* career and their marriage were unhesitatingly more important to her. He was selfish but also aware and intelligent, and she was the most beautiful thing that had happened to his life. It worked both ways. She chose her role; if she had not, each of them would have been far less complete a person. They loved each other unwaveringly for twenty-three years.

With her insight and knowledge, she was ever conscious of his moods, smoothing them like hands on a brow. She remained his staunchest supporter as well as "translator" between his daughter and him. There must have been times at the Ranch when she found him difficult and felt cut off from both her husband and their friends. But whenever a shadow crossed his face, an encompassing hug and kiss, a comforting question, a warm laugh were there to allay the worry or the pain. His doctor had now prescribed the use of oxygen every day as he had more pronounced difficulties with his breathing.

Spring vacation arrived with investigations in hand as to which house and where should be rented during the summer. After careful research into Swiss boarding schools, one French-speaking one was chosen, and we looked forward with excitement to the South of France vacation and my European enlistment, which Ronnie must have regarded as a heaven-sent opportunity of losing the piercing California accent. My sole sustained interest over the years of grade school had been that of writing, strongly punctuated—inevitably—with acting, which my father had always quietly discouraged. The reasons behind this were never clarified. Perhaps he could not reconcile the dangers and discomforts of the profession as a life with which his daughter could be safely and happily involved. On the other hand, perhaps it was because I was dreadful in the school plays. Benita always maintained that I was bound to end up marrying some awful trumpet player before any occupation took over, and there the conversation would end in a burst of laughter.

* * *

One evening in May, 1958, Ronnie wasn't feeling particularly well and quietly disappeared to bed before dinner. Benita rang for his doctor who, after an examination, suggested bringing him to the hospital for treatment the following day if the condition persisted.

Feeling worse by the following afternoon, he was taken in, accompanied by Benita who returned to collect me for a visit that evening. Ronnie, well supplied with tubes, was unable to talk much, but cheerfully bridged the gap with a wealth of expressions and finger signs. Eventually, noticing the time, he told me to head for home so that I would not miss my favorite television program. Benita, finally satisfied by the doctors that everything was under control, that he was "responding well to treatment" and would sleep soundly, drove home later that night.

In the early hours of the morning he took an unexpected turn for the worse, and Benita rushed back to his hospital room. He died—very easily, very peacefully—with her beside him.

A weighty feeling of emptiness overwhelmed San Ysidro. The little church by the ocean in Montecito was filled to bursting with both local friends and many who had driven up from Hollywood. A crowd filled the street outside the entrance. Dick Barthelmess and Bill Powell had flown in from New York and Palm Springs, respectively, to escort Benita into the brief service she had requested. Bach and an abundance of flowers filled the wood-beamed interior of the church.

The Santa Barbara cemetery contains none of the gloom that usually accompanies the word. Its rolling green expanse, studded with enormous oaks and crisp flower borders, is more reminiscent of a private park. The purple mountains form the backdrop; directly in front the Pacific waves lap the cliffs; beyond the Channel Islands the sun sets. An appropriate resting place for Ronnie—surrounded by the countryside he loved, with a quotation that had long been a mutual favorite, chosen by Benita, engraved upon the black marble stone:

"Our revels now are ended. These our actors,
As I foretold you, were all spirits, and
Are melted into air, into thin air;
And, like the base-less fabric of this vision,
The cloud-capped towers, the gorgeous palaces,
The solemn temples, the great globe itself,
Yea, all which we inherit, shall dissolve
And, like this insubstantial pageant faded,
Leave not a rack behind. We are such stuff
As dreams are made of, and our little life
Is rounded with a sleep." *

* Prospero in *The Tempest;* Act IV, Scene 1.

Finale

I am closing with quotations from two of Benita's letters. The first was inspired by some offensive remarks made in a biographical article in *Films in Review* and was written a few weeks before Ronnie's death in the spring of 1958:

"There is one glaring inaccuracy on which I feel impelled to comment. This is the fatuous supposition that a man of Mr. Colman's intelligence is at present languishing by his fireside wistfully longing for parts which are no longer forthcoming due to his age. It is perfectly apparent to him, if not to you, that people are born, they live, they grow old and they die, and Mr. Colman has not cornered the market in this respect, as you appear to suggest. Nor are his diverse interests in life contingent upon remaining thirty-five for all eternity. Ronald Colman is not and never will be the less magical for being mortal."

In 1959 Benita, living in Europe, replied to Al Weingand's letter regarding an inscription for a Colman memorial about to be erected at San Ysidro by some of his friends:

"I wish it could be something which had about it some of the poignance of Ronnie's ineffable charm and romance

· 279

so that someone young reading it would feel a little bewitched, a little feather across his face, a little wink of all the dark glitter Ron had about him. He had a way of tilting his head that was quizzical and delightful, and I would like to find something in that mood."

During the summer of 1967, not long before she died, Benita, George Sanders, and I were in Los Angeles. One afternoon she and I drove by the Summit house. The long, tree-lined driveway had a new building in its stead, so we drove up the back entrance, only to discover that the immediate surroundings (fishpond, silver birch, Chinese plum, swing, rose garden, pergola) were now smothered with Better Homes. The vintage mock Tudor stood newly encircled. We trespassed from the car at the end of the drive and took in the strangeness; then, beyond the front door, we saw in the living-room window the curtains Benita had chosen over twenty years earlier.

"Where does it all go?" she murmured, and before anything had time to answer, we drove quietly away.

I hope very much that some of it went into this book.

Filmography and Theatrical Career of Ronald Colman

(The plays are in italics; the films are listed in the order of their release.)

ENGLAND

1912 Member of concert party "The Mad Medicos," later called "The Popinjays"

1916 *The Maharani of Arakan*
The Misleading Lady

1917 *Partnership*
Damaged Goods
A two-reeler film, never released

1918 *The Little Brother*
The Live Wire (understudy to lead)
The Bubble
The Live Wire (lead)

1919 The Toilers
Skittles
A Daughter of Eve
Sheba
Snow in the Desert
A Son of David

1920 Anna the Adventuress
The Black Spider
The Great Day

U.S.A.

1920 *The Dauntless Three*

1920/
21 *The Green Goddess*

1921 Handcuffs or Kisses
The Silver Fox
The Nightcap

1922 *East Is West*
East of Suez
La Tendresse

1923 $20 a Week
The White Sister

1924 Tarnish
Romola
Her Night of Romance

1925 A Thief in Paradise
His Supreme Moment
The Sporting Venus
Her Sister from Paris
The Dark Angel
Stella Dallas
Lady Windermere's Fan

1926 Kiki
Beau Geste
The Winning of Barbara Worth

RONALD COLMAN

1927   The Night of Love
       The Magic Flame
1928   Two Lovers
1929   The Rescue

TALKIES
       Bulldog Drummond
       Condemned
1930   Raffles
       The Devil to Pay
1931   The Unholy Garden
       Arrowsmith
1932   Cynara
1933   The Masquerader
1934   Bulldog Drummond Strikes
       Back
1935   Clive of India
       The Man Who Broke the
       Bank at Monte Carlo
       A Tale of Two Cities
1936   Under Two Flags

1937   Lost Horizon
       The Prisoner of Zenda
1938   If I Were King
1940   The Light That Failed
       Lucky Partners
1941   My Life with Caroline
1942   The Talk of the Town
       Random Harvest
1944   Kismet
1946   The Late George Apley
1948   A Double Life
1950   Champagne for Caesar
1950–
   52   *Halls of Ivy* (radio series)
1955–
   56   *Halls of Ivy* (television
       series)
1956   Around the World in Eighty
       Days
1957   The Story of Mankind

Acknowledgments

The following people contributed to making this book possible, and to them I extend my most grateful thanks:

Elizabeth Allan
Irwin Allen
Mary Astor
Jack Benny
Joan Blondell
Charles and Pat Boyer
Clive and Millie Brook
Clarence Brown
Mrs. Nigel Bruce
Frank Capra
Charles Chaplin
Marc Connelly
Gladys Cooper
Noel Coward
John Cromwell
George Cukor
Constance Cummings
Douglas Fairbanks, Jr.
John Ford
William Frye

Lillian Gish
Neil Hamilton
Muriel Martin Harvey
Helen Hayes
Celeste Holm
Arthur Hornblow
Isabel Jewell
Edith Lester Jones
Henry King
Jesse Lasky, Jr.
Jerome Lawrence
Mervyn LeRoy
Bessie Love
Myrna Loy
Joseph Mankiewicz
Margo
Frances Marion
Percy Marmont
Sarah Marshall
Raymond Massey

May McAvoy
Tim McCoy
Milton and Barbara Merlin
Lewis Milestone
R. J. Minney
David Niven
Laurence Olivier
Vincent Price
Aileen Pringle
Irene Rich
Dorothy Rodgers
Artur Rubinstein
Victor Saville
Irene Selznick

George Stevens
Donald Ogden Stewart
Blanche Sweet
Heather Thatcher
Ruth Waterbury
Alvin Weingand
William Wellman
Lois Wilson
Shelley Winters
Fay Wray
Jane Wyatt
Loretta Young
Darryl Zanuck

My grateful appreciation to the following people and organizations who made it possible to track down and see Colman films, and others who allowed me the use of their libraries for research:

Kevin Brownlow
Regina Cornwell and the Museum of Modern Art, New York
Brenda Davies and the National Film Archive, London
William Everson, New York
Alex Gordon and 20th Century-Fox TV, Hollywood
John Hampton and The Silent Movie, Hollywood
Leslie Halliwell and Grenada Television, London
Cyril Hayden and ATV, Elstree
Allan Howden and the BBC, London
Philip Jenkinson
Ray Mander and Joe Mitchenson Theatre Collection, London
David Shepherd and the American Film Institute, Washington
Pierre Sauvage and the Cinemateque, Paris
The British Film Institute, London
The Motion Picture Academy, Hollywood
The Lincoln Center Library, Film Dept., in New York City
    (where I was also given generous help by Dion McGregor)
The Victoria and Albert Museum, Theater Collection, London
Marc Ricci and The Memory Shop, New York

Acknowledgments

The London Scottish headquarters in London made it possible for me to research the events of 1914 in which my father was involved, and I'm grateful for their help and the use of their library. H. J. Hutchings and Norman Chapman, two of the three current surviving members of "A" company, generously answered my requests for firsthand information, and my special thanks to A. Seton, who shared Ronnie's war up until Messines night, after which time they never met again. Perhaps our meeting, fifty-eight years later, somehow made up for that.

Thanks to John Wykert and Elizabeth Karaman, who let me stay for many months in their New York apartments while researching. Thanks to Lorraine Chanel for her time and assistance in Hollywood, to Carlos Clarens for his assistance with the early (British) research and his invaluable enthusiasm, also that of John Russell Taylor.

Thanks to Raymond Chatham for some good grammar and good ideas, and to Pru Reading for a lot of typing.

Finally, my deepest thanks to John Kobal. Without his knowledgeable help and untiring encouragement, this book would neither have been started nor completed.

Bibliography

Mary Astor, *My Story*. New York: Doubleday, 1959.

Felix Barker, *The Oliviers*. London: Hamilton, 1953.

Daniel Blum, *A New Pictorial History of the Talkies*. New York: Putnam, 1968.

Daniel Blum, *A Pictorial History of the Silent Screen*. New York: Grosset & Dunlap, 1953.

Kevin Brownlow, *The Parade's Gone By*. New York: Knopf, 1968.

Lillian Gish, *The Movies, Mr. Griffith and Me*. Englewood Cliffs, N.J.: Prentice-Hall, 1969.

R. J. Minney, *Hollywood by Starlight*. London: Chapman & Hall, 1935.

During the twenties and thirties period in this book, I have often quoted from *Photoplay,* an American fan magazine founded by James Quirk (previously editor of *Popular Mechanics*), who was sufficiently familiar with the film business not to be taken in by the usual press agent stories. He lent *Photoplay* an accuracy unique in fan magazines. It set a high standard for journalism and published works of Robert E. Sherwood, H. L. Mencken, George Jean Nathan, and Donald Ogden Stewart.

The following publications also proved enormously valuable for background, reference, interviews, reviews:

· 287

RONALD COLMAN

Bioscope
Cinema (1937)
Dramatic Mirror and Theater World
Focus on Film (esp. Jeffrey Richards article, Sept.–Oct., 1970)
Film Weekly
Films in Review
Films and Filming (esp. Julian Fox articles, 1972)
Motion Picture
Modern Screen
Motion Picture Classic
Movie Classic (esp. Joseph Henry Steele articles, 1937 and 1945)
The New York *Clipper*
The New York *Star*
The New York *Herald Tribune*
The New York Times
Picturegoer
Picturegoer Annual
Picture Play
Screenland
The Stage (U.S.A.)
The Stage (London)
The Theatre Magazine
Variety

Acknowledgments are due to the following companies for the reproduction of still photographs:

Columbia
20th Century-Fox
First National
MGM
Paramount

RKO
United Artists
Universal-International
Warner Brothers

Index

Index

Index

Index

Index

Clara Crenshaw
September 29, 1975